When Napoleon's first parliament met in Paris at the beginning of 1800, English commentators ridiculed the fact that one chamber could speak and not vote while another could vote and not speak. Even the ceremonial of the opening sessions was derided as "a burlesque upon French legislation!" Yet the parliamentary system was to survive, with drastic modifications, to the end of the Empire.

This is the first comprehensive study of Napoleon's parliaments. It explains the constitutional framework with the complex and much misunderstood method of election by lists and electoral colleges. It analyzes the composition of the parliamentary assemblies, detailing the age, political background and social status of the members without neglecting their individual personalities. Napoleon's own ideas about representative government are revealed, most transparently perhaps in his comment on the purge of the Legislative Body in 1802: "There were some good workmen among them. The only trouble was, they all wanted to be architects." Above all, this book is concerned with the actual working of parliament and its involvement in the important measures of the regime – the reorganization of local government and education, the Civil Code, the Concordat, the Legion of Honour. Parliament played a significant role in political developments, from the creation of the Life Consulship and then the Empire to the overthrow of Napoleon, when it finally emerged as an active source of opposition.

Irene Collins makes lively use of contemporary material, including memoirs, newspapers and parliamentary reports, and her book will be a major contribution to our understanding of this momentous period in French history.

Napoleon and his Parliaments

For Jo

Napoleon and his Parliaments, 1800–1815

Irene Collins

St. Martin's Press
New York

ISBN 0–312–55892–9

Library of Congress Cataloging in Publication Data

Collins, Irene.
  Napoleon and his parliaments, 1800–1815.
  Bibliography: p.
  Includes index.
  1. France – Politics and government – 1799–1815.
  2. Representative government and representation – France – History. I. Title.
  JN2777.C64 1979   320.9′44′05   79–12634

ISBN 0–312–55892–9

Contents

Introduction: The Idea of Parliamentary Government

The first parliament of Napoleon's Consular régime met in Paris on 1 January 1800. The date was not particularly significant in the Republican calendar then in use in France, where it appeared merely as the 11th day of Nivôse in the Year VIII, but its significance in a wider context no doubt appealed to Napoleon, who had once said to his friend Bourrienne: 'My only wish is that my time may mark the beginning of the era of representative government.'[1]

Political representation was not a new concept, either in theory or in practice, when Napoleon made this remark. Assemblies of estates, bearing some resemblance to later parliaments, had developed throughout western Europe as early as the twelfth to fifteenth centuries. The men who sat in them were noblemen, clergymen, or rich townsmen, and very often they sat by virtue of their office or status rather than because they had been elected; but they claimed to represent at least the whole of their order, and it could be argued in the context of the times that these orders embraced the only influential elements in the community. Sometimes wider claims were made. The burgesses were thought of as representing all the inhabitants of the towns and their surrounding regions, the nobles as representing the entire population of the countryside. In 1484 the chancellor of France described the Estates General at Tours as representing the whole of the French people.[2]

In France great assemblies of estates were summoned by King Philip the Fair and his successors from the early fourteenth century onward. They never flourished as vigorously as in some other countries, chiefly because they failed to produce the financial assistance for which the king had called them together. Even when a grant of money was agreed upon, the deputies within each estate quarrelled about the allotment of taxes between the various provinces. Provincial estates proved to be more effective, and a multiplicity of these assemblies came to be a part of the normal procedure whereby the king raised money and the deputies watched over the interests of powerful social groups. Attempts

1 Bourrienne, *Mémoires* I, p. 321.
2 Myers, *Parliaments and Estates*, p. 24.

were made by rulers in the sixteenth century to revive the Estates General as a support to the crown against religious dissension, but they were not successful, and from 1614 the Estates General did not meet again until 1789.

During the seventeenth century, the glories of Louis XIV's reign put a premium upon absolute monarchy. Many even of the provincial estates abdicated their power to the royal bureaucracy. Those which were allowed to survive were on the periphery of the kingdom, in such provinces as Brittany, Burgundy, and Languedoc. They seemed something of an anachronism at the time, and it was only later that they were regarded as bastions of the nation's liberty. This was in the eighteenth century, when the glories of absolute monarchy had been eclipsed by its burdens. The king had increased his power at the cost of granting tax exemptions and economic privileges of various kinds to aristocracy, clergy, municipal oligarchies, trade corporations, and a great many other organized groups. As a result he could not raise enough money to pay for his wars. The poor groaned under heavy taxes which fell exclusively on them, and at the same time they were reduced to near starvation by the backwardness of agriculture and the inadequacy of the economy. For the first time, writers such as Voltaire and Montesquieu began to see the political system which operated in England as preferable to their own. England managed to fight wars and establish an empire without ruining her finances; her aristocracy did not refuse to pay taxes and her economic expansion was not hampered by privileged gilds. The standard of living of all classes seemed to be rising. Parliament respected traditional institutions such as monarchy, aristocracy and the church while protecting liberty of the individual and equality before the law.

In the later decades of the eighteenth century, many people in France hoped that a revival of the Estates General would result in parliamentary government not unlike the British. In 1788, when the crown was facing bankruptcy, Louis XVI agreed to summon the Estates General, and bowing to the climate of opinion, which recognized the importance of the lower house in the British parliament, he allowed the Third Estate as many representatives as the other two estates put together. At the same time, however, he insisted on so rigid a definition of membership for the noble estate that no commoners, however wealthy, were ever likely to be able to rise into its ranks. This caused so much resentment that when the long-awaited Estates General met in May 1789, representatives of the Third Estate were determined that it should declare itself a National Assembly with power to draw up a new constitution. With the aid of popular convulsions – the attack on the Bastille, widespread peasant riots, and the forcible removal of the King from Versailles to Paris – they succeeded. The French Revolution had begun.

The idea of the people as a constituent power owed much to the American example, as did the subsequent definition of the role of the king.[3] In the constitution which was slowly hammered out during the next two years, the king was described as the representative of the nation, charged with the direction of its executive power. For legislative purposes there was to be an elected assembly which it was hoped would be composed of enlightened and responsible men whether commoners or nobles. To this end, elections were to be indirect, and voting was confined in the first instance to men who paid at least a small amount in the new direct taxes. These were to vote, in the ratio of 100 to 1, for delegates who must be men owning or enjoying considerable amounts of land (about 50,000 Frenchmen qualified out of a population of some 7 million adult males). The inventors of the system, such as the Abbé Sieyès, argued that voting was not a right inherent in the individual, but a function, which the nation should bestow upon persons who could carry it out properly.

Representation, though no longer based on estates, was not yet based on the collective mass of individuals. Out of 745 members of the new Legislative Assembly, 247 were described as representing the territory of France, most of the departments electing three each and Paris one; a further 249 were described as representing the population, though in fact they were allotted among the departments not in accordance with the number of inhabitants but in accordance with the number of primary voters; and the remaining 249 represented the nation's wealth, each department being allotted a number of these seats in accordance with the amount of money its inhabitants paid in direct taxes. Since the last two criteria tended to reinforce each other, the Legislative Assembly elected in September 1791 turned out to have an overwhelming majority of members from among the educated middle class of the towns, mainly lawyers who had already served in local government or as judges and magistrates in the new courts.

Many of the deputies already suspected, not without reason, that the King was plotting with the aristocracy and clergy to destroy the Revolution. That so great a division could arise between assembly and king was due in part to the almost total separation of powers which was built into the Constitution of 1791. The King could not choose his ministers from among the members of the assembly, and nothing like the cabinet system which had been growing in England since the days of Walpole could develop in France. A fear that Louis XVI was about to invite foreign armies to invade the country led France to declare war on Austria and Prussia in April 1792. War, however, increased popular anxiety rather than allaying it: large numbers of aristocrats and priests were arrested as suspects, and in August 1792, after a mob had attacked the Tuileries, the King was suspended from his functions. The Legislative Assembly, which was supposed to last for two years before being

3 On the people as constituent power, Palmer, *The Age of the Democratic Revolution* I, 213–35.

renewed, resigned its powers after barely a year and called for a new constituent assembly, the Convention, to be elected.

For the election of the Convention a franchise almost amounting to universal male suffrage was employed. But although votes had been given to about 5 million adult males, only 1 million went to the polls. The rest were kept away either by apathy or complacency, or by the fact that voting involved attendance at an electoral assembly for several days in, perhaps, a distant town. These factors, combined with an indirect system of elections, produced the same kind of middle-class assembly as before.

The Convention declared France a republic one and indivisible, and set about the task of governing it until such time as a new constitution could be produced. A struggle for power immediately began between the two rival groups of politicians ultimately known as Girondins and Jacobins. The former, though they had been to the forefront in advocating war, seemed reluctant to take the ruthless measures necessary to wage it succesfully, and this enabled their opponents to denounce them as traitors. With the aid of another popular rising the Girondins were expelled from the Convention in May 1793. In their desperation they had associated themselves with federalist and even royalist revolt in the provinces, and it became a major concern of the Terror to hunt them down.

The constitution accepted by the Convention a month later reflected the extent to which Jacobins were influenced by the ideas of Rousseau. The French people was declared to be sovereign, and its sovereignty could not be alienated, either to a monarch or to a parliament. A representative assembly was to be elected for the purpose of formulating laws, a task which the people could clearly not perform for itself, but laws emerging from the assembly were to be regarded merely as 'proposals' and immediately submitted to the people in a form of referendum. The assembly was to be elected by all male citizens over the age of twenty-one. Population was declared to be the sole basis of representation, and this was carried to the extent that the country was to be divided into constituencies of 40,000 inhabitants, each electing a single deputy. The constitution declared that the people would nominate its deputies 'immediately', a term which many commentators have interpreted to mean 'directly', but since election was envisaged as taking place in assemblies, some sort of indirect system was inescapable, and indeed, further articles referred obscurely to 'groups of primary assemblies' choosing 'electors'. The 'electors' were to designate candidates for an executive council, producing a vast list from which the legislative assembly would choose the final twenty-four names.

The ambiguities in this constitution were never clarified, for the simple reason that it was never put into effect. The execution of the King in January 1793 shocked Europe and provided a link for the formation of a vast coalition of powers against France. Threatened with invasion on four fronts the Convention declared a state of emergency and continued to govern the country as before. A Committee of Public Safety, consisting of twelve men chosen from within the Convention, supervised the executive, published decrees, and proposed laws to the Convention. Separation of powers had been abandoned almost unnoticed.

The rule of the Committee of Public Safety, especially when Robespierre became its most prominent member, was the nearest France had ever got to dictatorship; and since there could be no doubt that the Committee's ascendancy rested on popular approval, many people came to believe that Jacobinism, with its appeals to popular sovereignty, led automatically to dictatorship and terror. Attempts by the Committee to regulate the economy in such a way that everybody obtained a livelihood produced the added fear that the Jacobins aimed at an equalization of property, or at least at taking excessive property from the rich and giving it to the poor. Once the superlative organizing abilities of such members of the Committee as Carnot had resulted in victory against the armies of the First Coalition, and terror no longer seemed to be necessary, the Convention turned against the Jacobins. Robespierre was denounced and guillotined in July 1794, and the Committee was dismantled shortly afterwards.

In 1795 the Convention produced yet another constitution, that of the Year III of the Republic, designed to restore political power to the main stream of the middle class. Indirect elections were once more prescribed, and a property qualification was reimposed upon the franchise. Men who were taxpayers, and over the age of twenty-one were entitled to vote for electors, who must be over the age of twenty-five and owners of property yielding annually a sum equivalent to 100–200 days' wages, the amount varying according to the locality. From the Jacobin Constitution, only the idea of population as the sole criterion of representation was preserved. Deputies were specifically told that they represented the whole of France, not just the department in which they happened to have been elected.

No property qualification was imposed upon deputies, it having been discovered by now that this was unnecessary to produce a middle-class assembly. The Constitution provided France for the first time with a bicameral legislature: a Council of Five Hundred, composed of men over the age of thirty who had resided in France for ten years before election, was to have the function of proposing and discussing laws, and passing them on if it saw fit to a Council of Elders, where they would be discussed again and finally passed or rejected. The latter Council was to consist of 250 men, over forty years of age, married or widowed, who had been resident in France for fifteen years before election. One third of the membership of the Councils was to be renewed each year. The constitution thus introduced for the first time a system of 'partial' elections designed to avoid massive swings of opinion as a result of ephemeral circumstances.

Executive power was placed in the hands of a Directory of five members, chosen by the Elders from a list of five candidates presented by the Five Hundred. They must be chosen either from among the members of the legislature or from among the ministers. One Director, designated by lot, was to retire each year and a new one to be chosen. The Directors were to sit as a council and direct the ministers, no one Director being responsible for any one sphere of activity. They could communicate with the legislature by messenger, but neither they nor the ministers could sit in parliament. It was hoped that these provisions would recover the advantages of separation of powers without the disadvantages.

The operation of the system was dogged from the start by the irresponsible attitude of the majority of France's middle-class property owners, who reacted violently to any suspicion that Jacobins or royalists were likely to obtain power yet would not go to the polls to ensure the election of moderate republican deputies. In 1797 large numbers of royalists, and in 1798 large numbers of Jacobins were successful in the partial elections to the Councils; the Directors annulled the elections and expelled the unwanted deputies in the *coups d'état* of Fructidor of the Year V (September 1797) and Floréal of the Year VI (May 1798). In 1799 the election of more Jacobins gave Sieyès, who had made a hobby of studying and devising constitutions, the opportunity to plan the overthrow of the régime.

Meanwhile the successes of French armies had resulted in the creation of six sister republics – the Batavian (Dutch), Helvetian (Swiss), Ligurian (Genoese), Cisalpine (North Italian), Parthenopean (Neapolitan) and Roman Republics – outside France's frontiers. All were given constitutions similar to France's own of the Year III, though in most cases with wider franchises designed to win the support of local revolutionary groups, which were pro-Jacobin. French army officers, promoted in the days of Carnot and the Committee of Public Safety, and resenting bitterly the inefficiency of the Directory, also tended to be Jacobin in their sympathies. By contrast Napoleon Bonaparte, who was younger than most senior officers, was believed to be above 'party' affiliations.

It would be unwise to attach too much significance to Napoleon's remark to Bourrienne expressing devotion to the idea of representative government. Like most young men, Napoleon followed the trends of the time and doubtless thought that he believed in them. His early letters are full of half-baked notions derived from eighteenth-century philosophy. At the age of sixteen or seventeen he read a French translation of Barrow's *History of England* and made notes indicating approval of Simon de Montfort and of the triumph of parliament over the Stuarts. In October 1788, he was planning to write an essay pointing out that Frankish kings had been elected by the nation and that absolute monarchy was therefore a usurpation.[4] When the French Revolution

4 Napoleon, *Manuscrits inédits*, Hall, *Napoleon's Notes on English History*.

broke out he was serving as a second lieutenant in the small garrison town of Valence. He deplored the local food riots, which his regiment was summoned to put down, but approved of the work of the National Assembly and was one of the first to join the local Society of the Friends of the Constitution. There is no reason to suppose, however, that the details of France's ephemeral constitutions made any more impact upon him than they did upon the majority of France's citizens.

During the next few years his search for an army career, and sometimes simply for a livelihood, connected him first with Paoli, the democratic leader of Corsica, whom he hoped would support France in the war against the First Coalition; then with the Jacobins, for whom he helped to put down rebellion at Toulon; then with the post-Jacobin reaction, during which he put down a popular rising in Paris. His big chance, as general in command of an expedition to Italy in 1796, was given him by Barras, whose immoral and self-seeking behaviour had already done much to bring the whole Directorial régime into disrepute. From none of this would it be advisable to make political inferences, however. Victorious in North Italy, Napoleon presided over the creation of the Cisalpine and Ligurian Republics and insisted on preserving them when the preliminaries of peace were signed with the Austrians at Loeben. Having been acclaimed as a liberator by the Italians, he would not have wanted to barter their freedom in exchange for the Rhineland, which some of the Directors had in mind. In Egypt the following year he ruled as an enlightened despot, arranging everything from street lighting to hospital provision by governmental decree. The divan which he set up was for consultative purposes only, though it might ultimately, he thought, 'accustom the Egyptian notables to the ideas of assembly and government'.[5] When he arrived back in France towards the end of 1799 it would seem fair to say that he had no fixed ideas about government except that it ought to conform to a general view of progress.

5 Charles-Roux, *Bonaparte, Governor of Egypt.*

1

Brumaire and a new parliamentary system

In the last years of his life, Napoleon tried to make some of his hearers believe that he had only granted parliamentary government to France because the people wanted it. For instance, Rear-Admiral Sir George Cockburn said that Napoleon had told him on the voyage to St Helena that he had never believed representative government to be a wise thing for France but that 'his situation at the moment required him to yield this point to the popular feeling.' At the end of 1799, however, there was no evidence at all that the people wanted a parliamentary system. They undoubtedly wanted a constitution, as a guarantee that government would proceed according to fixed rules and would safeguard property and individual liberty, but there was a widespread desire that within the constitution complete governmental power should be given to General Bonaparte. After ten years of revolutionary ferment, the nation, wrote Miot de Melito, was tired of assemblies and speeches, and was 'greedy for government'. If Napoleon yielded to anyone, it was to the politicians, not to the public.[1]

As Napoleon approached the *coup d'état* which was to make him First Consul of the French Republic, he knew that he needed the help of the politicians. They were, almost without exception, extremely unpopular, but only they could make his seizure of power appear legal, and he was aware that the discredit into which the existing régime, the Directory, had fallen was due in large measure to the fact that the governing clique had too often acted illegally. Moreover he had enough sense to realize that he could not run a government alone, or with the sole help of the army; and in the country at large he knew hardly anyone. The Council of Elders and the Council of Five Hundred must be involved in his seizure of power if their members were to be used by him afterwards, and the only way he could hope to manoeuvre the Councils was by allying with one or other of the two groups which were opposing the Directorial régime.

Napoleon gave the impression in his memoirs that he was approached by one of these groups, the neo-Jacobins, and that he turned them down

1 Cockburn, *Diary*, p. 50; *Gazette de France*, 17 Dec. 1799; Miot, *Mémoires* I, p. 275.

because he would not subsequently have wished to set up a Jacobin régime. If the approach was serious the disenchantment was probably mutual. By the autumn of 1799 the orators of the Manège, as the revived Jacobin party was called, were beginning to realize that their small, unpopular group could not hope to dominate a *coup*, and that in these circumstances their best bet was to maintain the flabby Constitution of the Year III, which for all its faults might still one day be bent and interpreted to produce a genuinely democratic republic.[2]

This left only the 'revisionists' as possible allies for Napoleon. These were men who were anxious to maintain the oligarchic régime set up in 1795 but had come to the conclusion that this could not be done by retaining its formula, the Constitution of the Year III. If the essence was to be preserved from continuous onslaughts by Jacobins and royalists, the formula must be 'revised'. The revisionists had the advantage of including in their number two key legislators, Daunou and Boulay de la Meurthe, and of being led by Sieyès, who was not only the most respected constitutional expert in the country but actually a Director. They needed a tame general to carry out their *coup*, and were attracted to Napoleon because of all the generals he seemed 'the most civilian'. An alliance between the two was such a foregone conclusion that only the most shortsighted of the men in authority seem to have been taken unawares.[3]

In the course of the *coup d'état* Napoleon discovered that the politicians, though universally despised, presented an awe-inspiring spectacle when gathered together in a body. His speech to the Council of Elders, denouncing a plot against the Republic and demanding dictatorial powers while a more effective constitution was drawn up, became so disjointed that the editors of the *Moniteur* had a job to piece it together for the morrow's official report. Worse followed, for in the Council of Five Hundred he was shouted down and had to be dragged fainting from the hall. He admitted to Bourrienne, when they got home from the scene, that he had been 'intimidated by those b. . . s' and that he would sooner address soldiers than lawyers. All would have been lost had not his brother Lucien, who was President of the Five Hundred, covered up for him by pretending that Jacobin deputies had attacked him with daggers. On hearing this, the guards had cleared out the supposed culprits with the sword, and Lucien had gathered together a docile rump which gave Napoleon the powers he wanted. The air of legality thus given to the dictatorship of Brumaire was an important factor in getting its decrees accepted when they were first read by puzzled officials in the provinces.[4]

2 Napoleon, *Memoirs*, p. 354; Wolloch, *Jacobin Legacy*, pp. 395–6.
3 Joseph Bonaparte, *Mémoires* I, p. 77. Napoleon, since his return from Egypt, had deliberately cultivated the impression that he was an 'intellectual'.
4 Marmont, *Mémoires* II, p. 98; *Moniteur*, 11 Dec. 1799; Bourrienne, *Mémoires* II, p. 367; Chavanon and Saint-Ives, *Pas-de-Calais*, p. xvi; Viard, *Côte d'Or*, p. 20.

The drawing up of the promised constitution was a complicated business in which Napoleon displayed less mastery than either his admirers or his critics afterwards claimed. The Elders and the Five Hundred each chose a commission of 25 of their members, who in turn chose panels of 5 and 7 members respectively. The panels were meant to confer with Napoleon and the other two temporary consuls, Sieyès and Ducos. In fact, everyone waited to hear from Sieyès, who had for a long time been airing his views regarding a perfect constitution and had given his friends the impression that he had actually drawn up a desirable scheme. Boulay, who had been chosen chairman of the panel of the Five Hundred, undertook to sound him out, and was disappointed to learn that all he possessed was a mass of notes. He did his best to bring the great man's thoughts to fruition by taking down a draft at Sieyès's dictation, and this was accepted by the panels as a basis for discussion.

Napoleon had been warned by Sieyès's equivocal friend Roederer that the plans for the executive power were unlikely to suit him. He wisely reserved his fire for this part of the discussion, which meant that the plans for the legislative power went through with only one notable modification (whose author is unknown). When the time came for discussing the executive power, Napoleon got his own way chiefly because Sieyès and Daunou, the other 'expert' member of the gathering, disagreed, the former wishing to divide authority and the latter to concentrate it. Boulay intervened decisively with the opinion that they would all be betraying their 'mission' to the nation if they failed to give supreme power to General Bonaparte. The latter thus emerged as First Consul for ten years, head of the executive authority, with two colleagues in a mere advisory capacity and no 'Grand Elector' to watch over him as Sieyès had prescribed.[5]

The Constitution of the Year VIII, heralded by drums and fanfares, was read out to the assembled populace of Paris at various points in the city on 16 December 1799. Registers were opened for a public vote, and when the majority in favour was seen to be enormous Napoleon anticipated the approval of the rest of the nation and promulgated the Constitution on 24 December. It came into operation at 8 o'clock in the evening on the following day.[6] Articulate opinion seized with enthusiasm on the fact that complete executive power had been given to Napoleon, who as First Consul could appoint and dismiss ministers at will. Separation of powers was to be almost total; ministers could not be chosen from among members of parliament, they could not enter parliament except (in the case of the Minister of the Interior) to read a report at the beginning of a session, and they could not present bills to parliament. The initiative in legislation had been given to Napoleon, who was

5 Napoleon, *Memoirs*, p. 384; Boulay, *Boulay*, p. 116; Bourdon, *La Constitution*, pp. 13–31.
6 Again, the date had no official significance, since Christmas Day was not recognized by Republican France.

to draw up bills with the help of a Council of State and designate three members of the latter to present each one to parliament. This was another aspect of the Constitution which met with whole-hearted approval, for there was tremendous confidence in Napoleon's legislative abilities, presumably arising from accounts of his activities in Malta and Egypt. The remaining legislative provisions of the Constitution met with little comment.[7]

These stipulated that there were to be two legislative chambers: a Tribunate with 100 members aged twenty-five or more, and a Legislative Body with 300 members aged thirty or more. Members were to receive a salary: 15,000 francs a year for a Tribune and 10,000 francs for a Legislator.[8] From the Year X onwards, one fifth of each chamber was to be replaced annually, the out-going members of the Tribunate being immediately re-eligible and those of the Legislative Body after one year. There was no suggestion that the members of either body should be elected by the people. The entire membership was to be nominated by the Senate (a self co-opting body) from a list of some five or six thousand names supplied by the nation. The two chambers were to have entirely different functions. The Tribunate was to discuss each bill presented to it by the Council of State, and choose three of its members to expound its opinion to the Legislative Body. The latter, having heard the three Tribunes and also listened to speeches by the three Councillors who had been chosen to present the bill, was to vote, without any discussion on the part of its members, by secret ballot. A bill receiving a majority vote was to be promulgated by the First Consul as law ten days later, unless it was quashed in the meantime by the Senate as unconstitutional. The Legislative Body was to meet annually on the 1st day of Frimaire (22 November), its session lasting no longer than four months.

The main difference between these provisions and Sieyès's proposals was that the Tribunes had no power to introduce bills. It was at a late stage in discussion of the Constitution that the entire initiative in legislation, including the power to propose amendments, had been removed from the Tribunate and conferred upon the First Consul.[9] This limitation upon the powers of the Tribunate, combined with the brevity of the parliamentary session and the complete silence to which the Legislative Body was doomed, received favourable comment from publicists. To such an extent had former assemblies abused their powers of initiative that people looked forward to being rescued from a welter of proposals and counter-proposals. Metaphors were exhausted in condemnation of politicians who had 'swamped the country in the frightful deluge of laws inundating it'.[10] Much of the trouble was attributed to the

7 Text in Duguit and Monnier, *Les Constitutions*, pp. 304–13.
8 Salaries had been paid to members of parliament since 1792.
9 Boulay, *Théorie*, p. 60
10 Gaudin, *Réflexions*, p. 9

fact that France had had a legislative assembly or 'law factory' in existence all the year round.[11] The right of discussion given to the Tribunate was less appreciated than the silence imposed on the Legislative Body. 'The Tribunes are getting 15,000 francs for talking – it is too much. The Legislators have 10,000 francs for keeping quiet, which is really not enough,' wrote the *Ami de la Paix*.[12]

English commentators jumped to the conclusion that the Constitution would produce tyranny.[13] Yet there was little in its provisions to suggest that the government would be able to prey upon the legislature. The members of the Tribunate and the Legislative Body were not to be chosen by the government but by the Senate, which was a sort of supreme court standing above both the executive and legislative powers. The Senate was to consist in the first place of 60 members, two of whom (the out-going consuls Sieyès and Ducos) in consultation with the new Second and Third Consuls (Cambacérès and Lebrun) were to choose another 29. The ensuing 31 were to co-opt the rest. Thereafter, for the next ten years, the number would be increased annually by two, the Senate itself 'electing' each member from a list of three candidates presented by the Tribunate, the Legislative Body, and the First Consul respectively. The Senators were placed in a position above the fear or favour by being appointed for life, allotted a salary of 25,000 francs a year, and declared ineligible for any other post in the state. Cabanis shrewdly pointed out during the making of the constitution that despotism could only ensue if the First Consul allied with the Senate. This seemed a remote possibility, rendered even more remote when Sieyès, who had soon fallen out with Napoleon for seizing too much executive power, was made President of the Senate. Napoleon, like his brother Lucien, looked upon the Senate as a possible 'nest of conspirators'. He particularly disliked the idea of twenty vacant places, which he thought might be used, as time went by, to co-opt enemies of the government.[14]

The government was given no members sitting in either the Tribunate or the Legislative Body. Roederer afterwards came to regard this as a weakness, and suggested to Napoleon that five members of the Council of State should sit permanently in each chamber, but nothing came of the proposal.[15] In any case the Council of State, though not a parliamentary body, was not really a part of the government either, since it had no executive functions and ministers were not at first allowed to sit in it. (Later, when they gained entry, they were not allowed to speak.) The Council was a body of about forty men, hand-picked by Napoleon for the express purpose of drafting laws and decrees. Topics on which

11 *Décade philosophique*, 20 May 1800.
12 *Ami de la Paix*, 11 Jan. 1800.
13 Maccunn, *The Contemporary English View*, pp. 20, 41–2. An exception was Pitt, who thought that it would inaugurate 'a moderate, American type of government'.
14 Bourdon, *La Constitution*, p. 83; Boulay, *Théorie*, p. 61.
15 Roederer, *Journal*, p. 340.

legislation was required were communicated to it by message from the ministers or from Napoleon, who subsequently chaired the meetings at which drafts were discussed.

Napoleon frequently went to some trouble to cultivate friendly relations with members of parliament, but he never tried to cultivate a party. He once told Talleyrand to invite members regularly to dinner, but he apparently envisaged it being done indiscriminately, in batches. During the Life Consulate, Napoleon himself invited deputies to receptions at St Cloud, but any number of them could put down their names to attend, and all that happened to them was that they stood in the long gallery while the great man passed by. He liked to notice especially the ones who came from annexed territories. 'How are things in Geneva?' he would ask Pictet, much to the latter's amusement, every time he saw him.[16]

The members of the Legislative Body could neither hope to win the favour of the government by supporting its measures in the chamber nor fear to incur its disfavour by voting against them, since the members could not make speeches, and voting was done in secret. The Tribunes were more vulnerable, but even in their case rewards or punishments could only be of an individual nature. There was no government party enjoying the fruits of office and no opposition party vying to take them over. A man who showed by his speeches that he was likely to be useful in an official position might be removed from the Tribunate and made a Councillor of State, but such places were not legion and after a time they became dead men's shoes. In any case a genuine politician might not want such a transfer.[17] Portalis once told those members of the Tribunate who were in general favourably disposed to the government that they should refrain from criticizing its measures, but there was very little reason why they should do so.[18]

English commentators made fun of one chamber which could speak and not vote and another which could vote and not speak. Being accustomed to two houses of parliament whose functions duplicated each other they would have been surprised to learn that many Frenchmen regarded the English system as a waste of time. The French were equally critical of the fact that in England members of parliament voted on a measure after they had committed themselves to one side or the other by speaking on it, 'thus becoming, by a sort of political monstrosity, both judges and parties in the same cause'.[19] Their own Legislative Body, they said, was more like a court of law, in which a jury gave an impartial verdict after hearing both sides of the case. Sieyès himself had referred to his conception as 'a properly organized judicial tribunal'.

16 Napoleon, *Lettres inédites* (Lecestre) I, pp. 247–8; Pictet, *Journal*, pp. 105–6, 108–9.
17 For example, Duveyrier, *Anecdotes*, p. 311.
18 Thibaudeau, *Mémoires*, p. 218.
19 *Journal de Paris*, 13 Jan. 1800.

Chaptal, Napoleon's Minister of the Interior, who became very critical of some other Napoleonic measures, remained of the opinion that it had been 'a great idea to erect the Legislative Body into a tribunal before which Councillors and Tribunes argued the law.[20]

Napoleon was aware of the ridiculous aspect of an assembly of three hundred men who were not allowed to speak, but the idea of an impartial tribunal appealed to him. Though he frequently referred to the Legislators with scorn and often treated them with utter contempt, he had a grandiose vision of them in his mind, derived from classical literature. He pictured a body of wise, serene, predominantly elderly statesmen, sitting in something which looked like a temple, preferably on a hill. He would so much have liked them to have been on a hill. In fact they met in the Palais Bourbon, which provided an impressive assembly hall ('one of the most elegant and beautiful rooms in Europe', an English visitor called it)[21] but was built on low ground on the left bank of the Seine. In 1805 Napoleon had a ramp built, 'almost similar to the Capitol at Rome', so that he could enter the building in greater state for the official opening of the parliamentary session.[22] In 1806 work was begun on a new façade with twelve corinthian columns raised above ground by twenty-nine steps, but Napoleon was still not satisfied. In 1808 he suggested that at least a monument might be erected on the heights of Montmarte to celebrate the wonderful partnership between himself and the Legislative Body, but the Legislators were not keen on their part in the enterprise, which was to provide the money.[23]

Though Napoleon in no sense invented the parliamentary system of the Year VIII, it suited his ideas well enough to survive, albeit with massive modifications, to the end of the Empire. In spite of the arrogant remarks he made on a number of (fleeting) occasions, there is no reason to suppose that he ever contemplated entirely personal rule. At the height of his power he could still say seriously to Metternich, whom he met at Dresden when he was on his way to attack Moscow: 'I do not desire absolute power.' With regard to the Legislative Body he said he wanted 'more than forms'.[24] He was hostile to Eugène's parliament at Milan, but this was because he despised the Italians: to Jerome, when the latter became King of Westphalia, he sent a letter with the magnificent opening sentence, 'You will find enclosed the constitution of your kingdom,' and concluding with the advice, 'Be a constitutional king.'[25]

Napoleon had a fair knowledge of the English parliamentary system, to which his close questioning of the MPs who visited him at Elba bore witness. He had acquired it chiefly from following newspaper reports of

20 Bourdon, *La Constitution*, p. 41; Chaptal, *Mes souvenirs*, p. 215.
21 Yorke, *France in 1802*, p. 209.
22 *Gazette de France*, 4 Mar. 1806.
23 Napoleon, *Lettres inédites* (Lecestre), no. 366; Cambacérès, *Lettres inédites* II, pp. 622–5.
24 Metternich, *Memoirs*, p. 151.
25 Napoleon, *Correspondance*, nos. 8986, 9015, 9024, 9028, 13361.

the careers of opposition members – Fox, Holland and Whitbread – whom he regarded as friends of France; but with characteristic confidence he regarded himself as an expert on the whole of the constitution, and was indeed not without ability to make some shrewd comments.[26] He was obviously worried from time to time to see the English parliament playing a large part in producing governments, because he would not have wanted such a system to develop in France. Unlike most Frenchmen he was not prepared to dismiss the English example with contempt, but preferred to excuse himself for deviating from the pattern by expatiating on the differences between the two nations. The Englishman, he said, 'lives on a damp soil, under a sun which is almost always cold, drinks beer and porter and consumes a great deal of milk food'; the Frenchman 'lives under a clear sky, drinks a fiery, exhilarating wine, and lives on food which excites his senses to action'. The Englishman is therefore proud, the Frenchman vain; the Englishman is concerned only to preserve his own rights, the Frenchman demands equality with others. 'How can one dream of giving the same institutions to people so different?' he demanded of his Council of State. In England, he said on another occasion, the members of the opposition thought only of being bought over by the crown; in France, given a similar position, they would seek to abolish the monarchy.[27]

Parliament, Napoleon came to believe, should have two functions, financial and legislative. In the tradition of the Enlightenment, financial accountability was a sign of good government, and Napoleon persisted to the end of his reign in summoning the Legislative Body annually to lay his accounts before it.[28] 'If your meeting, gentlemen, had for its sole object the examination of the accounts we have the honour to present to you, its importance would be immense,' said his spokesman Molé in a speech to parliament in 1813. 'The administration can err; it can be corrupted. It is necessary that deputies from all parts of the Empire should come at least once every year to receive in this capital an account of the public revenues.'[29] By 'accounts', Napoleon meant both a statement of last year's expenditure and an estimate of next year's needs. The latter were normally met for the most part by taxation, but it was not for the purpose of granting taxes that Napoleon summoned parliament regularly. From 1804, when he reverted to a system of indirect taxes, he needed no new source of revenue, and it was only for new taxes, he said, that parliament's sanction was required.[30]

Towards the end of the reign a disgruntled deputy complained that

26 Kerry, *Bowood papers*, p. 87; Lean, *The Napoleonists*, p. 163; Bertrand, *Cahiers, 1816–17*, p. 186, 1821, pp. 59–60.
27 Pelet, *Opinions*, pp. 62–3; Thibaudeau, *Mémoires*, p. 226.
28 The session of 1809 admittedly did not open until 3 December, and there was a purely formal pause before the opening of the session of 1810 on 1 February. The session of 1812 did not begin until 14 February 1813.
29 *Arch. parl.*, 11 Mar. 1813.
30 Pelet, *Opinions*, p. 147.

parliament had become a mere accounting body, so restricted were its legislative duties. Napoleon's idea of legislation was Rousseauesque: only fundamental statutes were worthy of the name law and came within the competence of parliament. Detailed matters of day-to-day administration were properly the subject of governmental decrees, the members of the Legislative Body being incompetent, on account of their long residence in the provinces, to deal with them.[31] During the first two or three years, fundamental laws were weighty and numerous: the administrative system, the judicial system, the educational system, the Civil Code, were only a few of the matters that occupied the attention of the parliaments of the Consulate. As the years went by, the need for such legislation diminished. 'We have presented few bills this year,' said Ségur on behalf of the Council of State at the closing of parliament in 1811. 'After the making of the Code Napoléon, the Codes of Procedure and Commerce, and the Criminal Code, when all is organized in the Empire, it is natural that the work of administration should increase and that of legislation diminish. Creation ends, life begins.[32] The change might not have been so drastic had not Napoleon's temperament led him to restrict more and more his view as to what constituted a subject for fundamental legislation. In 1800, parliament debated a bill allowing the government to create special courts in the departments at its discretion; in 1804, Napoleon dismissed the opinion of the Council of State that a law would have to be passed by parliament if the government were to be allowed to appoint senior police officials in the principal towns of France as it saw fit. In 1802 a bill creating the Legion of Honour was placed before parliament; in 1808 new titles of nobility were created by decree. The flow of fundamental legislation never entirely dried up, however: a Rural Code was on the stocks when the Empire fell.

It was also in the spirit of Rousseau that Napoleon expected the French nation, if it was in any sense a community, to produce an assembly which would co-operate with the general will, expressed by himself. His spokesmen, presenting bills drawn up by the Council of State to the Legislative Body, frequently used the metaphor of the family, with Napoleon as the father summoning his children to a conference, at which they could express their opinions while manifesting a general willingness to accept the father's decision and respect his ultimate responsibility. The Legislators, as Napoleon continually pointed out to them, were not representatives of the people but deputies of the departments. When Josephine, receiving the members of the Legislative Body during one of the Emperor's absences, referred to them as representing the nation, Napoleon announced flatly in the *Moniteur* that she had said no such thing (although the offending phrase remained

31 Pelet, pp. 146, 150; Miot, *Mémoires* II, pp. 130, 133. The only exception Napoleon made was in regard to property transactions (see below, pp. 112–13).
32 *Arch. parl.*, 25 July 1811.

in the parliamentary record). The nation, he said, was sovereign, and could not be represented. Its will, however, was embodied in the various constituted authorities, of which the Emperor was the chief and the Legislative Body came fourth in line, after the Senate and the Council of State. In 1809 he thought of having a senatus-consultum drawn up to make the point quite clear.[33]

It took a little while for politicians to settle into the Napoleonic routine. The first two or three years of the Consulate saw a good deal of bickering, and adjustments had to be made on both sides. Napoleon, for his part, agreed to present his financial demands in one annual budget, and to draw up bills which were less vague in terminology and less sketchy as to detail than his earliest efforts. Meanwhile the minority of politicians who wanted a totally different system were got rid of, with the approval of the majority. Though many men professed afterwards to have disliked the system there was no weighty opposition to it from 1803 until the last year of the Empire.

33 *Arch. parl.*, 19 Nov. 1808; *Moniteur*, 15 Dec. 1808; Napoleon, *Correspondance*, no. 15978.

2

Personnel and Procedure

The four hundred men who sat in the first parliament of the Consulate were chosen in a tremendous hurry. The Senate, which was supposed to nominate them, was formed during the morning of 25 December 1799; notices were sent out to such of the new Senators as could be found in Paris to assemble in the afternoon; at 4 o'clock Sieyès was formally elected President and on taking the chair he read out lists of nominees for the Legislative Body and the Tribunate, which were approved by a show of hands.[1]

Obviously a great deal of work had gone on behind the scenes. Gohier, one of the two recalcitrant Directors arrested by Napoleon during the *coup d'etat*, tells us in his memoirs that no sooner did people realize that new parliamentary bodies were to be nominated than place-hunters besieged the offices of the Luxembourg where the Senate was to sit, for all the world like the crowd at the drawing of a lottery. 'Our unfortunate country was like a town taken by assault and given over by the victorious general to pillage,' he wrote. An article in the *Moniteur* suggests that there was some truth in the ex-Director's account: 'Ever since the Constitution created a large number of richly endowed places, what an upheaval there has been! What unknown faces hasten to show themselves! What forgotten names stir again in the dust of the Revolution! What proud republicans of the Year VII make themselves small in order to get an interview with the powerful man who can place them! What talents are exalted, what meagre services exaggerated, what bloody occupations disguised!' In future years the Senate would be required to make its nominations from a national list, but no list would be ready until the Year X, and meanwhile the business was a free-for-all.[2]

Contemporary opinion varied as to how much Napoleon had to do with the nominations. Roederer and Girardin, both of whom were to some extent in Napoleon's confidence, said that he left the matter entirely to Sieyès. On the other hand Bourrienne, Napoleon's secretary, published

1 *Arch. parl.*, 24–6 Dec. 1799; Thiry, *Le Sénat*, p. 74.
2 Gohier, *Mémoires* II, p. 63; *Moniteur*, 24 Dec. 1799.

lists of recommendations which he said were drawn up by Lucien Bonaparte and Regnault de St Jean d'Angély at Napoleon's request. Aimé Martin recalled an ill-natured anecdote about Benjamin Constant, who were supposed to have been so anxious to become a Tribune that he visited Sieyès and Napoleon in turn, swearing to each that he was an enemy of the other. Occasionally someone remembered Talleyrand, who with his usual talent had managed to remain *persona grata* with both Sieyès and Napoleon-when the feud broke out between them.[3]

An analysis of the lists published on 27 December suggests that the influence of all three men had been at work. Of 300 nominated to the Legislative Body, 240 were drafted in from the Councils of the Directory.[4] There were, officially, 750 members of the Councils, and it cannot have been absolutely clear which ones were well disposed towards the new régime. A few glaring mistakes were made: two men who were nominated indignantly refused membership, while another, who was on leave of absence at the crucial time, found himself unjustly black-listed.[5] Of the remaining 60 nominees, 31 had been members of the Councils in previous years and had either been expelled in the purge of Fructidor of the Year V or simply dismissed by lot in the annual retirement of a third of the members. Another 8 had been members of the Constituent Assembly of 1789–91, 5 of them being especially likely to be remembered by Sieyès and Talleyrand as clergy who had sworn the oath required by the Civil Constitution. Of the 21 men who had never sat in any previous assembly, 4 were relatives of Napoleon and one of Sieyès. Two were diplomats, presumably known to Talleyrand (1799 was a bad time for the diplomatic corps, owing to the activities of the Second Coalition, and there were a number of good men in need of temporary employment). Talleyrand may also have been responsible for nominating the banker Fulchiron, who had directed a loan to facilitate a projected invasion of England in 1797. There were two more bankers, both fairly recently established in Paris: Claude Périer, who while still residing at Grenoble had played a resounding part in the local opposition to royal tyranny in 1788, and Charles Gabriel Rousseau from the Ardennes, whose family had been heavily engaged in army contracting throughout the Directorial period.[6] Teissier was a businessman whom the Bonaparte family had known at Marseilles. Seven were scholars of some renown, members or associate members of the Institute where Sieyès was a leading light. Cochon-Duvivier, a medical officer in the

3 Thiry, *Le Sénat*, p. 74; Dutruch, *Le Tribunat*, p. 30; Bourrienne, *Mémoires* III, pp. 9–12, 30–52; Reinhard, *Lettres*, p. 112; Girardin, *Mémoires* II, p. 259.
4 Every historian who writes on this subject produces slightly different numbers. The information given in the following paragraphs, unless attributed otherwise, comes from lists in the *Archives Parlementaires* and from biographical details in Bourleton *et al.*, *Dictionnaire des parlementaires français*.
5 Bourrienne, *Mémoires* III p. 33.
6 Bergeron, *Banquiers* I, pp. 109, 129.

navy, was a relative of the former Minister of Police. The nomination of Latour d'Auvergne, a grenadier captain of legendary courage, was presumably a flight of fancy, perhaps on the part of Napoleon. Only one member, Saint-Pierre Lespéret, remains unexplained: he appears on official lists simply as a member of the administration in his department of Gers.

In nominating the members of the Legislative Body, attention had had to be paid to Article 31 of the Constitution, which said that there must be at least one member from each department. The Tribunate gave greater freedom of choice; nevertheless, 69 members came from the Councils and another 5 from previous legislatures, leaving only 26 places for new men. Of these, 5 were attached to the diplomatic corps, and one was Tallyrand's private secretary. Six were scholars or publi-cists of repute; another 7, like many of the men chosen from the Councils, were intellectuals-cum-politicians who had frequented the salons of Auteuil and learnt to look upon Sieyès as a future saviour.[7] Garat-Mailla belonged to the same circles and also had an uncle in the Senate. Desmousseaux, a member of the Paris administration, was warmly recommended to Napoleon by his informants; Miot and Duveyrier[8] had known Napoleon in Italy, Leroy in Egypt; Jubé had rendered timely service at the head of the guards who cleared out the obstreperous members of the Five Hundred on 19 Brumaire.

The publication of so many names taken from previous legislatures led to an immediate outcry in the press. The *coup d'état* had been welcomed because it promised to save France from factions, and here were the same old politicians still in their places. The *Diplomate* ridiculed the men who had managed to touch a parliamentary salary for the past eight years and now found themselves reappointed for another five. A week later it was still harping on the same theme, parodying the Litany: 'Des éternels conventionnels, délivrez-moi, Seigneur.'[9] The *Gazette de France* affected surprise that republicans could produce only these well-worn figures – 'a few hundred individuals who have exploited France for ten years and want to preserve the privilege'.[10] Napoleon's friends immediately denied that he had had anything to do with the nominations, and public support for Napoleon as against parliament grew up at once, never to be dissipated till 1813.

As the months went by and the Senators took up their duties more effectively, nominations to vacant places in parliament were made by the Senate. Mme la Comtesse de Chastenay-Lanty, in Paris for the winter and seeking to repair the family fortunes after the ravages of the Revolution, failed repeatedly to obtain a seat in the Legislative Body for her father, in spite of courting several Councillors of State and even the

7 Gobert, *L'Opposition*, pp. 8–17, 74–7.
8 Bertrand, *Cahiers, 1821*, p. 50.
9 *Diplomate*, 9 Dec. 1799, 8 Jan. 1800.
10 *Gazette de France*, 30 Dec. 1799.

Third Consul.[11] The Senate sat *in camera* and published no report of its proceedings, but several newspapers professed to know how the business of nominations was accomplished. 'Each member [of the Senate] proposed as many names as there were places, plus one,' said the *Journal du Soir*. 'The election was then made by means of successive reductions.' A preliminary list made in this way was bound to be lengthy, continued the *Journal*; on this particular occasion, ninety-three candidates were said to have been nominated, including several whom the *Journal* could specify as persons of note. The *Journal des Défenseurs de la Patrie*, meanwhile, denied that such information could be genuine: rival newspapers, it said, published fictitious lists in the hope of influencing Senators on behalf of the persons named.[12]

When the Legislative Body met for the first time there were 285 members present. This was a good turn-out in view of the fact that some of the members were quite unable to appear: for instance, it took two months before Belleville, chargé d'affaires at Genoa, was able to write accepting nomination. Some who had administrative jobs in the provinces waited to see if they could get secondment from the head of their department, the Constitution having said nothing about the incompatibility of administrative posts and legislative duties.[13] It was a little while before the membership became fully established. The head of the Bonaparte contingent, brother Joseph, declined membership in order to take up a diplomatic assignment; Latour d'Auvergne preferred to continue in his military calling. There were one or two sudden deaths, and a few happier translations to posts in the civil service. By March an informed observer might properly have started to judge the collective character.

It was a predominantly middle-aged assembly. Out of 280 men whose ages are known, 113 were in their forties and 93 in their fifties. At the two extremes, 50 were in their thirties and 23 in their sixties. Tarteyron, who took the chair at the first meeting as the oldest member present, was over seventy. All the members, including the handful who had belonged to the noble order during the *ancien régime*, had shown their commitment in some unmistakeable way to the Revolution, for Napoleon was at this time very much afraid of men who might have leanings towards royalism.[14] About 130 had had precisely the same kind of career – a legal training, followed by advancement in the various legal/administrative posts created in the provinces by the Revolution, culminating in election to one of the Councils of the Directory. Another score or more had been local doctors or merchants before election to the Elders or the Five Hundred. The Constitution of the Year III, which

11 Chastenay, *Mémoires* I, pp. 424–7.
12 *Journal du Soir*, 20, 23 Apr. 1800; *Journal des Défenseurs de la Patrie*, 23 Apr. 1800.
13 *Procès-verbal, Corps législatif*, 1 Jan., 13 Jan., 12 Mar. 1800.
14 Bourrienne, *Mémoires* III, pp. 58, 108.

required 700 legislators replaceable by one third annually, had of necessity swept into the Councils of the Directory anybody with the slightest ambition or talent for a parliamentary career, and it was doubtless the presence in the Legislative Body of 159 men who had never sat in any other assembly than those of the Directory which gave rise to the accusation that it was a gathering of nonentities. The judgement needs modification. Over a hundred members of the new chamber had sat in earlier assemblies of the Revolution, and the fact that they survived was not always due to colourlessness. Thirty-four had suffered persecution under the Terror and either been imprisoned or obliged to lie low, while on the other side of the coin 11 were regicides. Some had had eventful lives: Maupetit, who had had himself carried from his sick-bed to the Jeu de Paume to swear the famous Tennis Court Oath; Lenormand and Bodinier of Calvados, who had played leading parts in federalist revolt in 1793; Bréard, a member of the Committee of Public Safety in its early days; Bollet, who with Barras had attacked the Commune on 9 Thermidor; Auguis, who had led the troops of the Convention against the rebels of Prairial; Baraillon, wounded while tending the victims of Vendémiaire; Poultier, one-time army officer, civil servant, actor, monk, teacher, who had sat in the Convention with the Mountain, voted for the death of Louis XVI, shouted Robespierre down on 9 Thermidor, suffered capture by the rebels at Toulon, and returned to Paris to found a newspaper under the Directory. The members from newly acquired departments to the east of France were men who had encouraged revolution in Belgium or Liège, helped to hold back invading forces in the Rhineland, or promoted the annexation of Savoy to France. Only three members, however, were likely to have been known to the public by name: Rabaud and Vergniaud, for the sake of their more famous brothers guillotined under the Terror, and the Abbé Grégoire for his own sake, as a persistent supporter of both revolution and religion since the outbreak of the former in 1789.

In the Tribunate the average age was slightly lower: only 14 of the 100 members were over fifty. The rest were fairly evenly divided between the thirties and forties, none being below thirty though the entry qualification allowed for it. Twenty-nine of the 100 had sat in assemblies before the fall of Robespierre; 9 were regicides. A high proportion, at least 30, had suffered imprisonment or persecution of some kind during the Terror: it formed a bond between them and made them into something of a select group. Compared with the Legislators there were more whose names were likely to be known by the public: Bailleul, for instance, who had escaped from Paris at the expulsion of the Girondins but was brought back in irons and imprisoned in the Conciergerie; Chabaud-Latour, who had been on the point of mounting the guillotine when he escaped in his wife's garments; Chauvelin, one-time ambassador of the Republic at the Court of St James's; J.-M. Chénier, brother of the famous poet and himself the author of several brilliantly successful plays – a controversial figure whom some people held responsible for his brother's death; Courtois, author of a violent report against Robespierre and responsible for the denunciation of many Jacobins after Thermidor; Ginguené and J. B. Say, editors of an erudite but strongly independent newspaper, the *Décade Philoso-phique*. The entire hundred were men who, if not Parisians already, were prepared to take up permanent residence in Paris, for the Tribunate had been designated by the Constitution as the proper body for receiving petitions from the people and had therefore not been confined to a short session annually like the Legislative Body. The members of the latter were by contrast provincial men, most of whom returned to their local occupations after a brief spell in parliament, and lived and died in the locality where they were born.

As far as procedure was concerned, again a few weeks elapsed before a pattern emerged. The main lines were laid down in a bill passed by the Legislative Body on 9 January, and the details were filled in by standing orders adopted by each chamber on the 17th. A certain amount of ceremonial was insisted upon, to the amusement of foreigners who attended parliamentary sessions during the Peace of Amiens. The meetings of both the Legislative Body and the Tribunate took place during the afternoon only, the members of each body assembling beforehand in rooms adjacent to their respective halls and proceeding to their meeting in double file, between guards of honour drawn up at the salute and to the sound of drums beating to arms. An irreverent account of the scene in the Tribunate was given later by the Englishman Henry Redhead Yorke in his letters home:

> After we had waited about twenty minutes, during which time two or three individuals peeped through the folding doors opposite to us much in the same way as a head is sometimes seen through the green curtain at Drury Lane in the act of exploring the house, a sudden crash of drums as a signal was heard, and the folding doors vanished as if touched by the wand of Harlequin. The drums then beat a salute, and the scene that opened presented us with a very fine perspective of soldiers presenting arms. In a minute or two the procession commenced, with six men in fancy dresses, whose appearance was a burlesque upon French legislation.[15] They were dressed in grey coats and pantaloons, with scarlet waistcoats and red half-boots. Upon their heads a round hat turned up in front with a blue feather, a red sash round the waist, and a good-sized stick in their hands. Next followed the President, his round hat garnished with three upright tri-coloured feathers; he wore a mazarine-blue coat embroidered in silver, breeches to match, and a white silk waistcoat bound in by a silk tricolour sash with silver fringes. Behind followed the secretaries, and a motley group [of Tribunes] whose appearance provoked great merriment amongst

15 These were the gentlemen ushers.

us. Most of them were in full costume, like the President, but some with worsted, others with black silk, stockings. They wore pantaloons and half-boots, and several had whole-boots with dirty brown tops.[16]

The order to wear uniform had been made by the provisional government of Brumaire: dark blue coats embroidered with gold at the collar and cuffs for the Legislators, and light blue embroidered with silver for the Tribunes, the expense to be borne by the members. The day had gone, said a contemporary newspaper, when people expected their legislators to dress like workmen.[17] At the opening of the Tribunate, Riouffe objected to a costume which divided legislators from the sovereign people, and went on to say that if a uniform was obligatory at least it should consist of 'a long, large, simple garment, easy to put on, like a robe or a mantle', not a tight coat which pinched when worn on top of other garments and was altogether exhausting in the heat of the city. He was told, however, that orders for the cloth had already been placed with the manufacturers and that he must not waste time discussing a frivolous topic. Patterns were circulated, measurements taken, and the cost docked off members' salaries over a period of three months.[18]

At the beginning of each month the members balloted for seats, an arrangement which was supposed to emphasize the absence of party. They also elected a president from among themselves, and four secretaries chosen from a list of members (sixty in the case of the Tribunate) who had volunteered their services for the job. What with one thing and another a good deal of balloting went on. It was done by roll-call, beginning with a different letter of the alphabet each time. The members individually mounted a platform, crossed in front of the secretaries' bench where they received a white disc for 'yes' and a black disc for 'no', placed the appropriate disc in an urn and discarded the other, and descended to their places by steps at the farther side. The discs in the urns were then solemnly counted by the secretaries in full view of the President and members. To a Norfolk squire who witnessed the process in 1803, the secretaries' bench with its array of urns and a set of scales painted below it was reminiscent of an apothecary's shop with the apprentices behind the counter.[19] The most complicated balloting of all took place when the chambers decided on their candidates for a place in the Senate, an event which occurred once a session in accordance with the Constitution and on other occasions when a Senator died. For each nomination there was first of all a *scrutin d'indication*, which might produce as many as thirty names. This was followed by a *scrutin d'élection*, which might have to be repeated several times before one of the nominees acquired an absolute majority of votes. In the middle of

16 Yorke, *France in 1802*, p. 207.
17 *Bulletin des Lois*, 24 Dec. 1799; *Rédacteur*, 5 Jan. 1800.
18 *Arch. parl.*, 2 Jan. 1800; *Procès-verbal, Corps législatif*, 19 Mar. 1800.
19 Greatheed, *Journal*, p. 81.

February 1800, when the session of the Year VIII was well advanced and there were four nominations to make, the Legislative Body reduced the required interval between ballots from three days to twenty-four hours, but the process would still not have been completed in time had not the government for other reasons prolonged the session.[20]

As early as the first month there were complaints in the newspapers about absenteeism. A committee of the Tribunate charged with drafting standing orders proposed that money should be deducted from the salaries of members absent more than twice a month without leave, but this suggestion was discarded in favour of a reprimand delivered by the President and recorded in the minutes.[21] A good deal of time was taken up each day by the President reading out letters of apology for absence. This was followed by the reading out of petitions, which were invariably sent straight to the government, and by the formal acceptance of books and pamphlets submitted by authors for inclusion in the library. An hour or more usually elapsed before the more important duties of the day began.

The actual process of legislation commenced with the First Consul sending a message to the Legislative Body to say that at such-and-such a time on the following day Councillors of State would arrive to present a bill. They did not always, in fact, arrive on time, and Legislators might then be seen strolling about outside the Palais Bourbon waiting for a hasty summons to resume their places.[22] On arrival the councillors of State, usually three in number, were ushered to places on the right of the President's chair, and when called, all three mounted into the tribune. One of them read out a speech stating the government's reasons for presenting the bill, and then read out the bill itself, however long, and announced the date on which discussion of it should commence. This date referred not to the examination of the bill by the Tribunate but to the encounter between Councillors and Tribunes in the Legislative Body, and the time allowed for reaching this crucial stage was usually short – nine days for an important subject like the administrative reorganization of France, two days for a routine matter. A copy of the bill was therefore carried at once to the Tribunate, where the lengthiest work was to be done.

When a bill arrived at the Tribunate it was sent to a committee of between five and seven members, chosen by the officers from lists on which members had indicated their line of interest (judicial, administrative, or financial). The committee drew up a report, which one of the members read to the Tribunate, advising acceptance or rejection of the bill. The meeting was then thrown open for discussion. Members who wished to speak had to give their name to the President, indicating whether they intended to support or oppose the bill, and the President

20 *Arch. parl.*, 14 Feb. 1800.
21 *Arch. nat.*, AF^{IV} 1329; *Arch. parl.*, 7, 17 Jan. 1800.
22 *Arch. nat.*, AF^{IV} 1329.

summoned them in the order in which he had received their names. (Standing orders said that they were to be summoned to speak alternately for and against, but this regulation was never followed.) They were not allowed to speak from their places, but had to mount a rostrum, a procedure which put a premium on reading long, prepared speeches, delivered without reference to the arguments of previous speakers. When the Tribunate first opened, Thiessé rebuked a colleague for making such a speech, but within a few weeks the practice had become so common that Sédillez felt obliged to apologize for speaking from notes which he had not had time to write out more fully.[23] Protests were made if a member tried to interrupt the speakers on the pretext of asking a question, for there might not be enough time to hear all those who had handed in their names. Sometimes the meeting itself demanded closure of the discussion, on the grounds that enough arguments had been heard, or that speakers were tediously repeating each other, or that there were other bills awaiting attention.

When the President had closed the discussion a straw vote was taken to elicit the majority opinion. The Tribunes mounted the platform and deposited their *boules blanches* or *boules noires*, which were then counted. The result was often referred to in newspapers as passing or rejecting the bill, but in fact the Tribunes had no power to do either of these things. Whatever their opinion, they had to choose three delegates to return the bill to the Legislative Body with an account of their views. There was much competition to be given this task. It was eventually decided that at least two of the three delegates should be chosen by ballot; the third should be the man who had delivered the report of the committee on the bill, provided that the majority of the Tribunate had agreed with the report, and if not, the third delegate also was to be chosen by ballot.[24]

The debate before the Legislative Body was conducted with great ceremony. The semi-circular hall of the Palais Bourbon provided an impressive setting, with its mosaic floor, tiered seats, and marble pillars supporting the public gallery. Facing the members, the President sat in a raised box, flanked on either side by statues of famous legislators and statesmen of ancient Rome. Below him was the orators' bench, of solid mahogany inlaid with gold. Each speaker was solemnly conducted to the rostrum by two ushers. A Tribune spoke first, then a Councillor, until as many of the six had been heard as wished to speak. The Tribunes were expected to expound the views of the minority of their assembly as well as those of the majority, although in some cases no one of the three had supported those views himself. They were not, however, expected to invent new arguments: on one unusual occasion, when Thiessé enlarged upon the minority view, he was reprimanded next day by one of

23 *Arch. parl.*, 2 Jan., 14 Mar. 1800.
24 *Arch. parl.*, 6 Jan. 1800.

the Councillors of State who insisted that the President should have called him to order.[25]

The Legislators might well have wondered why they were constrained to listen to the Tribunes at all, since the proceedings in the Tribunate were open to the public, reported in the press, and communicated almost verbatim in a printed hand-out to the members of the Legislative Body before the debate began. The *Journal des Hommes Libres* not surprisingly described a state of boredom in the Legislative Body, the members ruffling their papers, playing with their tassles, and showing every sign of impatience to end the session.[26] The only opportunity for novelty in the debates was in the replies made by the Councillors of State, but since they, like the Tribunes, read prepared speeches, repetition could hardly be avoided. Often, too, a Councillor was heard refuting at length some argument which had been expressed in the Tribunate but which none of the three delegates had bothered to report. The Legislators themselves were not only debarred from speaking but from making any sign of approval or disapproval. At the end of the debate, voting took place by the now familiar method of balloting. The President then pronounced a set formula announcing the number of white and black discs in the urns and the consequent acceptance or rejection of the bill.

On rare occasions the delegates from the Tribunate, instead of opening the debate before the Legislative Body, appealed for an extension of time in which discussion could continue among their colleagues. The appeal, in accordance with a law of 10 March 1800, was addressed to the government in the person of the three Councillors of State, who gave their opinion as to whether an adjournment should be allowed or not and asked the Legislators for a decision. The Legislators were not allowed to specify the length of the adjournment, however; nor were the Tribunes allowed to ask for a specified number of days. The government in this matter clung jealously to its right to decide ultimately on the time factor, which it regarded as intimately connected with its right of initiative in legislation. Thiessé, who once encouraged his fellow Tribunes to think that they could appeal for an extra four days in which to discuss a controversial bill, was accused by the Council of State of 'political heresy' and regarded with suspicion thereafter.[27] Napoleon had taken care to appoint as one of his Councillors of State the pedantic Boulay de la Meurthe, whose detailed knowledge of the Constitution enabled him thus to guard the government's interest at every turn.

25 *Arch. parl.*, 3, 4 Feb. 1800.
26 Quoted in the *Rédacteur*, 29 Mar. 1800.
27 *Journal de Paris*, 20, 21 Mar. 1800.

3

The First Two Sessions of Parliament, 1800–1801

Mme Reinhard, the wife of one of France's leading diplomats, wrote a long letter to her mother from Paris on 8 January 1800, in which she said that Napoleon regarded the parliamentary assemblies as 'harmless toys, with which well brought up children could amuse themselves while he got on with more serious matters', and that it never occurred to him that the children would cause trouble. Other evidence suggests, on the contrary, that he was distinctly apprehensive. In a letter to the Senate acknowledging the nominations it had made to the two parliamentary bodies, he expressed somewhat pointedly the hope that the men it had chosen would forget past opinions and give up criticizing the Constitution.[1]

By the time parliament met, Napoleon must have known that Sieyès was an irreconcilable enemy. An attempt had been made to buy him off by arranging for him to receive a large estate near Versailles as a gift from the nation, but this had merely destroyed his public reputation without curbing his appetite for intrigue.[2] Placed in the Senate, he was somewhat cut off from the two parliamentary assemblies; but as a member of the Institute he was still closely in touch with the group of intellectual politicians he had cultivated in the salons of Mme Helvétius and Mme de Condorcet at Auteuil. A number of these gentlemen had been placed in the Tribunate, where their powers of expression could be used to the greatest advantage. They had all supported the *coup d'état* of Brumaire, but they were an independent lot, and some of them were already annoyed about the amount of power Napoleon had allotted to himself. There was Laromiguière, a distinguished philosopher and popular teacher, who had refused a place in the Senate; Andrieux, a successful lawyer and appeal judge, an expert in the French language and a writer of charming comedies, who as a member of the Council of Five Hundred had made himself the defender of freedom of education and liberty of the press; Ginguené, poet and literary critic, who had been Director of Education for two years under the previous régime and

1 Reinhard, *Lettres*, pp. 113–14; Napoleon, *Correspondance*, no. 4468.
2 Thiry, *Le Sénat*, pp. 48–9.

admired its secularizing tendencies; Chazal, a regicide who had none the less protested against the expulsion of the Girondins from the Convention, and had continued in the Council of Five Hundred to support contradictory policies as the spirit moved him; Thiessé, noted for his acid speeches; Ganilh and Garat-Mailla, recently taken up by the Auteuil group as promising parliamentarians; the volatile J.-B. Chénier; and above all Daunou, whose constitutional ideas had been treated by Napoleon as unceremoniously as those of Sieyès, an who had refused a place in the Council of State at more than twice the salary in favour of a seat in the Tribunate. Napoleon, though a great talker himself, disliked and distrusted men whom he accused of indulging in an excessive amount of talking. Perhaps it was because he was expecting trouble from the Auteuil group that as soon as opposition appeared he denounced it as 'systematic'. Applied to so egocentric and undisciplined a collection of individuals the accusation was wide of the mark.[3]

The Tribunate began its activities by electing Daunau as its president for the first month with 76 votes out of 78, but the first sign of trouble in debate came from outside the Auteuil group. Duveyrier was a newcomer to parliamentary life, and perhaps, as another newcomer Miot de Melito afterwards said, he merely wished to make a mark.[4] He certainly seized one of the earliest opportunities to mount the rostrum and deliver a speech whose passionate tone was in excess of the circumstances which prompted it. Of the two buildings formerly used by the Councils of the Directory, one, the Luxembourg, had been assigned to the Senate, leaving the Palais Bourbon for the Legislative Body. The Tribunate had been somewhat hastily accommodated in the Palais Egalité, once the Palais Royal, the town house of the Duc d'Orléans. Opened up as a pleasure ground for the public in the last years of the *ancien régime*, the character of the place had rapidly deteriorated, and the galleries were full of brothels, gaming dens, and low-class dance halls. Sniggering comments were inevitably made upon the choice of such a location for the Tribunes of the People, but Duveyrier, taking up the challenge, professed to find inspiration in the revolutionary associations of the palace gardens:

> I for my part render homage to the free and popular conscience of those who wanted the Tribunes of the People to sit among the people, the soldiers of liberty to be placed on the scene of their first triumph. I thank them for having enabled us to see from this rostrum the spot on which the generous Camille, giving the signal for a glorious movement, took up this national cockade, our most handsome trophy and most beautiful ornament. I thank them for enabling us to see the place where, if anyone should dare to speak

of an idol of fifteen days, we would remember that men saw overthrown an idol of fifteen centuries.[5]

There was an immediate outcry in the press against this apparent insult to Napoleon. What, it was asked, had Duveyrier himself ever done for his country? An anonymous writer in the *Rédacteur* challenged him to give an account of himself, 'for I know not who you are, or where you have come from, or where you have been; and no one has been able to tell me.' A correspondent to the *Gazette de Hambourg* thought that the Tribunate was already beginning to resemble the Council of Five Hundred in its irresponsible speeches and offensive remarks. Girardin took it upon himself in the Tribunate to reprimand Duveyrier: an imprudent word, he said, could ring round France and cause disturbances which gave foreign powers the impression that the new government was insecure and incapable of making peace.[6]

Napoleon, never a man to shirk an issue, sent for Duveyrier and asked him what he thought he was doing. Duveyrier pretended that his words had been misheard or misinterpreted, and the incident was officially allowed to drop.[7] By then a more serious issue had arisen. On 2 January the government introduced its first bill, outlining procedure for the presentation and passage of bills through the legislature. The proposal that the time schedule should be fixed by the Council of State immediately aroused suspicions among some of the Tribunes that attempts would be made to rush bills through parliament and perhaps even circumvent the Tribunate altogether; Article 11 of the bill put forward the sinister suggestion that if the Tribunate had failed to give an opinion on a bill by the time the debate was due to take place, silence should be construed as approval. Objections were just beginning to be voiced when Démeunier, the leader of a working party charged with drawing up a set of standing orders for the Tribunate, presented his draft scheme, and saw fit to preface it with an exposition of the role allotted to the Tribunes by the Constitution. In addition to their legislative functions, he pointed out, Article 28 gave them the duty of referring to the Senate any actions of the executive power which appeared unconstitutional. 'The Tribunate is thus instituted to serve as a barrier against excesses of the ministerial power,' he said.[8]

In this way, the idea got abroad that the Tribunate regarded itself as having a right and duty to oppose the government at every step. Roederer, a member of the Council of State who had taken upon himself the role of promotion manager to the new régime, enquired rhetorically in his newspaper the *Journal de Paris*: 'Is it true that the Tribunate is an "organized opposition"? Is it true that a Tribune is condemned always

5 *Arch. parl.*, 3 Jan. 1800. The reference is to Camille Desmoulins's speech on 12 July 1789 leading to the attack on the Bastille.
6 *Rédacteur*, 5 Jan. 1800; *Gazette de Hambourg*, 16 Jan. 1800; *Arch. parl.*, 5 Jan. 1800.
7 Bertrand, *Cahiers, 1821*, p. 50; Duveyrier, *Anecdotes*, pp. 312–20.
8 *Arch. parl.*, 4 Jan. 1800.

to oppose the government, without reason or consideration? To attack all it does and proposes? ... If that were the role of a Tribune it would be the vilest and most hateful of roles.' The *Publiciste*, along with other journals alerted by Roederer, declared that a body permanently opposed to the government would be condemned by public opinion.[9] Unabashed by the warning, Guingené and others pressed the attack upon the procedural bill in the Tribunate that very afternoon. They were eclipsed by Benjamin Constant, one of the newcomers to the political scene, who seized this opportunity to make the first great parliamentary speech of his career. The obvious aim of the government in wishing to keep the time schedule in its own hands, Constant said, was to 'wing bills through', and to rule by pleas of urgency. The Tribunes should not abdicate their constitutional duty because a journalist like Roederer gave a false impression of them. The Tribunate was not instituted to oppose *all* bills but to oppose *bad* bills, of which this was clearly one.[10]

The speech caused such a stir that the cold-blooded Chauvelin chided Constant for dazzling the Tribunes with too much eloquence, and Riouffe, a fervent admirer of Napoleon, not only replied that afternoon but rose again the following day and attacked both Constant and Duveyrier with such vehemence that he was three times called to order. Newspapers came out with suggestions that Napoleon should purge the parliamentary bodies of all opponents and start afresh. Constant had made the speech on the advice of Mme de Staël in the hope that Napoleon would recognize his talents and promote his career, but the reverse happened. Reports of the great man's anger flew around Paris, and politicians who had been invited to a dinner party by Mme de Staël that evening to fête her protégé discreetly sent excuses. Napoleon never forgave Constant. The storm did not immediately break, however, for the government decided to minimize the importance of the affair. After all, the bill that had provoked the trouble was approved in the Tribunate by 54 votes to 26. An officially inspired article in the *Moniteur* on 8 January attributed the opposition to ill-advised perfectionists who had condemned the whole bill on account of a few minor defects. Sieyès, who had hurriedly withdrawn to the country, crept back to Paris, and everybody involved breathed again. Mathieu, reporting for the Tribunate to the Legislative Body, gave the impression that opponents were only trying to get the government to use a little tact when exercising its powers over the time schedule, and with this the bill was passed by 203 votes to 23.[11]

The outcry from the public over this affair, though probably manu-

9 *Journal de Paris, Publiciste*, 5 Jan. 1800.
10 *Arch. parl.*, 5 Jan. 1800.
11 Gobert, *L'Opposition*, pp. 87–9; Miot, *Mémoires* I, p. 277; *Gazette de France*, 12 Jan., *Décade philosophique*, 10, 20 Jan. 1800; Reinhard, *Lettres*, p. 114; *Arch. parl.*, 6, 9 Jan. 1800.

factured to a large extent by Roederer, chastened all but the more ebullient spirits in parliament, for a time at least. The majority timidly rejected an opportunity to enlarge the powers of the Tribunate in the matter of petitions. Article 83 of the Constitution, which allowed any private individual to address a petition to any of the constituted authorities, designated the Tribunate as an especially appropriate body for receiving such communications. At first the Tribunate did no more than read out the petitions it received and send them straight to the government, but on 28 January Huguet suggested that a commission should be set up to select those petitions which were of national importance and reserve them for proper discussion in parliament. Constant enlarged on the proposal, saying that all petitions should be discussed and given a recommendation before being sent to the government. Both suggestions were vigorously opposed by Girardin, who reminded his hearers of the tumultuous times when 'a child of twelve, admitted to the bar of the House, told the representatives of the nation that he spoke in the name of 30 million; when women, frequenters of the galleries, dictated laws; when madmen demanded the law of the maximum and, on May 31st, the heads of the purest republicans'. Bérenger reminded colleagues of the need to reassure the public as to the non-subversive character of the Tribunate, and Huguet's proposal, along with Constant's amendment, was thrown out by a large majority.[12]

The Legislative Body necessarily began life more calmly than the Tribunate, since there was bound to be a lapse of time before the government's first measure reached the stage of debate. Meetings were several times adjourned after a formal opening. An attempt by Crochon to modify the rule of silence imposed upon the Legislators by claiming that they had a right to compose an explanation when passing or rejecting a bill was shouted down.[13] When the first debate eventually took place, it proved to be something of an anticlimax, for the first government speaker was wordy and ponderous and the second almost inaudible, and the one Tribune who expounded the views of the opposition did so in a flat and almost apologetic manner. As soon as the vote was taken members drifted away, and there were too few left to carry out routine business later in the afternoon. Under these circumstances an agitation begun by some of the members for an increase in salary was unlikely to find much support.[14]

Greater excitement was experienced at the beginning of February when the government's second important measure, to reorganize the Tribunal of Cassation, was debated at length. The Tribunal was the spiritual descendant of the Parlement, and as such was disliked by many lawyers, who at the same time were on the look out for attempts by the government to interfere with the independence of the judiciary. The bill

12 *Arch. parl.*, 1, 7 Feb. 1800.
13 *Arch. parl.*, 8, Jan. 1800.
14 *Arch. parl.*, 9 Jan. 1800; *Arch nat.*, AF[IV] 1329.

at first sight, however, gave little cause for complaint, and speakers in the Tribunate had been at a loss to find fault with it. Only on the fourth day of discussion, when members had applied for and received an extension of time, had Thiessé, followed by Ganilh, discovered reasons for attacking the bill root and branch. The former based his criticism on a group of articles which allowed the Tribunal, instead of the legislature as hitherto, to indict judges for neglect of duty, while Ganilh concentrated on an article which allowed the government to uphold decisions of the Tribunal vis-à-vis the lower courts by framing an 'interpretative law'. Together the two Tribunes had found the bill destructive of civil liberty and subversive of the Constitution. Other speakers had clamoured to join in, but the President had already closed the list. A vote had been taken revealing 44 members in favour of the bill and 42 against. Fireworks were expected in the Legislative Body.[15]

The display began calmly with a speech by the Tribune Mouricault stating the reasons why the majority in the Tribunate had approved the bill, and a speech by Berlier, Councillor of State, indicating the merits of the bill from the government's point of view. It was the second day which the *Ami des Lois* described as 'brilliant'. Thiessé, believing that more could have been made of the opposition in the Tribunate if there had been more time, spoke for three hours, during which he not only enlarged on arguments already used but produced new ones, denouncing the bill as an attack upon the system of justices of the peace. Berlier demanded an adjournment, and having apparently spent the evening preparing another speech he proceeded on the morrow to restate the reasons why the Tribunate had approved of the bill. He prefaced this extraordinary behaviour by telling the President of the Legislative Body that he should have called Thiessé to order for not sticking to his brief. In spite of these efforts the bill was rejected by a majority of 95, but whether this was because members were genuinely impressed by Thiessé's arguments as one of them afterwards maintained, or because as a body they were annoyed by Berlier's officiousness, cannot be said for certain.[16]

The bill had been announced by the government as part of a much larger reorganization of judicial procedure, and defeat could therefore be explained away by saying that presentation of the complete measure would vindicate the government's sincerity. In fact the bill for the reorganization of the judicial order, presented to the Legislative Body on 5 March 1800, was approved by the Tribunate with 59 votes to 23 and passed by the Legislators with 232 votes to 41, although the government had openly refused to take Thiessé's criticisms into account. It was a lengthy and comprehensive work, creating a complete hierarchy of courts, defining the jurisdiction of each, and establishing the number and salaries of the judges. The Council of State, said its

15 *Arch. parl.*, 26–9 Jan. 1800.
16 *Ami des Lois*, 5 Feb. 1800; *Arch. parl.*, 2–4 Feb., 23 Nov. 1800.

spokesman Emmery, did not flatter itself that it was proposing the best imaginable judicial organization, but only the best that could be achieved in the time available. Similar appeals to the urgent need for legislation to restore order and security to France had already undermined opposition to the bill reorganizing the administrative system. Speakers on that occasion had revealed numerous impracticalities in the proposed division of territory, but Daunou had ended a critical report to the Tribunate with the words: 'My committee cannot ask you to *approve* of the bill, because of its many defects, but it must ask you to *consent* to it, because you would be unwise to wait too long for the bill to be perfected.' Sédillez believed that only when the most urgent measures had been passed would members escape from the invidious position of criticizing bills on the one hand and voting for them on the other. The lack of power to amend legislation was a serious drawback to most critics: there cannot have been many members like Huguet, who was prepared to reject a bill of 80 clauses because he seriously objected to one article. Under these circumstances the size of the opposition vote on some of the government's more important bills was quite surprising. Twenty-five Tribunes out of 96, and 63 Legislators out of 280 voted against the administrative law, though it proved to be one of Napoleon's most famous and characteristic pieces of legislation. Unfortunately there is no means of knowing whether the opponents were impressed by serious arguments of principle, such as those put forward by Duchesne, Gillet and Ganilh against the despotic tendencies inherent in the proposed system, or whether they were motivated by one of the many local grievances that had arisen over boundaries and the choice of *chefs-lieux*.[17]

More remarkable still was the fact that 20 Tribunes and 22 Legislators were prepared to vote against a conscription bill at a time when the campaign against Austria was about to commence. Even Benjamin Constant was moved to say that the Tribunate ought not to be the first of France's assemblies to deny the country the means of repelling its enemies. Opposition persisted, however, around two points: the fact that men previously granted exemption were to be called up unless again exempted under the new regulations, and the fact that decisions as to who was or was not qualified for exemption were to be left to the recruiting authorities. Unfortunately the point on which opposition might on principle have been the most telling proved with the majority of parliamentarians to be the most popular part of the bill. Article 2 allowed 'all who could not support the fatigues of war', and 'all who were recognized as being of more use to the state by continuing in their work or study', to 'replace themselves by a substitute'. The system of substitutes was not new, having commonly operated in connection with militia service under the *ancien régime*; and experience indicated only too clearly that men who had the means to buy substitutes would do so

17 *Arch. parl.*, 12–14 Feb., 14–15 Mar. 1800.

whether they were unfit for military service or in reserved occupations or not. The government spokesman Lacuée fully realized this, but pretended that the practice would stabilize society by creating a new bond between rich and poor. 'Is there a rich man who could refuse support, protection, succour, friendship even, to the one who has braved for him the intemperance of the seasons and the burdens of war?' he asked. 'The kind of adoption and patronage which will be established between the substitute and the substituted will have effects far more lasting and far happier than any in the annals of our history.' Benjamin Constant admitted that the system created an embarrassment for egalitarians, but added obscurely that it could perhaps be justified while France 'still had many ills to cure'. A few democrats salved their consciences by drawing attention to Article 3, which allowed the 'indigent' (defined at first as men paying less than 25 francs in direct taxes and subsequently amended to 50 francs) to claim exemption on grounds of infirmity or family responsibility *without* having to buy a substitute, but no one attacked the system of bought substitutes altogether or, oddly enough, pointed out the injustice of requiring any man, however rich, to buy a substitute if he were genuinely debarred from service through ill-health. Portiez, one of the duller wits in the Tribunate, was evidently under the impression that *all* the indigent were to be exempt from military service simply because they were indigent, and spoke against Article 3 on the grounds that hordes of paupers would be able to subvert the social order while the rich were away on military service.[18]

Opposition was more coherent and successful when revolutionary principle coincided with the interests of property owners, as happened when the government tackled a complicated land problem. Ever since 1789 there had been uncertainty as to which rents and dues had been abolished on the famous night of 4 August and which had not. A law of 17 July 1793 had failed to resolve the problem, chiefly because many people found obscurity to their advantage. The government now tried to reiterate the distinction between rents and dues which were of feudal origin and those which were not, proposing that on state property, tenants, or failing them an outside party, should be allowed to buy out the non-feudal impositions at fifteen years' purchase. No attempt was to be made to collect arrears of payment (all such rents and dues having been universally ignored over the past decade), but money was urgently needed for the war, and the government believed it was on to a good thing. The proposal, however, raised a storm of protest from men who had bought land, outright as they thought, and could now imagine themselves obligated for rents and dues by the previous owners. The integrity of the government was not questioned, but the wording of the bill, which did not distinguish clearly enough between feudal and non-feudal obligations, was said to leave loopholes for the restoration of the entire feudal system. Benjamin Constant condemned the bill as

18 *Arch. parl.*, 26 Feb., 4, 5, 6, 8 Mar. 1800.

'dangerous, equivocal, favouring feudal pretensions under another name, and likely to cause the ruin of citizens through the host of law-suits it rendered inevitable'. Chazal painted an equally terrible picture of the consequences – 'judgments, executions, seizures, desolation, despair, sterility, poverty, all the vices and crimes of feudalism in the bosom of the motherland'. Fifty-nine out of 88 Tribunes voted for the bill to be rejected, and the government withdrew it rather than face defeat in the Legislative Body.[19]

Revolutionary principle by itself failed to carry the majority. A famous revolutionary law of the Year II obliged fathers of families in their wills to divide all but a tenth of their property equally among their children. When Boulay de la Meurthe, introducing a bill to extend the discretion to a quarter of the property if there were fewer than four children, said that it was desirable to set alongside the revolutionary principle of equality the more natural principles of individual liberty and paternal authority, the more ardent republicans in the Tribunate were roused to anger. Andrieux denounced the bill as creating an opportunity for reactionary fathers to penalize their revolutionary sons, and as a first step towards the restoration of primogeniture. His speech created enough of a stir for the debate, which should have opened in the Legislative Body on the following day, to be put off for five days, but much of the time granted to the Tribunate was wasted on a ridiculous quarrel as to whether or not a speech on equality of inheritance made by Mirabeau in 1790 should be dug out of the archives and given a formal reading. The debate in the Legislative Body attracted an unprecedented number of visitors. The Councillors of State approached the subject more cautiously than before, contenting themselves with pointing out that parents had for years been resorting to fraud in order to will a little extra property to deserving children, and that the bill offered them an opportunity without placing them under an obligation. The bill passed by a majority of 213 votes to 43.[20]

The first session ended, however, with a complete triumph for the opposition, albeit on a matter of small practical importance. A bill to allow the government to authorize a toll when making a concession to a private company to build a bridge or cut a canal was rejected by large majorities in both assemblies. The reason was ostensibly theoretical: a toll was a tax, and should not be levied without the consent of the legislature. Principle again coincided with self-interest, however: opponents of the bill were able to frighten property-owners in parliament by suggesting that, if the bill passed, the government would force private owners to sell their land to speculators, who would 'overrun France with canals and bridges.'[21]

Shortly before the end of the session, Councillors of State appeared in

19 *Arch. parl.*, 9, 14, 15, 17, 18 Mar. 1800.
20 *Arch. parl.*, 17, 19, 20, 25 Mar. 1800; *Journal de Paris*, 26 Mar. 1800.
21 *Arch. parl.*, 27, 29 Mar. 1800.

the Tribunate and the Legislative Body to announce that war was about
to commence. They read out decrees calling soldiers to the colours and
creating a reserve army 'to be commanded directly by the First Consul'.
Blame for the renewal of hostilities was placed, both by the Councillors
of State and by various Tribunes who made speeches on the occasion,
entirely upon Britain, and any visitor to parliament could have been
excused for not realizing that the fighting was in fact to be against
Austria. In spite of Napoleon's professed desire to hang back from the
war, no one seemed to be in any doubt that he would leave at once for
the front: the Tribunate voted an address expressing the hope that he
would 'return as victor and peacemaker'. Napoleon said in his memoirs
that his hesitations were due to a clause in the Constitution forbidding
the Consuls to command armies in the field; but there was no such
clause. It is more likely that he still wished to be recognized as a civilian
ruler ('I do not wish to be the general,' he told Miot de Melito), and also
that he did not want his political enemies to know, sooner than they
need, that he was about to leave them with a clear field for their
intrigues. In the event, 'intrigues' was probably too strong a word.
Napoleon left Paris on 5 May. During the next two months, interested
politicians met regularly to decide what arrangements to make if he
were killed. Such discussions were natural enough, however, and the
Tribunes named by Miot de Melito as taking part in the meetings (Adet,
Girardin, Bérenger, Lebreton, Gallois and Miot himself) were not men
noted for opposition. More sinister, perhaps, was a meeting said to have
taken place among Sieyès's friends at the end of May, at which discussion passed over what to do if Napoleon were killed and lingered upon
how to take advantage of a swing in public opinion if Napoleon were
defeated. The evidence for such a meeting having taken place is slight,
but the police reported every rumour to Napoleon and doubtless
increased thereby his sense of insecurity and his distrust of politicians in
general.[22]

The Tribunate, meanwhile, seemed to fall over backwards in its
attempts to behave discreetly. The legislative session, after a pro-
longation of ten days, ended on 31 March, and the Legislators, exhorted
by Boulay de la Meurthe to meditate on the wonderful difference
Napoleonic laws had already made to France, departed to their homes.
The Tribunes were not entitled to go, because the Tribunate, as the
voice of the people, was designed by the Constitution to remain in
permanent session. But on what business were they to occupy themselves? Now was the time, said Chénier, for the Tribunate to establish
itself as the great forum of debate. Issues of national importance should
be discussed, and suggestions for future legislation should be sent to the
government under Article 29 of the Constitution, which allowed the
Tribunate to 'express its wishes on abuses to be corrected and improve-

22 *Arch. parl.*, 8 Mar. 1800; Miot, *Mémoires* I, pp. 273ff, 286–7, 290–92; Girardin,
Mémoires I, pp. 175–88; *Arch. nat.*, AF[IV] 1329.

ments to be made in all branches of the public administration.' 'Do not vacate your posts,' urged Chénier, 'Let the people see that you are occupied with their affairs.' All attempts to carry out this advice were thwarted by the less zealous or more timid members, however. To start with, the Tribunate decided to meet only once a fortnight, and even for these meetings there was a constant fear that a quorum would be lacking, as a steady flow of members applied for leave of absence to visit their families. Then a petition which was regarded as being of special interest since it came from the citizens of St Domingue was looked at by a commission, but the commission recommended that no exception should be made to the self-imposed rule of sending petitions direct to the government. Chazal asked the Tribunate to express a desire for the law of inheritance to be amended, but the majority rejected the suggestion on the grounds that the law of inheritance was a part of the civil code currently under discussion in the Council of State, and the Tribunate must take care not to infringe the government's right of initiation. Isnard, on the same day, suggested that the Tribunate could be looking at the figures necessary for next year's budget, but this idea too was discarded. A committee examined a law suit which had been dragging on for some time in the courts to see if the government, which had interfered at several points, could be accused of unconstitutional behaviour, but reached the conclusion that it could not. A request by Sédillez for the Tribunate to consider expressing a desire for the abolition of the death penalty merely provoked another member to protest against speakers who introduced dangerous topics without due notice. At the very end of the vacation the Tribunate adopted a suggestion by Démeunier that representatives who were chosen to expound the Tribunate's view in debate before the Legislative Body should not in future include members who had supported the minority opinion.[23]

Nevertheless there were signs from the very beginning of the second parliamentary session that the opposition meant business. The police had been reporting to Napoleon since the beginning of October that his enemies were plotting a *coup*, to be carried out as soon as parliament met. Napoleon had returned to France victorious after Marengo, but the final peace for which the nation craved had not yet been secured: France's armies might still be defeated, and in such an eventuality the troops, it was suggested, might rise on behalf of some other general. There was an air of fantasy about most of these rumours, and of comic opera about police attempts to spy on members of the Tribunate as they assembled in their reading room and library, but forecasts of more concerted opposition in parliament were borne out by events. Siméon, newly appointed to the Tribunate in place of a member who had died, told his friend Thibaudeau that the Tribunate resembled the Councils of

23 *Arch. parl.*, 19, 31 Mar., 13, 22 Apr., 6, 22 May, 21 July, 4 Aug., 7 Nov. 1800. Officially, of course, the Tribunate did not know which members had voted with the minority, but only which members had spoken for it.

the Directory in the days before the purge of Fructidor: there was a revolutionary party, he said, full of zeal and energy, and an amorphous mass of other members who were feeble and silent. Siméon himself was one of the men who had been proscribed from the Council of Five Hundred as a royalist at Fructidor: when hs took his seat in the Tribunate he was under the impression that former revolutionaries like Chénier and Bailleul looked at him askance.[24]

The session opened with unaccustomed liveliness in the Legislative Body, where Charles Rousseau, the member for Ardennes, rose to suggest a change in procedure. Now that the minority view of the Tribunate could no longer be expounded by one of its own adherents, the Legislative Body must take its own steps to ensure that the minority was properly heard, he said. Members must pay more attention to the printed reports of proceedings in the Tribunate, and if, as frequently happened, these arrived too late to be read before the debate took place, the vote must be postponed until they had been perused. Also, members must be prepared to allow all three Tribunes to speak, and not be in such a hurry as they had been in the past to close the discussion. Rousseau proposed, in fact, that demands for closure should be forbidden, and that all the speakers, both for the government and the Tribunate, should be encouraged to speak as many times as they wished. The proposal was merely regarded by most members, however, as impugning the honour of the legislature (when had they ever demanded a premature closure of discussion? etc.) and the assembly moved angrily to next business.[25]

Rousseau, however, rose again, this time to propose that when the Legislative Body chose its candidates for places in the Senate, each nomination should be accompanied by a sentence explaining the reasons for putting the candidate forward. This proposal might have been commended on the grounds that it was the practice followed by the First Consul, but Rousseau, who was not apparently a man of tact, preferred to hint that members were simply putting forward their own friends, and that as a result the Senate most often chose the military men nominated by Napoleon. His speech provoked shouts of protest, and when, next day, a report of it was discovered to have been printed along with the rest of the proceedings, Rousseau was made to pay the costs himself.[26]

There was more in Rousseau's proposal than met the eye, however. A similar suggestion had been made by Parent-Réal in the Tribunate the day before, and at the same time vigorous efforts were being made by the opposition in both parliamentary bodies to secure the election of Grégoire as a candidate for the Senate. The presentation of so notorious a supporter of France's breach with the Papacy, especially if accom-

24 *Arch. nat.*, AF[IV] 1329, F[7] 3688[21]; Thibaudeau, *Mémoires*, p. 20.
25 *Arch. parl.*, 23, 28 Nov. 1800.
26 *Arch. parl.*, 27, 28 Nov. 1800.

panied by an attribution, would be an embarrassment to Napoleon at a time when his thoughts were turning towards a Concordat. In the event, Grégoire's candidature achieved little success in the Tribunate but was only narrowly defeated in the Legislative Body.[27]

The complicated in-fighting that always accompanied senatorial nominations was still in progress when the Tribunate asserted its independence in an astounding fashion by voting for the rejection of a government bill by 85 votes to 5. It was a small bill listing the types of documents to be deposited in the Archives Nationales, and its offending nature was not immediately obvious. The committee of the Tribunate which examined it first saw nothing wrong with it. The warning was given later in discussion by Bouteville, an experienced parliamentarian of moderate but staunch liberal views, who pointed out that before Brumaire the Archives Nationales had been under the direction of the legislature, that the government had taken over control by a mere decree, and that parliament was now being asked for a law to supplement a patently irregular act. The unconstitutional character of the government's behaviour would have warranted an appeal to the Senate, but it was not this which roused the anger of the Tribunes. They fastened instead upon the slipshod fashion in which the bill had been drawn up, presenting an opportunity for the Tribunate to vent all its spleen upon the Council of State.[28]

In the previous session there had been a great deal of criticism of the condition in which bills had arrived from the Council of State. Factual inaccuracies were numerous: in the course of discussing the administrative law it was discovered that an out-of-date atlas had been used for drawing up the divisions of territory. A bill to allow the state to sell off some of its ground rents was proved to be mathematically so bad that the government withdrew it indefinitely. Factual errors were accompanied by obscure statements, such as the clause in the conscription bill which offered exemption to 'all who could not support the fatigues of war'. Proper administrative machinery was seldom set up: a bill to relieve the ordinary courts of claims for maritime prizes forgot to provide any other courts or tribunals to which claimants could go. These deficiencies were frequently attacked in the Tribunate with zeal and venom. 'It is time that care was taken to draw up bills worthy of the great nation they are designed to rule,' declared Thibault on 27 March. Members of the Council of State believed that the attacks were inspired wholly by jealousy, since Napoleon was known to take pride in his Council, allowing the members a great deal of freedom in discussion and giving them precedence over the Tribunes and Legislators at official gatherings. (They also received twice the amount of salary – 25,000 francs a year.) In the debate on the Archives bill, Councillor Regnault de St Jean d'Angély appealed to the Legislative Body to rise above petty

27 *Arch. parl.*, 25, 28, 29, 30 Nov., 3, 5, 6 Dec. 1800.
28 *Arch. parl.*, 29 Nov., 2 Dec. 1800.

considerations, but the speakers from the Tribunate claimed that they had none but the loftiest motives for their opposition, and the bill was rejected by 209 votes to 58.[29]

The Archives bill was not an issue likely to stir the public, however. More interest was aroused by two bills presented within a week of each other, the one to cut down the number of justices of the peace in France from 6,000 to 3,600, and the other to transfer their responsibilities for law and order to special 'security police' appointed by the government. The reasons given by the government were the need for economy and the lack of educated men in rural areas to carry out the duties of JP. Opposition in the Tribunate was fierce and comprehensive, and attempts by one or two speakers to defend the bills met with open disfavour. Economy would be negligible, it was said, because the area to be covered by each JP would be larger and would necessitate more expenditure on travel; the duties of a JP required not education but common sense, and there was enough of this to go round; and since the number of paid officials was rapidly increasing it was not in the interests of liberty to decrease the number of justices, who were elected, and place their more important functions in the hands of appointees of the First Consul. For the first time, an examining committee unanimously advised rejection of a bill. The government withdrew both measures, and exalted spirits were jubilant. Others, however, began to fear a reaction from the public. 'The entire mass of working people are for the government, and there is general discontent with the conduct of the Tribunate and the Legislative Body,' wrote a police reporter. The government's withdrawal was purely tactical, for it intended to present the bills again, in conjunction with a measure designed to deal with the robbery and vandalism rampant in many areas of France.[30]

Before presenting this crucial bill, Napoleon decided to try and soften up the opposition. He had often said to members of the Tribunate: 'Instead of declaiming from the rostrum, why don't you come and talk with me privately? We could have family conversations like we do in the Council of State.' He now arranged for several members – Daunou, Andrieux, Duveyrier – to be brought round separately to see him. In private conversation he was without doubt at his best ('If ever I thought it would be useful to win over a few of the recalcitrant, I had only to get them to come to the Privy Council and discuss things, and they would speak like the rest,' he told Bertrand on St Helena), but on this occasion his only success was with Duveyrier, who was not, after all, a very determined opponent of the government, although the police had had their knife into him ever since the 'idol' speech. Daunou indignantly rejected all offers to make him a Councillor of State or a Director of

29 *Arch. parl.*, 16 Feb., 16, 27, 28 Mar., 4. Dec. 1800.
30 *Arch. parl.*, 27 Nov., 2, 3, 5, 6 Dec. 1800; *Journal de Paris*, 6 Dec. 1800; *Arch. nat.*, AF[IV] 1329.

Education, whereupon Napoleon flew into a temper and described the entire Tribunate as 'unbearably insolent'.[31]

Affairs had reached this point when an attempt was made to blow up Napoleon's carriage as he was driving to the opera on the night of 24 December. Fouché produced strong evidence to prove that the plot was the work of the royalist rebel George Cadoudal, but Napoleon brushed it aside: he was already proceeding against royalist rebellion with all the means at his disposal and could afford to use the opera plot for other purposes. He persuaded the Senate to decree the deportation of 130 men known to the police as Jacobins. None were members of parliament, but any attempt by the legislative bodies in the near future to deny Napoleon the means of restoring law and order might be construed as collusion. Public opinion surged up in favour of Napoleon as a result of the plot, and became more enthusiastic than ever when the government announced that an armistice had been signed with Austria. The Legislators rushed off in a body to congratulate the First Consul. The Tribunate, however, refused even at this juncture to be carried away, and spent a day electing a deputation, of which it unanimously agreed that one member should be Moreau, the brother of the general whose recent victory at Hohenlinden could be said to be at least as important as Napoleon's at Marengo.[32]

The government threw down the gauntlet on 7 January 1801 by presenting in one afternoon the two bills on JPs and police and a third bill allowing the government at its discretion to set up special tribunals of a semi-military nature to deal with crimes generally described at the time as 'brigandage'. The first two bills were accepted by the Tribunate with respectable majorities, a number of opposition members having decided to reserve their fire for the third bill. A speech by Benjamin Constant incorporating new arguments, and suggesting that the desired economies could be made, and a better class of men attracted to the job, if justices were unpaid as in England, provoked from Girardin an accusation of 'formed opposition', which Constant indignantly denied.[33]

Meanwhile Duveyrier reported for the committee on the special tribunals bill. To most people's astonishment he appealed to his fellow politicians to show confidence in the government by awarding it the powers it requested. Napoleon's personal approaches, though amounting, it seems, to no more than flattery, had obviously paid off.[34] In spite of this setback, nineteen Tribunes handed in their names to speak

31 Thibaudeau, *Mémoires*, p. 198; *Arch. nat.*, AF[IV] 1329, F[7] 3829; Gobert, *L'Opposition*, pp. 154–6; Guérard, *Daunou*, p. 85; Bertrand, *Cahiers, 1816–17*, p. 259.
32 *Arch. parl.*, 2, 3 Jan. 1801.
33 *Arch. parl.*, 17, 21–4 Jan. 1801.
34 Duveyrier was summoned to read his speech to Napoleon before delivering it in the Tribunate. Later he was encouraged to think he had achieved an important amendment by being allowed to strike out Article 32, which was particularly badly worded. 'What fool invented that article?' exclaimed Napoleon, forgetting that it was himself. Abrantès, *Mémoires* II, p. 79; Gobert, *L'Opposition*, p. 175.

against the bill. Constant, one of the first to be heard, listed all the major grievances and denounced the bill as both unconstitutional and unnecessary: unconstitutional because although the legislature could suspend the rights of the individual when safety required, it could not allow the government to suspend those rights as and when it liked; unnecessary because the ordinary laws were already sufficiently severe. So many and so vague were the crimes allotted to the special tribunals, he said, that the latter would have more to do than the ordinary courts. Prefects would prefer them to the ordinary courts because their judges, unlike ordinary judges, could be removed from office by the government if their judgments were unfavourable. Daunou enlarged on the unconstitutional nature of the bill by arguing that if the legislature wished to suspend individual liberty it could do so only by suspending the whole of the Constitution (a course of action which would clearly be unpopular), but later speakers, at a loss to find new arguments, could only resort to rhetoric. Ginguené accused the government of reverting to the Terror; Chénier accused it in general terms of abandoning the Revolution: 'Let the government rally more whole-heartedly to republican principles, to republican institutions, to republican opinion. . . .Let the reins of government be confided to republican hands, and public spirit will improve. The ordinary laws will be sufficient because they will be carried out.' In the end, after hearing 20 speakers altogether, members voted to close the discussion without hearing the remaining 18 who had handed in their names. To the intense disappointment of the opposition, the vote was counted at 49 for the bill and 41 against. Guingené was beside himself, and made a number of injudicious threats which were duly reported to Napoleon by the police; Daunou swore he would no longer sit in an assembly so devoid of concern for liberty. Benjamin Constant, who had resigned his position as reporter to the Legislative Body on a minor bill in the hope of being able to make a great opposition speech on this one, was thwarted of his ambition.[35]

Supporters of the bill in the Tribunate had made little attempt to deny the criticisms put forward by the opposition but had argued simply on the grounds of necessity, seeing more danger in abuse of liberty than in excess of authority. In the debate before the Legislative Body the most impassioned speaker was the Councillor Français de Nantes, who urged his hearers to descend from any 'metaphysical' heights they may have scaled and envisage the prisons full of ferocious vagabonds and brigands – men so vile, he said, that they were no longer worthy of regard as human beings. This was apparently going too far for some of the Legislators, but the bill passed by 192 votes to 88, and the majority decided that the speeches made in its favour should be published for the general good. Napoleon was less pleased by the outcome than annoyed by the opposition. It was he who had invented the term 'metaphysician'

35 *Arch. parl.*, 25 Jan.–3 Feb. 1801; *Arch. nat.*, F⁷ 3829; Guérard, *Daunou*, p. 89.

as a form of abuse, to describe those of his opponents who judged by abstract principles rather than by utility. There were twelve or fifteen of them, he said, 'who wanted drowning'. . . .They are vermin that have got under my skin. . . .They needn't think I shall let myself be attacked like Louis XVI. I shan't stand for it.' He approved of the speech by Français de Nantes and told his fellow Consuls, when they deplored the line he had taken, that it was worth losing a few votes to let people know some home truths.[36]

As the session proceeded, bills were presented thick and fast; discussion of one was frequently interrupted to take up another, as urgency required. Some were routine. Others were non-controversial but not unimportant, such as those outlining a new system of election for JPs, establishing commercial banks, and 'reuniting' with France four departments on the left bank of the Rhine. (This last bill, whose passage through parliament was accompanied by cries of *Vive la République!* at every stage, nevertheless got three negative votes in the Tribunate and one in the Legislative Body.)[37] On two occasions the opposition was roused to renewed efforts. A bill to revise procedure for taking appeals to the Tribunal of Cassation was rejected by the Tribunate by 71 votes to 19, chiefly on the advice of Thiessé who proved that it would not achieve either the economy or the efficiency declared to be its motives. In spite of an adjournment to give the government time to prepare its case, the bill was defeated in the Legislative Body by 195 votes to 91. Almost at the same time a bill to consolidate different portions of the public debt and sell 120 million francs worth of national land was criticized in the Tribunate by Benjamin Constant in a speech bristling with financial detail, and after some obscure passages of arms, in which Tribunes accused each other of impugning France's honour and undermining her credit, the bill was rejected by 56 votes to 30. The result was greeted with applause from the public galleries, which were promptly cleared by order of the President. For the first time three opponents of a bill, Benjamin Constant, Bailleul, and the fearless Ganilh, were sent to harangue the Legislative Body, which unaccountably adopted the bill by a large majority.[38]

All these excitements tended to distract attention from what was, perhaps, the most constructive endeavour of the Tribunate during these first two sessions – the development of a reasoned critique of the government's financial procedures. Article 45 of the Constitution charged the government with the task of directing the income and expenditure of the state 'in accordance with the annual law fixing the amounts of the same'. On 4 March 1800 the government introduced a bill whereby the direct and indirect taxes authorized for the Year VIII were to continue to be levied in the Year IX, when it was calculated they

36 *Arch. parl.*, 6, 7, 10 Feb. 1801; Thibaudeau, *Mémoires*, p. 204.
37 *Arch. parl.*, 8, 9 Mar. 1801.
38 *Arch. parl.*, 12–16, 18–20 Mar. 1801.

would bring in some 400 million francs. This, said Defermon, the Councillor introducing the bill, would be enough to cover expenses unless war was still being waged, in which case the government could ask for more. In the Tribunate a committee of seven members under the economist Arnould unanimously advised rejection of the bill on the grounds that it was not a 'budget'. Further financial provision was bound to be required, said Arnould, because taxes would be difficult to collect in the rebellious western departments; why did the government not cover its obvious needs at one move?

> It was the intention of the Constitution that there should be annually a system of finances for that year; that this system should be the result of balancing receipts and expenses of every kind for a given year; that this system should be a whole and not remain a collection of atoms floating in space and accidently colliding with the laws that attempted to give them coherence; because the system of finances must be the rational and agreed work of the Legislative Body and the Tribunate as well as of the government, and for this purpose they must one and all be able to judge the proportions and suitability of all parts of the general plan.

In the ensuing discussion, shortsighted members expressed delight with a government which seemed reluctant to ask for money: nevertheless the bill was approved by only 45 votes to 40.[39]

In the Legislative Body, however, a very large majority, 214 to 19, accepted the bill, and the government saw no reason to mend its ways.[40] On 28 February 1801 Defermon, in a bill consisting of eight brief clauses, repeated the previous year's procedure, proposing to prolong the taxes of the Year IX on the grounds, this time, that they would yield enough revenue for wartime expenses though not, perhaps for the reconstruction that would be required with the advent of peace. The bill was again criticized by a committee of the Tribunate on the grounds that it was not a 'budget', though the reporter Chassiron announced that the committee this time was willing to accept the bill as a necessary expedient while war was waging. Not so the Tribunate's engineering expert, Isnard. He had supported the government in the previous year on the grounds of expediency and was not prepared to do so again. If this hand-to-mouth policy continued, he said in the course of a remarkable speech, Article 45 of the Constitution would be 'annihilated' and the national representation would become 'a chimera' as far as finances were concerned; the Directory had been bad on receipts but had gone a long way towards establishing proper forecasts of expenditure, and he could hardly believe the present government when it said that such predictions could not be made again. The government blamed most of its difficulties on the shortness of the parliamentary session, which ended six months before the calendar year; but a writer in the *Décade*

39 *Arch. parl.*, 4, 10 Mar. 1800.
40 *Arch. parl.*, 16 Mar. 1800.

Philosophique (perhaps J.-B. Say) pointed out that it would always be possible to divorce the financial year from the calendar year and begin the former as soon as parliament was prorogued. None of these arguments bore much weight outside the Tribunate, however. While the latter body voted for the bill with a majority of only 26, the Legislators produced only a single opponent among 229 members voting.[41]

The second session closed on 21 March 1801. From a strictly factual point of view, opposition during the first two sessions had amounted to three bills rejected by both the Tribunate and the Legislative Body; one bill rejected by the Tribunate but passed by the Legislative Body and another *vice versa*; and six bills (two of them dealing with very minor matters) withdrawn by the government because of opposition in the Tribunate. Of the latter, two had been presented again in almost the same form and passed without much trouble. Such a record could hardly be said to amount to much, in all conscience. Thibaudeau thought that at a time when members of parliament were still accustomed to revolutionary ways, the government had been lucky to get off so lightly; the damage done, he pointed out, was slight compared with the extent to which the government had increased its power by such measures as the Local Government Act.[42]

Napoleon, however, did not see the situation in this light. A great many of his measures had been criticized, if only by a few speakers in the Tribunate, and he was almost as much upset by this as by outright defeat. His friends sometimes asked themselves why Napoleon seemed positively to welcome criticism from the Council of State yet could not abide it from the Tribunate, and came to the conclusion that it was because the proceedings of the Tribunate were public. It was indeed one of Napoleon's temperamental weaknesses that he was extremely sensitive to any attack on his public image, and particularly to any attack which he thought made him look ridiculous. At the same time he professed to be able to accept constructive criticism, whether delivered in public or not, and it is fair to remember that a few men, such as Bouteville, Isnard and Arnould, who patiently criticized bills without rhetoric and without apparently any ulterior motive, did in fact escape his anger. He had some grounds for saying that most of the criticism in the Tribunate was destructive. For this the Constitution, which deprived parliament of the right to amend legislation, was chiefly to blame.[43]

41 *Décade Philosophique*, 21 Mar. 1801; *Arch. parl.*, 28 Feb., 8, 9, 10, 12 Mar. 1801.
42 Thibaudeau, *Mémoires*, pp. 194, 205.
43 Thibaudeau, p. 198; Bourrienne, *Mémoires* IV, p. 299.

4

The Lists of Notables

Of all the constitutional arrangements suggested by Sieyès and carried bodily into the Napoleonic régime, the most extraordinary was that which substituted for elections a system of lists. It involved a total rejection of one of the basic ideas of representative government, namely that rulers should be chosen by those whom they are to rule. The rejection was deliberate: Sieyès believed that a ruler chosen by his subjects could never have sufficient authority over them.[1] This applied, in his view, to local officials and national executives alike. His system was therefore comprehensive: it was designed to produce a whole range of officials, from the lowest to the highest. It was also intended, curiously enough, to be democratic; for although Sieyès believed that authority could come only from above, he was equally sure that confidence could come only from below. The people should indicate which men they were prepared to trust in office, and by 'the people' Sieyès meant the entire adult male population.

The unit which started the operation was to be a new territorial division called a 'grand commune' or 'communal arrondissement', of which there were to be several forming a department.[2] The adult males of each communal arrondissement would elect a tenth of their number on to a communal list; these 'communal notables' would elect a tenth of their number on to a departmental list, and the 'departmental notables' would elect a tenth of their number on to a national list. From the first set of lists, communal officials would be chosen; from the second set, departmental officials; and from the national list, which would contain five to six thousand names, the consuls, ministers, high court judges, and members of parliament. The choosing, at least of the higher echelons, would be done by a lofty magistrate of exemplary disinterestedness, called the 'grand elector'. It is often suggested that Sieyès intended to give this dead-ended position to Napoleon, and the latter himself may

1 Bourdon, *La Constitution*, p. 71.
2 Boulay, *Théorie*, p. 12. The communal arrondissement was usually referred to afterwards as the commune. It should not be confused with the municipality, the smallest unit of local government, which was also usually called the commune.

have feared as much, but there is no evidence to this effect. Mme Reinhard thought he intended to appoint Roederer or Boulay de la Meurthe, either of whom would have acted with suitable pedantry.[3]

When this proposed system was discussed by the commissions and panels appointed to draft the Constitution, there was a good deal of opposition, especially in the panels, to the idea of universal male suffrage. A property qualification was advocated, but Sieyès clung to the wider franchise and obtained a majority for his view among the members of the commissions. In other respects there seems to have been fairly general acceptance of the idea of lists. Only Daunou is said to have argued for a more orthodox system of elections.[4]

In the discussions held with Napoleon, the 'grand elector' (or 'fatted pig' as Napoleon called him) was eliminated from the picture, with the result that the system as it ultimately appeared in the Constitution of the Year VIII was different in respect of who was to do the choosing of officials from the lists. Article 20 of the Constitution gave the task of choosing consuls, members of parliament, high court judges, and treasury officials to the Senate; Articles 41, 58, and 59 bestowed on the First Consul the right of nominating ministers and Councillors of State from the national list and members of local administrations from the communal and departmental lists. The process of choosing from the lists was described as 'electing', a conceit which was maintained in official jargon throughout the Napoleonic period. Roederer went so far as to claim that the system gave France national representation for the first time. A member of parliament elected by a body of voters in a particular area of France could never truly be regarded as representing the whole country, he said; he could only rightly be regarded as the representative of the nation if he were *designated* by his fellow citizens but *elected* by a body of men (the Senate) who stood for the nation. Gohier, on the other hand, likened the 'lists of confidence' to the *cartes de civisme* issued during the Revolution, and complained that the nation's right to vote had been reduced to the doubtful function taken upon themselves by Jacobin clubs in the Year II. The lists were rendered completely fatuous in the eyes of the former Director by a clause in the Constitution which said that they were not to be drawn up until the Year IX, by which time all public functionaries of any importance would already have been appointed.[5]

The obscurities and difficulties inherent in the system sketched by the Constitution soon became apparent. What was to be the size of the communal arrondissements? If they were to be fairly large, as Sieyès' alternative name of 'grand commune' seemed to imply, was it permissible for elections to be organized in sections? To what extent were the

3 Reinhard, *Lettres*, p. 112.
4 Boulay, *Théorie*, p. 58.
5 *Arch. parl.*, 10 Feb. 1801; Gohier, *Mémoires* I, p. 49.

lists to be renewed periodically? What was to happen to officials already appointed, if their names were subsequently found to be not on the lists?

The answer to the first of these questions was pre-empted by the passing in February 1800 of an act dividing France into departments and arrondissements for the purposes of administration. Roederer denied that these arrondissements were necessarily the communal arrondissements to be used for elections, but no one else was in any doubt as to their double purpose. Pierre-François Duchesne, a barrister from Grenoble opposed the administrative act in the Tribunate on the very grounds that the arrondissements it created would be unsuitable for electoral purposes. They were based, he said, on the areas covered by tribunals of correctional police, and these had resulted from personal claims and local demands rather than from rational planning. Some covered 6 or 8 of the former cantons, others 35. The biggest might have 30,000 citizens eligible to vote in the first instance. How could the inhabitants of the countryside be expected to make a two day journey to the polls? Only townsmen would vote; the lists would be composed entirely of townsmen; all France's officials would be townsmen; the countryside would be 'frappée de nullité' as it had been during the *ancien régime.* It was Duchesne's first opposition speech, on a subject he was to make peculiarly his own.[6]

Duchesne's argument assumed that voting in each communal arrondissement would take place at one polling station only. The Council of State discussed this matter in October 1800, however, and came to the conclusion that in terms of the Constitution did not preclude division of the basic unit into sections. How otherwise could twelve thousand voters in an average-sized communal arrondissement choose twelve hundred of their own number? How many men would know twelve hundred others by name, let alone well enough to choose them advisedly from among twelve thousand? Though some kind of sectional arrangement seemed unavoidable, however, it was necessary to ensure that the lists were truly common to the arrondissement. If each section simply elected forty or fifty of its own men, they could hardly be regarded as representing the whole arrondissement, especially, thought the Councillors, if they came from a rural area. The answer, it seemed, was to have a mixed system, both sectional and communal, of which no fewer than four were put to the Council as possible drafts for the forthcoming bill.[7]

The difficulties that were obviously going to be encountered in forming the lists strengthened the hands of those experts who argued that the complete operation need only take place once. Article 11 of the Constitution referred to voters being summoned every three years to withdraw from the lists names they no longer wished to retain, and to replace

6 *Arch. parl.*, 13 Feb. 1800.
7 The discussion in the Council of State was reported at length in the *Journal du Soir*, 20, 21 Oct. 1800.

them with the names of other citizens in whom they had greater confidence; but this did not mean that the previous lists had to be nullified and the entire process started again. So, at any rate, argued Laloi, in opposition to a clause in the Archives bill which required the government to deposit electoral lists in the Archives 'every three years, after their renewal'. The Constitution, Laloi pointed out, did not use the word 'renewal': it referred to 'replacement', and obviously envisaged only repair work. This argument was displeasing to Roederer, who had constituted himself the high priest of the electoral mysteries and published newspaper articles of incredible length upon the subject at every conceivable opportunity. The lists once made must remain intact, Roederer opined, for how otherwise could the Senate or the First Consul be sure that an official appointed from a particular list had ever had the confidence of the voters? It may be necessary to refer back to lists ten or twelve years after they had been made. Meanwhile new lists would have been made every three years, and these would have been used when appointing new officials.[8]

This argument, though not really answering the question about renewal, may possibly have served to quieten fears of a wholesale dismissal of officials every three years. There remained, however, a good deal of anxiety as to the possible fate of persons appointed before the lists were drawn up at all. Article 14 of the Constitution stipulated that persons nominated to the Council of State, the Legislative Body, and the Tribunate at the outset were to be placed on the first lists *ex officio*. Of the numerous other 'officials' who swarmed about the capital and provincial cities of France, the same article said that 'only those designated by law' needed to be able to point to their name on a list, but whom exactly did this include? When the electoral operation began, civil servants were discovered to be forming syndicates to get themselves on to the lists, lest they should lose their jobs. So much for the pamphleteer, Dr Gilbert, who had welcomed the Constitution of the Year VIII on the grounds that it would put an end to the unseemly scrambling for places that had gone on during the Directory. When the Austrian minister Cobenzl enquired out of curiosity if it were true that persons not on the lists could become nothing, he was told that, on the contrary, they could become ambassadors.[9]

Details were eventually worked out and a bill specifying electoral procedures presented to the Legislative Body by Roederer on 10 February 1801. It stated that on 22 March 1801, and every three years thereafter, the council of each municipality was to form a register of voters, listing all males over the age of twenty-one who had resided for

8 *Journal de Paris*, 9 Dec. 1800. Napoleon once described Roederer as 'a ball which won't bounce'; Sainte-Hilaire, *Souvenirs* I, p. 347. In modern parlance he could best he described as a 'stuffed shirt'.
9 *Arch. nat.*, F⁷ 3829; Gilbert, *médicin*, *Du Pacte social*; Roederer, *Autour de Bonaparte*, p. 134.

one year within the municipality and were not paupers, bankrupts, criminals or hired servants. These municipal lists were to be sent to the sub-prefect of the arrondissement, who would divide the voters inscribed on them into 'series' – one series in a municipality which had between 51 and 150 voters, two in a municipality with 151 to 250 voters, three if there were 251 to 350 voters, and so on. The sub-prefect must also indicate the number of tens of voters in each series and hence the number of communal notables to be elected. A copy of the master list for the arrondissement was to be sent to each municipality by the end of April, and a polling clerk for each series was to be nominated by the sub-prefect from among the voters.

Voting was to begin in the middle of May and last a fortnight, the poll for each series being held in the house of the polling clerk. Each voter was to fill in two forms. On the first he was to write a number of names equal to the number of tens in his series, drawn entirely from persons outside his series; and on the second the same number drawn from persons inside. The counting was to take place publicly on 9 June, the polling clerk drawing up a single list from the two sets of forms, stating the number of votes received by each person named, and sending it to the sub-prefect. The latter was to combine the results from the various series within his arrondissement, publish a communal list, and send a copy to the prefect.

The second round of voting was to take place at the house of the oldest notary in the chief town of the arrondissement, starting in mid-July and lasting ten days. Each communal notable who presented himself to vote was again to fill in two forms, each with names amounting to a tenth of the communal notables within his arrondissement, the first being composed of names from outside the arrondissement and the second from inside. The counting was to take place publicly on 20 July, each sub-prefect sending his list to the sub-prefect, who was to compose a list of departmental notables and send it to the Minister of the Interior.

The third round of voting was to take place at the house of the oldest notary in the chief town of the department, beginning near the end of August and again lasting ten days. This time voters were required to fill in only one form, with names drawn only from the department, to a number double that of the notables to be provided by the department. From the combined lists of all the departments the Minister of the Interior was to draw up a national list composed of the winning tenth.

These were merely the main lines of procedure. The bill was complicated at every stage by details as to precisely how the *ex officio* names were to be fitted into the lists, how to deal with forms which contained too many names, what to do if too many people got the same number of votes, and so on. Special clauses were inserted for the current year, to cater for the euphoria engendered by the call-up of men for the war: for this one year only, voters in the first two rounds were to fill in a third form, naming one tenth of the persons listed as absent from the arrondissement on public service, the winning tenth being divided out among the final lists. Further clauses applied only to subsequent lists, the Council of State having decided after all that in future years repair work only was required, to make up for notables who had died, or left the area, or been deprived of their civic rights, or withdrawn from the lists because they had lost the confidence of voters. The bill notably failed to specify how the removal of unwanted names was to be accomplished if this were not to be done by the production of a totally new list. But even without this knotty problem, the bill presented formidable complications. Doubts were raised in the Council of State as to whether mayors and municipal councillors in remote areas would be able to understand it, but Roederer insisted that it was perfectly intelligible to anyone who read it in stages and did not try to absorb the whole thing at once.

Discussion of the bill began in the Tribunate on 22 February 1801. Coming shortly after the excitements of the Special Tribunals Act is was regarded by most politicians as a great bore.[10] No one could have attacked it in principle without committing the grievous sin of criticizing the Constitution, and the details were clearly beyond the grasp of most of the Tribunes. Only a few waded bravely into the morass. Savoye-Rollin and Démeunier, while supporting the bill in the main, criticized the clause which required communal notables to vote for a tenth of their own number and an equal number of persons from elsewhere: in an average-sized arrondissement this would mean that they had to write 120 names on each of the two forms, and in an arrondissement the size of Lyon, 400. The government hastened to withdraw the article in question and substitute one which required the communal notables to produce a tenth of the number relevant to their own *series* only; but this was criticized by Duchesne as prolonging the sectional arrangements into the second stage of voting and thereby making the whole bill, in his view, more unconstitutional than ever.

For the greater part of the discussion, Duchesne found himself the only opponent of the bill. He regarded the first stage of the proposed system as the least practicable. Who could imagine a simple farm labourer, his hand aching from the unaccustomed effort of writing out 15 names from the 150 in his series, going on to write down another 15 from a list of perhaps 500 names drawn from the municipality at large? Duchesne proceeded to outline a scheme of his own, based on much smaller units derived from the areas covered by justices of the peace.[11]

At the very end of the discussion Pénières, a diffident young man who was, however, distressed and puzzled at the lack of opposition to the bill, rose to his feet to try and fill the gap as best he could. The absence of a proper procedure for the renewal of the lists would mean, he said, that persons nominated in the Year IX would form a 'patriciate' – a suggestion which raised shouts of protest. It seemed a pity, Pénières continued,

10 Thibaudeau, *Mémoires*, p. 200.
11 *Arch. parl.*, 24 Feb., 2 Mar. 1801.

that at least the departmental notables could not meet in assemblies to produce their portion of the national list – a regret not shared by the majority of the speakers on the subject, who believed that electoral assemblies were a threat to law and order and that avoidance of them was one of the chief merits of the bill. Pénières was then hustled out of the rostrum by Tribunes anxious to applaud the arangements made for representing members of the armed forces. The Tribunate commended the bill by 59 votes to 26, and the Legislative Body passed it on 4 March by 239 votes to 36. Roederer, on behalf of the Council of State, went to a great deal of trouble to refute Pénières' forecast of a patriciate, although in conversation with Napoleon he had himself commended the proposed system on the grounds that the lists would probably turn out on the whole to represent rising levels of wealth. Even the communal notables, he thought, would be small proprietors, while the departmental notables would be men of considerable means, and the national notables the wealthiest citizens of all. It was suggested afterwards that Roederer was already looking forward to the hereditary Empire, and that he regarded the national list as a possible source for a new peerage.[12]

The great electoral operation was launched in March 1801 with a circular from the Minister of the Interior to the prefects, pointing out that the fate of the Republic would for a long time depend on the lists now to be made.[13] Prefects and sub-prefects contemplated their part in the proceedings with varying degrees of dismay. How could the mayors in a department like Ille-et-Vilaine be instructed in their duties, when the majority of them were illiterate? How were polling clerks to be found in a department like Finistère, where some municipalities could not produce a single person who could read and write? How were lists to be produced in a department like Bouches-du-Rhône, where printing costs were so exhorbitant that arrondissement funds would not run to paying for the special sheets prescribed by the Minister of the Interior? What was to happen if, as at Brest, the persons nominated to act as polling clerks one and all refused to serve?[14]

Petitions that were addressed afterwards to the Tribunate revealed innumberable difficulties encountered, especially by sub-prefects arranging about 12,000 voters into series and drawing up vast lists of communal notables. Boundaries of municipalities had changed a good deal in recent years; names of streets, let alone numbers of houses, were not always known; maps frequently failed to indicate whether a few score of voters, left over when a municipality had been divided into series, lived near enough to another remnant to be added to the same

12 *Arch. parl.*, 2, 4 Mar. 1801; Roederer, *Autour de Bonaparte*, p. 30; Thibaudeau, *Mémoires*, p. 74.
13 *Décade Philosophique*, 21 Mar. 1801.
14 Benaerts, *Le Régime consulaire*, p. 209; *Arch. nat.*, F^{IC}III Finistère (6), Bouches-du-Rhône (2).

poll. Names and numbers submitted in series returns were sometimes illegible; the same name might designate three or four different persons; government employees whose residence was in one municipality and place of work in another were often tracked down at a late stage, to the confusion of the mathematical calculations.[15] On 22 July a consular decree deferred for two months the dates on which the various lists were to be ready; even so, thirteen departments failed to complete the final round.

Innumerable claims addressed to the authorities after the event testify to the fact that many people had been eager to get themselves elected, especially on to the communal lists.

> Citizen prefect, I demand with the utmost urgency the rectification of a serious error, to say no more, which has deprived me of a right precious to all good Frenchmen – the title of communal notable. I live at Noviant-aux-près in the arrondissement of Toul. To be a communal notable there, 21 votes were enough. In the commune of D . . . alone I had 48 votes. Yet, citizen prefect, my name does not appear on the list of notables of my arrondissement! It is a sacred property that has been taken from me, and also from my fellow citizens, who have an irrefutable right to have me as one of their communal notables.

So ran one of the more impassioned appeals, addressed to the prefect of the Meurthe.[16] Names on the lists were accompanied by numbers of votes obtained, and it was simple enough for disappointed citizens to work out, rightly or wrongly, that they had themselves received more votes than the minimum number published on the list of successful candidates. Errors were often attributed to deliberate malpractice, when they were very likely due to ignorance. Polling clerks were accused of closing the poll before time to keep out unwanted voters; public readings were said to have taken place without due notice to avoid awkward enquiries. Some of the prefects themselves investigated complaints and rectified errors; others took the line that a list once publicly read could not be altered. Thus the prefect of the Meurthe corrected sixty-two errors in the communal list of a single arrondissement, while the prefect of Gironde refused to make any alterations although all names beginning with the letter L had been inadvertently omitted from the lists at Bordeaux.[17] Frustrated claimants seized the opportunity to send petitions to the Tribunate, denouncing their particular lists as unconstitutional and urging the Tribunate to refer their case to the Senate. The Tribunate, contrary to its usual practice, set up committees to look into the petitions, but ultimately came to the conclusion that it lacked the machinery for investigating the allegations. Even the Senate could only have annulled lists which it found unsatisfactory, not rectify errors – an outcome which

15 *Arch. parl.*, 20 Aug., 3, 24 Sept., 8, 24 Oct., 22, 23 Nov. 1801.
16 *Arch. nat.*, F[IC]III Meurthe (2).
17 *Arch. nat.*, F[IC]III Meurthe (2); *Arch. parl.*, 3 Sept. 1801.

would have annoyed the people whose names were on the lists without satisfying the petitioners.[18]

The proceedings in the Tribunate helped to convince many people in France that the whole operation had been fraudulent and that the lists were worthless.[19] The *Clef du Cabinet* announced that many local lists had simply been concocted by the mayors.[20] The Abbé Morellet, still anxious at the age of 74 to play a part in public life and hence to get his name on the national list, described the final election in Paris as rigged from start to finish.[21] In the Council of State the question arose as to whether or not the lists should be used when appointments to places were made in the near future. Roederer, in spite of having read all the complaints sent to the Tribunate, thought that on the whole the lists were good, and that complaints from a few aggrieved individuals were hardly a sufficient reason for violating the Constitution. Emmery was not convinced. He claimed personally to know of lists which were wholly bad, and he thought it was better to annoy the successful tenth of France's citizens by ignoring the lists than to annoy the unsuccessful nine tenths by operating them, especially since it could be claimed that the system violated the great revolutionary principle of careers open to talent. Napoleon began by describing the whole idea of lists as absurd, but came round to thinking that there would be no harm in operating them for two or three years 'to show willing'. He was impressed by a letter he had received from the Minister of the Interior, Chaptal, pointing out to him that even the worst lists contained enough worthy names from which to make the very few necessary choices, and he concluded, somewhat illogically, that operating the lists for a few years would show up their deficiencies and the system could then be abandoned. Several members of the Council challenged the last part of this argument, taking the view that using the lists, even for a short time, would validate the system and render it more difficult to change. Napoleon, as usual when crossed, dug himself in to the position he had at first adopted only tentatively. 'You all said that the system was inoperable and that only Roederer understood it,' he sneered. 'Well, the people have taken the trouble to understand and execute it. Now you want to annul it all, and show lack of respect for the people who have shown such respect for your law.' After this tirade the Council agreed almost unanimously that the lists should be used, and they were thus at hand when new members of parliament were needed in the Year X.[22]

18 *Arch. parl.*, 20 Aug., 3 Sept. 1801.
19 *Décade Philosophique*, 21 Mar. 1802.
20 *Clef du Cabinet*, 20 Aug. 1801.
21 Morellet, *Mémoires* II, pp. 109–10.
22 Thibaudeau, *Mémoires*, pp. 69–74; Napoleon, *Correspondance*, no. 5932.

5

The Purge

In the summer of 1801 a Concordat was signed between Napoleon and the Pope, bringing officially to an end the great dispute between Revolutionary France and the Catholic church. Negotiations had taken more than a year, and rumours of them had greatly agitated the members of France's parliamentary assemblies. Atheists and freethinkers regarded an approach to the Pope as a retrograde step; constitutional clergy and their supporters resented any effort to accommodate nonjurors; radicals of all shades feared a return to the politics of the *ancien régime*. Members of the Legislative Body returning to Paris in November after their lengthy vacation hastened to bring themselves up to date with the news; they fully expected Napoleon to present the Concordat to the legislature at an early stage in the session, and vigorous opposition was widely anticipated.[1] As a gesture of defiance they elected as their president Charles-François Dupuis, renegade priest and author (before the Revolution) of a celebrated work attacking religion. Excitement on this score proved to be premature, however, for although Napoleon found the elderly and scholarly Dupuis not at all difficult to get on with he nevertheless decided to defer the presentation of the Concordat to a more propitious time.[2]

The parliamentary session of the Year X opened at midday on 22 November 1801, announced by the firing of cannon. The Treaty of Lunéville with Austria (February 1801) and the signing of preliminaries of peace with Britain (October 1801) had brought a number of foreign diplomats to Paris, and Napoleon probably thought that ceremonial of a military character would impress them. Lord Cornwallis must have been considerably surprised when a casual visit he paid to the Legislative Body was greeted with a roll of drums as he entered and left the

1 *Arch. nat.*, F⁷ 3829, 3830.
2 Girardin, *Mémoires* III, p. 238. Napoleon told Bertrand on St Helena: 'Dupuis often dined with me; I treated him very well. He was astounded and shocked when I did not make him a Senator at least, but I couldn't because of his pronounced views against religion. He connected all religious systems with the system of Nature, with the epochs of the sun and its revolutions.' Bertrand, *Cahiers, 1816–17*, pp. 163–4.

gallery. On the whole such military trappings merely served to convince British visitors that France was living under a despotism.[3]

Members of parliament soon became aware that with or without the Concordat they were going to be presented with a formidable amount of legislation. Treaties of peace with no fewer than five foreign powers awaited ratification. A civil code and a new system of education were announced. Meanwhile bills authorizing local sales of land began to pour in – ten on 25 November, ten on 3 December, twelve on 15 December – each requiring discussion in the Tribunate and debate before the Legislative Body. On 27 November Dubosq proposed to the Legislators that they should at least to try to devise a speedier system of voting than the existing method, which required a roll-call after each debate. It was agreed that the Legislative Body could, if it wished, decide to vote on several bills at once, by placing discs in five or six urns, each marked with the title of the appropriate bill. The Tribunate adopted the same system, which had operated in the Council of Elders under the Directory.[4]

The Civil Code was to be presented in the form of a series of bills. Having sent the first to the Legislative Body on 24 November, the government interrupted the programme to send on five successive days the treaties signed between France and the USA, the Two Sicilies, Bavaria, Russia and Portugal. These were hardly likely to be thrown out in view of the general desire for peace, but a few intrepid opponents of the government put a spoke in the wheels here and there, and tried to show that France had abandoned the crusade for liberty. Mongez reminded his fellow Tribunes of the long and barbarous captivity inflicted by the King of the Two Sicilies upon the scholar Dolomieu; Ginguené, who did not speak in the Tribunate, seized the opportunity when reporting the latter's views to the Legislative Body to expatiate on the hideous brutality shown by the same king in putting down revolution in Naples in 1799. If Napoleon had expected unanimous acclaim for his efforts as peacemaker he was disappointed, for even the treaties with Bavaria and Portugal received one hostile vote each in the Legislative Body.[5]

The treaty with Russia, meanwhile, had raised a storm in a teacup. When the text was read out in the Tribunate, the ex-Jacobin Thibault jumped to his feet to protest against Article 3, which made reference to 'the subjects of the two powers'. Frenchmen, he said, were citizens, not subjects. He was ruled out of order for interrupting the reading, but further trouble was expected when discussion took place. When the time came, however, a government supporter Jard-Panvilliers managed to persuade the Tribunate that it was better to let off steam, on so delicate a matter as a peace treaty, in private than in public; disgruntled

3 *Gazette de France*, 24 Nov. 1801; Maccunn, *The Contemporary English View*, p. 52.
4 *Arch. parl.*, 30 Nov. , 2 Dec. 1801.
5 *Arch. parl.*, 26–30 Nov., 6–8, 10 Dec. 1801.

spectators were cleared from the galleries; and when the Tribunate reported its views to the Legislative Body the majority was said to have agreed with the reporter Costaz, that the word *sujets* in the treaty referred only to émigrés. Nevertheless, fourteen Tribunes had voted against the treaty.[6]

Napoleon's reaction was first of all one of incredulity and then of anger. How could anyone risk the renewal of war for the sake of a word? How could any intelligent person expect a treaty that had been negotiated under some difficulty with the Tsar to avoid terminology acceptable to him? Stanislas Girardin, one of the government's supporters in the Tribunate, was sent for. He did his best to minimize the importance of the incident. The government had very few regular opponents in the Tribunate, he said, and even these could be won over with a little 'management'. Napoleon at this point boasted of his approachability, but refused to have any dealings with 'curs' who would endanger peace for the sake of a word. He met them everywhere, he said, and he was looking forward to the day when he could expel them from the authorities of state. Girardin tried to persuade him that such drastic remedies were unnecessary as far as the Tribunate was concerned, since the majority could be relied upon to outweigh the malcontents; but Napoleon did not believe him. How could he be expected to rely on a majority that was not organized, he complained. Girardin assured him that it *was* organized; that there was a committee of government supporters consisting of himself, Siméon, Gallois, Adet, Jaucourt, Bérenger, Savoye-Rollin, and Chabaud-Latour; that it was this committee which had secured moderate membership for the various reporting committees set up so far, and had arranged for Jard-Panvilliers to suggest a secret session for the discussion of the treaty with Russia. Napoleon thought that the secret session had been a wise move: but then he changed his mind. If discussion had been held in public the nation would have known the names of the madmen who were willing to endanger peace for the sake of a word. . . . Thus he came back again and again to the same grievance.[7]

Meanwhile the government had run into quite unexpected difficulties with the Civil Code. Everything had started off well enough. Portalis, who presented the first bill, was famed for his oratory, and Napoleon, after reading the speech, did not see how anyone could oppose it. The bill consisted of a mere eight clauses, apparently uncontroversial in nature, dealing with the promulgation and application of laws. The committee set up by the Tribunate to report on the bill contained none of the more outstanding opponents of the government. Nevertheless the committee unanimously advised rejection of the bill, and its reporter, Andrieux, tore the measure to pieces in the most elegant speech of the session. The bill was out of place at the beginning of the Civil Code, he

6 *Arch. parl.*, 30 Nov., 6–9 Dec., 1801; *Arch. nat.*, F[7] 3830.
7 Girardin, *Mémoires* III, pp. 230–38.

said, for its stipulations applied to all laws and not just to the Civil Code. Its articles lacked coherence: the third could just as well have been placed second, the second third, the seventh eighth, or the last first. They were ungrammatical, in that they used the present tense for their injunctions instead of the imperative or the future. With the exception of the first article, they were not pronouncements of law but axioms of morality or principles of jurisprudence, like Article 2 which simply stated: 'Law is not retroactive.' In detail they were equally open to criticism. The first article, which read: 'Laws are executed throughout French territory by virtue of their promulgation by the First Consul; they are executed in each part of the Republic from the moment when their promulgation is known; it is reckoned to be known within the area of the appeal tribunal of Paris thirty-six hours after the date of promulgation, and in other areas at the same time plus two hours for every myriametre distant from Paris,' was both too vague and two specific, varying from reference to 'the date', which could be any time within twenty-four hours, to 'the moment', which implied a split second. Article 3, 'The law obliges all who inhabit the territory,' had been contradicted, Andrieux pointed out, by the second bill of the Civil Code, just received from the Legislative Body, according to which not all foreigners residing in France were to be subject to French law.[8]

The government's supporters were thrown into disarray by this devastating critique and appealed for time to prepare their case. Even so they made a poor job of it, and the bill was rejected by the Tribunate by 65 votes to 13. Portalis achieved rather better results in the Legislative Body, but his speech was lengthy and apologetic compared with Andrieux's incisive effort, and the bill was rejected by a majority of three.[9] Meanwhile not only the second but the third bill of the Civil Code had been presented to the Legislative Body. Both were long and detailed: the committee examining the second bill on behalf of the Tribunate took a fortnight to complete its report, leaving only four days for discussion before the final debate was due to take place. Several suggestions were made for speeding things up. Garry proposed that, for the Civil Code only, discussion should proceed article by article, with members speaking from their places. Duveyrier thought that this would lead to turmoil and suggested instead that the Tribunate should cut out the committee stage and allow all its members, divided into panels of twenty, to study a bill for four days and make a report on it before proceeding to general discussion.[10] These and other suggestions were lost sight of in the deluge of work. Local bills continued to arrive literally

8 Thibaudeau, *Mémoires sur le Consulat*, pp. 217–18; *Arch. parl.*, 24 Nov., 5 Dec. 1801.
9 *Arch. parl.*, 5, 9, 10, 12, 14, 15 Dec., 1801. Napoleon once said that Portalis would have been the greatest orator among the Councillors of State if he had known when to stop, but that he was like those musicians who take a lot of persuading to play and then cannot be got to leave the instrument. Sainte-Hilaire, *Souvenirs* I, p. 347.
10 *Arch. parl.*, 10, 16 Dec. 1801.

by the dozen: to the credit of the Tribunate its committees worked on them seriously, and sifted out one, for the compulsory purchase of land in Paris to open a cemetery, which Duchesne managed to get withdrawn by the government until further information regarding area and price was forthcoming.[11]

The second bill of the Civil Code dealt with possession and deprivation of civil rights. Discussion in the Tribunate focused upon two aspects: Article 13, which declared that any foreigner residing in France would enjoy the same rights as those accorded to Frenchmen living in the country to which the foreigner belonged; and Articles 26 to 28 which recognized 'civil death' as a judicial penalty, dissolving the culprit's marriage and causing his property to devolve upon his heirs. The former was seen by several speakers as a retrograde step, the Constituent Assembly at the beginning of the Revolution having opened France's doors to all foreigners in a spirit of brotherly love. Some went so far as to compare the new proposal with the exclusive attitude of the Romans, who allowed rights only to their own citizens. Others thought it was a sensible half-way measure, which would allow France to establish reciprocal relationships with countries connected to her by ties of commerce and at the same time to protect French property from exploitation by strangers. Siméon, reporting for a committee on the first half of the bill, thought that Article 13 might be acceptable if the rest of the bill were satisfactory. Civil death, however, was described by Thiessé, reporting on the second half of the bill, as an intolerable concept, which dissolved marriage regardless of the wishes of the partners, affected the civil status of children legitimately conceived, and confiscated property (albeit for the benefit of the heirs) in a manner reminiscent of the *ancien régime*. As though to make up for the sins of Andrieux, who had been accused by Councillors of State of destroying the work of months with a short burst of verbal fireworks, Tribunes now made laborious speeches of unprecedented length and dullness. Saint-Aubin regaled his hearers with a complete history of the rights of citizenship from ancient to modern times. Meetings went on so long that the minutes could not be got ready for the next day.[12]

Hardly surprisingly, the second bill was overtaken by the third. This was a very technical production dealing with the registration of births, deaths, and marriages, and seemed at first sight unlikely to arouse much interest. The meticulous Duchesne, reporting on behalf of the examining committee, advised acceptance. Benjamin Constant introduced a little excitment by attacking Article 60, which allowed the mother of an illegitimate child to name the father for purposes of the birth certificate. This was a useless concession to the mother, he said, because it did not allow her to bring an action against the father for maintenance; it stigmatized the man's conduct to no practical purpose; it allowed

11 *Arch. parl.*, 12, 13, 20 Dec. 1801.
12 *Arch. parl.*, 2, 16, 18, 20, 22–4, 26, 29, 30 Dec., 1 Jan. 1802.

women to make false accusations of which the men in question were not even informed. A few speakers took up the point, but Andrieux defended the clause in the only feminist speech since Brumaire, and the bill was accepted by the Tribunate with a large majority.[13]

While all this was going on, balloting kept taking place to produce candidates for the Senate. The two parliamentary bodies had come to regard this activity as a means of expressing opposition to the First Consul, who also presented candidates for vacant senatorships. The Legislative Body proved to be more single-minded than the Tribunate, and hence more successful. On 30 November it chose Grégoire as its candidate for the third time in succession, while the Tribunate, hovering between electing Daunou as a flamboyant opposition gesture and electing a government supporter as a tactical manoeuvre, found itself with a moderate candidate, Démeunier. If the First Consul had also presented Démeunier, whom he had seemed to favour a year before, the Senate would have been more or less obliged to take him, in accordance with its unwritten rule of electing any candidate nominated by two out of the three authorities. Napoleon, however, did not want to appear to be conceding to the wishes of the Tribunate. He preferred to accept Grégoire's election to the Senate, which he did with a moderately good grace. On 30 December the Legislative Body chose Daunou as its candidate for the second vacant senatorship. Daunou had been Napoleon's *bête noire* ever since he had seceded from the Tribunate over the special tribunals bill; if the Tribunate, which had still to vote on the issue, also presented Daunou as its candidate, the fat would be in the fire.[14]

On 1 January 1802 the Tribunate rejected the second bill of the Civil Code by a majority of 61 votes to 31. Later the same day it elected Daunou as its candidate for the Senate. Napoleon had already decided, in discussion with his Council of State, that if more than one bill of the Civil Code were lost in parliament he would 'take to winter quarters' and present no more bills until the following session.[15] He now decided to withdraw both the second and third bills before they reached the Legislative Body – this in spite of the fact that the third bill had received a favourable vote in the Tribunate. In a message to the Legislators on 3 January he regretted having to defer legislation awaited eagerly by the nation, but he realized, he said, that the time was not ripe for discussing these great measures with the calmness and singleness of purpose they required. In addition to the two bills of the Civil Code, he also withdrew a bill designed to restore branding as a punishment for forgery, which had been described to the Legislative Body by the government spokesman on 24 December as a necessary supplement to the laws against brigandage.

13 *Arch. parl.*, 23, 25–8 Dec. 1801.
14 Grégoire, *Mémoires* I, pp. 101–3, 432–6; Thiry, *Le Sénat*, pp. 78–83.
15 Thibaudeau, *Mémoires sur le Consulat*, pp. 222, 224; Thibaudeau, *Mémoires*, pp. 44–5.

The government-inspired press immediately took up the cry against irresponsible opposition in the parliamentary assemblies, and against orators who were carried away by their own eloquence. The practice of preparing speeches beforehand was held much to blame.[16] Napoleon's supporters puzzled their brains long afterwards for an explanation as to why the two parliamentary bodies had pounced with such vehemence upon the Civil Code. It could have been because they genuinely disliked such proposals as reciprocal rights and civil death, but nobody seemed to think so. Savary, who was Napoleon's aide-de-camp at this time, thought that the opposition was inspired by jealousy of the Councillors of State who had drawn up the Code. Cambacérès thought it was inspired by hostility to the First Consul in person. The police blamed Jacobin generals, returning from the wars. The Second Consul blamed émigrés who had been allowed to return to France in a fit of mistaken generosity. Napoleon believed that Sieyès had organized the whole manoeuvre in an attempt to destroy a constitution which had turned sour on him.[17] Locré, the secretary to the Council of State, was probably nearer the mark in suggesting that opponents were somehow or other hoping to obtain more power for parliament. A preliminary draft of the Civil Code had been published for general distribution during the summer of 1801; the appeal courts and the Tribunal of Cassation had been officially invited to comment; everybody's opinion seemed to have been asked except that of members of parliament, who were now expected to sanction the measure in an atmosphere of acclaim. If they refused to do so, they would perhaps teach Napoleon to take them into greater account in the future.[18]

If this was their plan, it certainly did not succeed. All pending legislation having been withdrawn, members of parliament were left kicking their heels. They continued to turn up daily, but sessions ended after the reading of correspondence; sometimes the members did not bother to sit down. Spectators in the public galleries jeered at their embarrassment, and turned up in large numbers to see what further entertaining moves the government might have in store.[19]

According to the Constitution a fifth of the membership of parliament was due for renewal in the Year X (23 September 1801–22 September 1802). At the time when Napoleon talked of going into winter quarters he seems to have intended to sit out the whole of the rest of the session and take up his legislative programme again in November 1802 when the new members would have arrived. It soon occurred to him, however, that the Constitution referred to renewal *in the course of* the Year X, not *after* or *at the end of* the Year X, and that action could

---

16 *Journal de Paris*, 5, 19 Jan. 1802.
17 Rovigo, *Memoirs* I, p. 294; Girardin, *Mémoires* III, p. 247; *Arch. nat.*, F⁷ 3830; Thibaudeau, *Mémoires sur le Consulat*, p. 223; Napoleon, *Correspondance*, no. 5922.
18 Locré, *Napoléon* I, p. 85.
19 *Arch. nat.*, F⁷ 3830.

therefore be taken at once. Just why he should have become so precipi-
tate is not clear: he said himself that there was no real hurry for a civil
code, France having got on quite well for a long time without one.
Perhaps he thought he had delayed long enough over the Concordat and
should present it as soon as possible. Or perhaps he was excited by a
further thought which suddenly came to him, to the effect that he need
not leave it to chance to decide which members of parliament should
retire, but could take steps to purge away unwanted individuals. The
Consitution did not say how the out-going members were to be chosen.
There was a general assumption that lots would be drawn, but Napoleon
hit on the idea that they could be chosen by the Senate. He was already
moving towards the idea that the Senate should be allowed to fill gaps in
the Constitution by special pronouncements known as senatus-con-
sulta, and this seemed a suitable place to begin. On 8 January he
departed for Lyon, leaving Cambacérès, the Second Consul, to fix the
matter.[20]

Napoleon had tested the loyalty of the Senators the week before he
left by warning them that he would regard the election of Daunou to the
Senate as a personal insult, and on 4 January they had elected his own
candidate, General Lamartillière. Nevertheless he could not have been
sure that they would comply with his wishes over the purging of the
parliamentary assemblies. Much depended on skilful management by
Cambacérès, who presided over the meetings, and on the influence of
Senator Tronchet, an elderly jurist who had played a leading part in the
early stages of the drafting of the Civil Code and was particularly
annoyed over the opposition. By 15 January Cambacérès was writing to
Napoleon to say that, thanks to the efforts of Tronchet in a secret
committee, the Senate had agreed to take on the duty of renewing one
fifth of parliament's membership, not by designating those who were to
go but by listing the four fifths who were to stay. The subtle difference of
approach was thought to render the business more in keeping with the
Senate's 'electoral' functions. Not all the Senators were happy about it:
Cambacérès mentioned a vote of 44 to 15 with Garat and Laroche
prominent among the opponents. The majority, moreover, needed
constant tending during the eight days at the end of January and
beginning of February when voting took place on individual names.
Napoleon wrote from Lyon insisting that public opinion required a swift
and thorough rooting out of the 'Medusa's head' which had appeared in
the parliamentary assemblies. He warned the Senators that no bills
could be presented next session, and perhaps for several sessions, if
'men such as Thiessé, Chazal, Chénier and Garat' remained in the
Tribunate. He never supplied a complete blacklist, however. He was
consulted about Daunou, whom some of the Senators were anxious to
save (after all, he had been presented as a candidate for the Senate by

20 Thibaudeau, *Mémoires sur le Consulat*, p. 221; Roederer, *Autour de Bonaparte*,
p. 104.

large majorities in both parliamentary bodies), but he was adamant that Daunou above all others must go.[21]

Members of parliament, meanwhile, waited with mixed feelings to see what would happen to them. Some went off home. Others were reported by the police to be hanging around in groups talking agitatedly. A few who were fairly sure they would be axed – Bailleul, Saint-Aubin, Chénier, Constant, Daunou, and Chazal – were said to be meeting in the house of Bailleul's mistress, a discreet residence at the back of a court-yard, to plan resistance. Bara was reported as saying that he wouldn't be a bit surprised if the entire 400 were sent packing.[22]

The lists of members who were to keep their places were communicated to the two parliamentary bodies on 18 March. An article in the *Journal des Débats* a few weeks previously had suggested that if the Senate had decided to list those who were to go instead of those who were to stay, the number would greatly have exceeded a fifth, and a reprieve would have been needed for some of those named, who would then have lived under a cloud. Cambacérès had written to warn Napoleon that the members chosen to remain included some doubtful characters, but it had been difficult not to cut out more than the number allowed. Whereas there had been much argument over the Tribunes, the Senators had been more or less unanimous over which of the Legislators should go, though it is not at all clear how they can have been so sure of the opinions of a body of men who met in silence and voted in secret.[23]

A list of the members eliminated from the Legislative Body[24] reveals nothing in itself as to why the sixty individuals had been less fortunate than their brethren. An occasional hint is forthcoming from police records, and a conjecture can sometimes be made from biographical information. The police had kept an eye on one Hardy from the beginning, and were constantly sending in reports of his subversive conversation; like Druhl, he had been known in the Council of Five Hundred for his antipathy to non-juring clergy. Leclerc was a notable atheist; Pilastre was a friend of the former Director Larevellière and may have shared his unorthodox religious views. It is possible that these four, along with such men as Dillon who was a constitutional priest, were eliminated as likely opponents of the Concordat. Grégoire was under the impression that nearly all the members who had supported his candidate for the Senate were eliminated.[25] Beerembroeck, one of the representatives from Belgium, had been reported to Napoleon by the police for expressing annoyance at the withdrawal of the Civil Code; like Clavière and Massa he was known to be one of the friends of Sieyès, another possible qualification for the blacklist. Mansard had been strongly recom-

21 Guérard, *Daunou*, pp. 87–8; Cambacérès, *lettres inédites* I, pp. 20–40; Napoleon, *Correspondance*, nos. 5911, 5922, 5923, 5927, 5931.
22 *Arch. nat.*, F⁷ 3830.
23 Cambacérès, *Lettres inédites* I, pp. 34, 39; *Journal des Débats*, 25 Jan. 1802.
24 No such list was ever published.
25 Grégoire, *Mémoires* I, p. 436.

mended to Napoleon at Brumaire for his integrity and learning (he was a distinguished lawyer), but he came from Chambéry and had voiced dislike of the creation of the department of Mont Blanc. Fabry, who came from Liège, was never entirely happy about the 'reunion' of his province with France. Albert, one of the representatives of the Bas Rhin, had been the subject of a protest from some of the other members at the beginning of the Consulate on the grounds that he did not really come from the Bas Rhin. Bassenge had collaborated with Ginguené on the *Décade Philosophique*. Crévelier, Faure, Meyer, and Poultier were regicides; but this cannot have been the sole reason for their elimination since eight other regicides remained. Some unfortunate members may have failed to find protection among the Senators simply because they were unknown; perhaps Blanc, for instance, who had always had difficulty in getting his name recorded properly (he habitually appeared as Leblanc). Curiously enough, Charles Rousseau, who had made a spirited attempt to achieve greater independence for the Legislative Body at the beginning of the fateful session, lived to fight another day.

The choice of Tribunes aroused more public interest and hence more contemporary comment. Daunou, Constant, Ginguené, Ganihl and Thiessé of course went; so did Thibault, who had made the first protest against the treaty with Russia, and Chénier, who had redeemed his somewhat equivocal reputation from the revolutionary years by persistent opposition to the Consulate. Chazal and Bara had also been prominent in opposition; Berthélemy less so, though Girardin seems to have thought of him as basically hostile to the government. Garat-Mailla had only spoken twice in the Tribunate, but both speeches had been quite remarkable for their independence and spirit. He was, as Girardin said, 'an excellent young man', and not even his uncle's intervention in the Senate could save him from elimination. Alexandre and Parent-Réal had seldom opened their mouths in the Tribunate, but both were friends of Sieyès. Parent-Réal had acquired the added disadvantage of admiring Daunou, his compatriot from the Pas-de-Calais; and Alexandre, when he was commissioner to one of the armies under the Directory, had reported unfavourably on General Lefèbvre, who was now a Senator and believed to be getting his own back. Isnard, also, had come into the Tribunate on the recommendation of Sieyès, and in his case this seems to have been his only offence (he was no relation of the former Girondin deputy of the same name). Légier, like Alexandre, had created antagonism during a former period of employment. Desrenaudes, once Talleyrand's private secretary, had turned out to be less diplomatic than his master; reported by the police as wholly won over to the opposition, he had had the temerity when debating the treaty with Bavaria to praise Napoleon's rival Moreau for the victory of Hohenlinden. Saint-Aubin was disliked more for his journalism than for his behaviour in parliament. Cambe had failed to put in an appearance at all during the current session, sending word that he was saving the expense of the journey from the Aveyron. His speech in opposition to the bill reducing the number of JPs reveals him as an unsophisticated countryman, and he seems to have been regarded as something of an eccentric by his fellow Tribunes. Courtois was a thoroughly suspicious character. Having gained possession of many of Robespierre's papers by somewhat dubious means, he had used the information to bring many of his former Jacobin associates to book after Thermidor. The radical press turned the tables on him at the beginning of the Consulate by accusing him of dishonest financial dealings, and a general impression was created that his presence was a disgrace to the Tribunate. Bailleul for some unknown reason was personally disliked by Napoleon, who had been very annoyed when he was elected secretary of the Tribunate for the usual short spell at the beginning of the session. He was by no means noteworthy as an opponent of the government inside the Tribunate, but the police were constantly reporting him for hostile comments outside. Duchesne survived the purge, possibly because his opposition had been most noticeably directed against the system of electoral lists, which many of the Senators also disliked. A more surprising name on the list of survivors was that of Andrieux.[26]

There was no protest from the public. The police had been reporting a generally hostile attitude to the parliamentary assemblies throughout the Year X: members, they said, were criticized for turning up late, for leaving early, for not wearing uniform, for earning easy money at a time when most people were having difficulty in buying enough bread. There were rumours from December onwards that the government was going to reduce the assemblies in size, and the general opinion seemed to be one of approval. Napoleon may not have been wrong when he wrote from Lyon that there was 'general indignation in France against the bad behaviour of the Tribunate'.[27]

Napoleon afterwards congratulated himself on the lack of vindictiveness he had shown towards the victims of the purge. A notice appeared in the newspapers early in May 1802: 'The government has just 'placed' several members of the Legislative Body, a great many of whom belonged to the opposition and were entirely contrary to the persons now at the head of affairs. Opinions are no longer taken into account; men of talent and integrity are rewarded regardless of what faction they previously belonged to.' 'There were some good workmen among them,' Napoleon once told Metternich. 'The only trouble was, they all wanted to be architects.'[28] At least half of the outgoing members of the Tribunate were given official posts, Isnard and Chazal becoming prefects, and Daunou archivist to the Legislative Body. Even Bailleul

26 Girardin, *Mémoires* III, pp. 237, 255–61; *Arch. nat.*, F⁷ 3829, 3830; Cambacérès, *Lettres inédits* I, p. 25; on Courtois, *Arch. parl.*, 23 Jan. 1800; *Journal des Défenseurs de la Patrie*, 27 Jan. 1800; *Journal des Hommes Libres*, 7, 17, 21, 27 Mar., 1800.
27 *Arch. nat.*, F⁷ 3830; Napoleon, *Correspondance*, no. 5917.
28 *Journal de Paris*, 3 May 1802; Metternich, *Memoirs* I, p. 78.

got a position in customs and excise, and Chénier, whom Bourrienne thought Napoleon particularly disliked for being a scribbler of republican verse, became an inspector of education until he disgraced himself again a few years later by publishing his *Epître à Voltaire*.[29] One in three of the outgoing members of the Legislative Body are known for certain to have obtained official posts, and the number in fact may well have been higher. Customs and excise was the biggest source of reward, but at least four men became judges, and the versatile Poultier was made a garrison commander. None, however, reappeared in Napoleon's parliaments at any time before the Hundred Days.

29 Bourrienne, *Mémoires* v, p. 94; Ménéval, *Mémoires* II, pp. 405–7. Napoleon was very angry with Chénier over this second fall from grace, but when, later, he received an appeal from Chénier who was ill and in financial straits he relented and gave him a pension.

6

The Supplementary Session of the Year X

Immediately after the purge, the government announced that the current legislative session had ended. However, since 'important laws, nécessary for the tranquillity and prosperity of the nation' still needed to be passed, the Consuls had agreed that the legislature should meet extraordinarily on 5 April and remain in session until 21 May.[1]

This allowed a mere fortnight or so for the Senate to 'elect' 60 new legislators and 20 Tribunes to replace the outgoing members. In fact it had already been working at the task for some weeks. The *Journal des Débats* revealed as early as 10 February that nearly 3,000 aspirants had sent in their names to such Senators as they thought might favour their cause, and that half of them had had to be dismissed without further consideration because they were not on the national list. Morellet, who was disappointed to find himself by-passed in favour of men whom he regarded as nonentities, attributed his lack of success chiefly to the fact that he had neither visited nor written to a single member of the Senate.[2]

Opponents of the government spread rumours to the effect that all the places were to be filled with émigrés and former nobles. Napoleon's only expressed wish was that a few prefects should be elected. When the lists were published they were found to consist mainly of the names of men who had already proved their loyalty to the régime either in judicial or administrative posts, as army officers, or by serving as members of local councils. The government denied that it had tried to recruit its own supporters, and maintained that the Senate had chosen strictly non-party men (sometimes thought to be the same thing). Two scholars, Chapuis and Toulongeon, added a certain amount of distinction to the list of new Legislators, while the Tribunes included three professors and a librarian. Most noticeable among the names for the Tribunate were those of Lucien Bonaparte, recently returned from a diplomatic mission to Spain, and of Carnot, ex-member of the Jacobin Committee of Public Safety and organizer of France's armies in the Year II. Why the latter had been chosen is not at all clear, unless it was thought necessary to

1 *Arch. parl.*, 20 Mar. 1802.
2 Morellet, *Mémoires* II, p. 111.

recompense the Pas-de-Calais for losing two local-born Tribunes in the purge by nominating another of its famous sons. When the session opened, an English visitor described Lucien Bonaparte and Carnot, along with Chauvelin from among the previous members, as being the only ones who presented a gentlemanly appearance, Lucien sporting silk stockings and Carnot 'a suit of black worthy of a courtier.[3]

Before the labours of legislation properly began, the Tribunate co-operated with Napoleon in producing a change in its own procedure. After lengthy discussion in private it ruled that henceforward all bills except declarations of war and treaties of peace and commerce should be sent for preliminary examination to one of three sections – interior, legislation and finance – into which the total membership was to be divided. The change has usually been regarded as inspired by Napoleon for sinister purposes, chiefly because the latter, during one of his outbursts of anger with the Tribunate, had said that it ought to be divided into sections to discuss matters with the Council of State, thus avoiding general discussion altogether. The *règlement* now adopted by the Tribunate, however, merely replaced preliminary examination of bills by committees of 5, 6, or 7 members, with preliminary examination by sections of 30 or more, and was in line with views expressed by some of the Tribunes in the previous session, to the effect that examination by very small committees was a waste of time since it left too many well-informed persons anxious to have their say. The *règlement* did not abolish public discussion by the general body of the Tribunate, though it was likely to take away some of the heat by involving interested persons beforehand. Further misunderstanding has arisen because Napoleon seized the opportunity to try out a suggestion made to him by Girardin for producing greater co-operation between Councillors and Tribunes. The Councillors who had drawn up a bill could, if they wished, he said, summon the appropriate section of the Tribunate for private discussion before the bill was presented to the Legislative Body. This, again, did not abolish general discussion in the Tribunate, and on the one occasion when it was tried (in connection with the Legion of Honour bill) it certainly did not inhabit opposition from parliament as a whole.[4]

The first measure to be presented to the legislature on 5 April 1802 was the Concordat. Portalis introduced the bill in a speech lasting 'two whole hours'.[5] He praised religion in general as the only possible source of morality, and Christianity in particular as a cultural and civilizing

3 *Arch. nat.*, F⁷ 3830; Napoleon, *Correspondance*, no. 5928; *Journal de Paris*, 29, 30 Mar. 1802; Yorke, *France in 1802*, pp. 207–8. The list for the Legislative Body contained only 59 names, apparently by an oversight. Sapey, a former diplomat, was added three weeks later.
4 *Arch. parl.*, 1, 11 Apr. 1802; Thibaudeau, *Mémoires sur le Consulat*, p. 212; Girardin, *Mémoires* III, p. 240. J. Godechot in his *Institutions de la France sous la Révolution et l'Empire* (2 vols, Paris, 1951) I, 490, confused these arrangements with later constitutional changes.
5 *Arch. nat.*, F⁷ 3830.

influence. Catholicism was undeniably the religion of the majority of Frenchmen, he said; a government which neglected so powerful a source of support did so at its peril. Negotiation with the Pope had been necessary because only he could heal the breach between constitutional and non-juring clergy, and only he could assure owners of national land that former church property would never be reclaimed. This did not mean that the Pope had been given a dangerous amount of influence over French affairs: as a minor foreign potentate he would always be dependent on France. Nor had the clergy been restored to political influence. Their activities were to be strictly controlled and their ambitions tempered by the toleration of Protestants and Jews. When Portalis had ended his speech, Regnault de St Jean d'Angély read out the text of both the Concordat and the Organic Articles, the whole being listened to with minute attention by a packed audience in the public galleries. A police observer received the impression that the reinstatement of Sunday as a day of rest in place of the less fequent *décadi* of the republican calendar was especially welcome.[6]

The text was sent immediately to the Tribunate, where it was classed as a peace treaty and referred to a special commission consisting of Siméon, Savoye-Rollin, Lucien Bonaparte, Arnould, Roujoux, and Jard-Panvilliers. Siméon reported to the Tribunate two days later. General discussion should have followed, but voices were raised demanding an immediate vote, the count resulting in a majority of 78 to 7 for the bill. The crowd which turned up to hear the debate in the Legislative Body next day not only filled the public gallery but invaded the body of the hall, whence it had to be expelled by the guards. The only speakers were Lucien Bonaparte and Jaucourt for the Tribunate. Lucien's speech was a résumé of Portalis's original discourse, delivered in a more flamboyant style. Jaucourt spoke very briefly on behalf of Protestant supporters who appreciated the toleration accorded to them by the bill. The vote was then taken, resulting in 228 for the bill and 21 against.[7]

It should not be too readily assumed that the 51 Legislators and 15 Tribunes who failed to vote had deliberately abstained, as a mark of protest.[8] It is more than likely that some, at any rate, of the missing members had not yet arrived on the scene. A great many of the men who had sat in the previous parliament had drifted off home during the process of the purge, not realizing that there was to be a supplementary session, and the police reckoned that some of them would not be able to return for a month or more. Meanwhile new members were not informed individually of their appointment: one of them, Ligneville,

6 *Arch. nat.*, F⁷ 3830.
7 *Arch. parl.*, 7, 8 Apr. 1802.
8 A. Gobert in *L'Opposition des assemblées pendant le Consulat* (Paris, 1925), p. 217, added them to the number of adverse voters to make an opposition of nearly a third of the total membership of parliament.

wrote to say that he could hardly abandon his post as prefect of the Haute Marne on the strength of a list in the *Moniteur*. Of the 51 members missing from the Legislative Body when the Concordat came on, 39 were newly appointed. In the Tribunate two new members were sworn in after the final vote had taken place.[9]

The opposition was nevertheless significant. Napoleon regarded the Concordat as his individual achievement, the Council of State having neither drawn up the clauses nor been allowed to discuss them. At the opening of the session Napoleon officially informed the members of the Legislative Body that he wished them to pass the Concordat unanimously. Of the twenty-eight opposition voters, one was undoubtedly Carnot, who was reported by the police to be 'fulminating against the Concordat' from the moment of arriving in Paris. Of the rest, a number were probably constitutional clergy, led by Grégoire from his position in the Senate. It cannot have been entirely pleasing to Napoleon that the only spontaneous expression of approval came from a Protestant member of the Legislative Body, Bassaget of the Vaucluse, who was allowed to make a speech on the subject the day after the vote was taken.[10]

The next major piece of legislation received more outspoken criticism. The education bill, in spite of being referred to one of the new 'sections' of the Tribunate, met with lengthy discussion in the general assembly, where it was condemned by Duchesne as abandoning the vast majority of the population to ignorance. Primary schools, Duchesne pointed out, were to be given no support, financial or otherwise, from the state, but were to be left to the initiative of municipal councillors in the communes, who must either allot local funds or charge fees. Among the greed and indifference of the countryside it was a delusion to think that they would provide one fifth of the places in schools free, as recommended by the bill. Meanwhile money was to be showered upon lycées and special schools, which the vast majority of the population would have neither the desire nor the means to attend. The state was to provide 6,400 scholarships, but entry for them was to be from secondary schools, which were wholly fee-paying. The number of scholarships could reasonably be cut down by two thirds and the money used to pay three or four primary school teachers in each group of communes. The Revolution, Duchesne continued, had been made neither by nor for particular classes of the population: all had co-operated in the conquest of liberty, and primary education was therefore a debt which the state owed to the nation.[11]

Other speakers criticized particular aspects of the bill without declaring themselves wholly against it. Chassiron thought that it ought to

9 *Arch. nat.*, F⁷ 3830; *Arch. parl.*, 11 Apr. 1802.
10 Thibaudeau, *Mémoires*, p. 159; Grégoire, *Mémoires* I, p. 107; *Arch. parl.*, 9 Apr. 1802.
11 *Arch. parl.*, 27 Apr. 1802.

have required the primary schools to teach agricultural techniques; Daru thought that religion ought to have been included at all levels; Jard-Panvilliers would have liked to have seen the provision of free secondary schools. Only Duchesne attacked the amount of control to be exercised by the government, and even he confined his criticism to the control of secondary schools, which he said should be free from interference since they were to receive no financial support. Carrion-Nisas joined him in asking outright for the rejection of the bill, but on the idiosyncratic grounds that it did not require teachers to be celibate, and that the teaching of modern foreign languages in the lycées would give pupils a preference for foreign countries. Some of the Tribunes who spoke before Duchesne supported the bill on the assumption that it would give real educational opportunities to the poor: if they were disillusioned by him they may have helped to produce the nine votes subsequently cast against the bill.[12]

The debate in the Legislative Body lasted two days. Fourcroy, who had once been a member of the Jacobin committee which aimed at free primary education and a liberal syllabus for secondary schools, spoke first for the Council of State, denying that there existed a government anywhere in the world which could find the money for free primary schools, and arguing that a government which gave free places in the lycées had a right to control all schools which gave access to them. Roederer, who followed him, defended the measure frankly on élitist and utilitarian grounds. The nation needed a modest number of well-educated and scientfically trained men, he said, and these the bill was designed to supply; the state had no right to spend taxpayers money on giving education to vast numbers of children who were unfitted for it. Siméon and Jard-Panvilliers reported in moderate terms for the Tribunate, and the bill passed by 251 votes to 27.[13]

In the early days of May the government presented its usual series of financial proposals. Tribunes made their now familiar plea for a proper budget, but without daring to suggest that money should be withheld from a government which had just given the nation the blessings of a general peace. The Legislative Body passed the bills with votes in the region of 250 to 10.[14] A bill to restore branding as a punishment for forging coins, which had aroused considerable opposition in the Tribunate before the purge, was now commended by the Tribunes with only 6 dissentient votes, and passed by the Legislative Body with 241 to 23, the chief excuse for restoring one of the 'indelible' punishments abolished during the Revolution being that transportation, envisaged as an alternative, had not yet been organized.[15] A bill to restore slavery in France's colonies passed almost without discussion, though with smaller

12 *Arch. parl.*, 26–8 Apr. 1802.
13 *Arch. parl.*, 30 Apr., 1 May 1802.
14 *Arch. parl.*, 1, 3, 4, 7, 11 May 1802.
15 *Arch. parl.*, 2 Jan., 8, 11, 12 May 1802.

majorities – 54 to 27 in the Tribunate and 211 to 63 in the Legislative Body. Adet, reporting for his section to the rest of the Tribunate, said that to persevere with the abolition of slavery would give France's commercial rivals an unfair advantage. 'L'humanité sans doute s'y oppose, mais la politique est forcée de la tolérer.'[16]

However, something like the old blaze of opposition reappeared when Napoleon launched his measure creating the Legion of Honour. Undeterred by a majority of only 14 to 10 in the Council of State, Napoleon gave notice of the forthcoming bill to the Tribunate's section of the interior, and accepted a couple of minor amendments. At 1.30 on the same day (15 May 1802) he nominated Roederer, Marmont, and Mathieu Dumas to take the bill to the Legislative Body at 2 o'clock, allowing Roederer only fifteen minutes to prepare his introductory speech before setting off. This haste can only have been due to a desire on Napoleon's part to prevent dissident Councillors from spreading their opinions too widely; it cannot have been due to the approaching end of the session, for the latter was put off for a fortnight without difficulty. The unseemly rush was continued throughout the proceedings. The debate before the Legislative Body was fixed for a mere four days ahead, allowing the Tribunate, already grappling with a full agenda, only half the afternoon of 15 May for discussion. In the Legislative Body, business already scheduled for the 19th was pushed into a morning session beginning at 9 o'clock and the first part of an evening session beginning at 7 o'clock. The debate on the Legion of Honour bill began at 9 in the evening and the vote had to be taken before midnight.

The bill was recommended to the Tribunate in glowing terms by Lucien Bonaparte, reporting as chairman of the section of the interior. Discussion began at once, with an attack by Savoye-Rollin on a bill which he described as a menace to public liberty. Its object, he said, was to create a privileged corps, endowed with special honours, special attributes, a special oath, a special organization, and funds to support it. The Legion would constitute a patriciate, which would ultimately become an hereditary nobility – worse, a nobility whose emphasis was on military glory, for who could suppose that the introduction of a few civilians would have any effect? Article 8 of the Constitution already provided for soldiers and civilians who had deserved well of their country to be rewarded individually: if they were formed into a Legion of Honour, this would imply that they had a monopoly of honour, which was rightly the patrimony of all Frenchmen.

This spirited attack was followed by a less successful speech from Chauvelin, who made a great parade of speaking extempore but who had been seen pacing the hall for a couple of hours before the meeting, preparing the speech in his head. Chauvelin had a reputation in his native Côte-d'Or as a radical, but he had not so far played a very distinguished part in opposition in the Tribunate. Ill-natured gossip

16 *Arch. parl.*, 18, 19 May, 1 June 1802.

accused him of coming into the open at last because he had fallen foul of Napoleon over the peace treaty with Russia. He did little more than repeat the points made by Savoye-Rollin; however, his hesitating manner gave an impression of sincerity, and a florid speech from Carrion-Nisas which followed, in defence of the measure, sounded silly by comparison. Lucien Bonaparte claimed the right as reporter to reply to opponents. He described membership of the Legion as a distinction rather than a privilege, since it carried no administrative or judicial power. Those who attacked the measure, he said, were not opponents of the bill so much as enemies of the government. Savoye-Rollin was not allowed to reply to this slander, but it may have served to irritate the Tribunes, for the vote immediately afterwards produced a majority of only 18 for the bill. Out of 94 voters, 38 had been against the bill. Since the opponents were a minority they could send no representative to the Legislative Body next day. The vote there nevertheless resulted in a substantial opposition count of 110, against 166 in favour of the bill. The result was a great surprise to Roederer, who had been rather proud of his own speech in support of the bill, and even more impressed by Mathieu's, which had been applauded in the public gallery. Napoleon had been warned by a number of well-wishers that the measure was 'premature' and would meet with opposition. He could not resist blaming the three spokesmen who took it to the Legislative Body for failing, in his view, to emphasize the right points, but he agreed that he ought to have waited a year or two before presenting the measure, and for once in his life he refrained from an outburst of anger against the legislative assemblies.[17]

17 Thibaudeau, *Mémoires sur le Consulat*, pp. 87, 92; Viard, *Côte d'Or*, p. 90; Roederer, *Autour de Bonaparte*, pp. 123–5; Bourrienne, *Mémoires* III, p. 200.

7

The Life Consulate

On 6 May 1802 Cambacérès, the Second Consul, sent for Chabot, the President of the Tribunate, and told him that government spokesmen would enter the Tribunate that afternoon to announce the signing of the peace of Amiens. It would be very appropriate, Cambacérès continued, if the Tribunate used its constitutional powers to express a wish favourable to the First Consul. Chabot hastened to consult Siméon, and together they performed a little pantomime. As soon as Regnier had announced the treaty, Chabot spoke in glowing terms of Napoleon's services to the country and to humanity. Siméon then took the rostrum and said that more was required than a mere speech from the chair: a formal address should be sent to the First Consul. Whereupon Chabot quitted the presidential seat and proposed that the Tribunate express a wish that the First Consul be given an illustrious token of the nation's gratitude. The proposal was adopted unanimously, though according to Girardin a number of members disliked the lack of definition in the proposal. Chabot himself, Girardin thought, was far from anticipating the life consulship. He imagined that the Senate would bestow the title of peacemaker upon Napoleon and give him a palace.[1]

On 10 May the Tribunate received notice that the Senate proposed to re-elect Napoleon Bonaparte First Consul for a further ten years after the original ten had finished. Duveyrier, while hinting that the Senate had not gone as far as Napoleon's well-wishers might have desired, proposed that the Senate's decision be accepted and printed in the minutes. On the next day, however, the Tribunate heard that Napoleon had conscientiously declined to accept an extension of power from anyone but the people, and that the nation was to be consulted by plebiscite on the (very different) proposal: should Napoleon Bonaparte be made First Consul for life? A register was at once opened in the Tribunate to receive the votes of the members, and so urgent was the desire to get it sent off to the First Consul that absentees were summoned individually from their homes to sign within twenty-four hours. The Legislative Body proceeded with more decorum throughout,

1 *Arch. parl.*, 6 May 1802; Girardin, *Souvenirs* III, pp. 265–6.

declining to associate itself formally with the wish concerning a signal honour for the First Consul on the grounds that the Legislative Body had no constitutional power to express wishes, and refusing to open a register to receive the votes of members until a sub-committee had recommended a suitable procedure. When the votes were presented to Napoleon, however, Viennot Vaublanc, the head of the deputation from the Legislative Body, made up for any previous shortcomings by addressing the last part of his speech to the First Consul alone, instead of to the Citizen Consuls together, an unprecedented form of flattery which greatly pleased Napoleon.[2]

The registers of both Tribunate and Legislative Body have unfortunately been lost to posterity. Rumour at the time had it that the only adverse vote was from Carnot, who insisted on adding to his signature, 'I hereby sign the warrant for my arrest.' It is more than likely, however, that Duchesne also registered a negative vote, for he was reported by the police on 12 May as openly disapproving of the life consulship. Information from a somewhat obscure source (a letter from an anonymous Parisian correspondent published in a London newspaper) suggests that Duchesne was shortly afterwards threatened with prosecution as an enemy of the government, but it is not clear whether this was because he had opposed the life consulship or because he had collaborated with his nephew, Camille Jordan, in publishing a pamphlet which Napoleon notoriously disliked. The pamphlet, *Vrai sens du vote national sur le Consulat à vie*, described the plebiscite as a contract between the nation and Napoleon, obliging the latter to grant more genuine representation to the people. It was seized at the printer's but reissued clandestinely, bearing the name of the author.[3]

The senatus-consultum of 4 August 1802 which made Napoleon Consul for life carried an appendix which prescribed certain changes in the structure of the parliamentary assemblies. The Legislative Body got off lightly, with what was virtually only a tidying up process. The total number of members was to remain the same, but henceforward each of the three hundred was to represent a particular department, the number of representatives of each department being decided according to population. The departments were to be classed in five 'series', each series renewing its parliamentary membership once every five years.[4] The Tribunate suffered a far worse blow, delivered in a single clause: 'By the Year XIII, the Tribunate will be reduced to fifty members. A half of the fifty will retire every three years. Until this reduction has been accomplished, members retiring will not be replaced. The Tribunate will be divided into sections.' In some ways, the most frightening aspect of this clause was its obscurity. Since the Tribunate had already been

2 *Arch. parl.*, 11, 14 May 1802; Bourrienne, *Mémoires* III, p. 313.
3 *Arch. nat.*, F⁷ 3830; *Une année de correspondance*, 23 Aug. 1802.
4 The senatus-consultum also prescribed new electoral machinery, which will be studied in the next chapter.

divided into sections, why mention them, unless they were to be given a different role? Rumour inevitably assumed that the Tribunate was to be phased out altogether.[5]

The senatus-consultum did not say how the Senate was to choose the members destined to retire from the two parliamentary bodies at the required intervals, but a supplementary decree of 30 August empowered the First Consul to nominate a chairman for the proceedings. On 31 August he nominated the scholar Lacépède, whose skill at flattering Napoleon was afterwards said to have 'carried too far the luxury of praise'.[6]

As far as the Legislative Body was concerned, the requirements regarding departments and series prevented too much attention from being paid to personalities. The senatus-consultum of 4 August had already classified the departments into series (widely dispersed, so that there should be nothing like a general election, even in one fifth of the country at a time). Later in August, lots were drawn to decide in what order the series should renew their deputations. Only in September were the existing members allotted to departments. They were assigned where possible to departments in which they resided, and only when this had been done was there scope for placing unwanted individuals in Series 4, the first to retire. Even so, Legislator Grouvelle was reported by the police as saying that 'intrigue' and 'cabal' had had a lot to do with the 'eliminations'.

For the Tribunate, things were different. The members themselves waited with a fatalistic air to hear their fate. (The 20 who had been elected after the purge held a dinner at which they toasted themselves with the words: 'May the twenty *new* Tribunes become *old*!')[7] On 4 September 1802 the Senate produced a list of 25 members who were to remain *in situ* until the Year XIX (1810–11). This meant that the Senate had 'elected' already, in the Year X, men who were to begin in the Year XIII a six-year stint under the new rules. Eighteen of the favoured 25 were men who had been placed in the Tribunate at the beginning of the Consulate and would thus have served eleven years by the time they went out. Not all of these favoured members were yes-men. Arnould, the economic expert, had many times complained of the lack of a proper budget; Garry and Grenier had made a number of opposition speeches during earlier sessions. More understandably the list included the names of Chabot and Siméon, and of Girardin, who had on many occasions acted as liaison between Napoleon and the Tribunate.

This list was followed by the names of 25 members who would remain for the first three years of the new system, retiring in the Year XVI (1807–8), and of 10 members who would retire in the Year XIII (1804–5). Another 20 were listed to retire in a mere two years' time, in

5 *Arch. nat.*, F⁷ 3830.
6 Napoleon, *Correspondance*, no. 6296; Chazet, *Mémoires* II, pp. 36–7.
7 Pictet, *Journal*, p. 104.

the Year XII, among them Bouteville, Portiez, Huguet and J.B. Say, who had more than once figured as opponents of the government, and Riouffe, whose exuberant support Napoleon was supposed to find embarrassing. The 20 whose names did not appear on any list were to retire in the Year XI. The choice of victims for this last category was regarded by some people as a second purge, but the majority seem to have been nondescript characters. The only ones whom the government might have been really glad to get rid of were Ludot, a noted radical journalist of the Directorial period, and Laussat, proscribed from the Council of Elders in the purge of Fructidor and still suspected of royalist leanings. Andrieux was also scheduled to disappear at this point, though he had been completely docile since escaping the purge of March 1802.

Four men whose opposition to the government had attracted attention in recent months met with varied treatment. Carnot was the luckiest, for the Senate decreed that men elected after the purge should stay in the Tribunate for their full five years, and Carnot, perforce, could not be obliged to retire until the Year XVI. Savoye-Rollin was listed to remain until the Year XIII, although rumour had designated him as one of those likely to be got rid of at once. Chauvelin was rather less fortunate, being scheduled to retire in the Year XII. Duchesne, to the approval of his admirers, did not wait to be 'shown the door', but resigned before the lists appeared. He wrote a sensational letter to the President of the Tribunate which was not, however, recorded in the minutes.[8] On leaving parliament none were shown vindictiveness except Duchesne. Carnot retired into private life, to emerge honourably and spectacularly during the Hundred Days. Savoye-Rollin was made prefect of the Eure; Chauvelin, having been offered a decoration in the Legion of the Honour which he declined, was made prefect of the Lys (he would have preferred the Côte-d'Or, but Napoleon said he owned too much land there and appointed Riouffe instead). Duchesne returned to legal practice at Grenoble, and when he was later chosen as candidate for the Senate, Napoleon refused to have him.

As usual there was a certain amount of administrative muddle. The 20 members whose names had not appeared on any list of candidates due to remain until the Years XII, XIII XVI and XIX, assumed that they at least had one more session to go, that of the Year XI. They were disabused of this notion when their pay stopped at the end of the Year X. The Tribunate consequently met for the Year XI with a maximum of 80 members. Those elected at the beginning of the Consulate could not, strictly, speaking, grumble at having to retire before they had completed five years, because the Constitution had made it clear that renewals were to begin after two years: nevertheless the government accorded the retiring members an indemnity, though it had done no such thing for the members purged in March. The sum of 3,000 francs fixed for the

8 *Arch. nat.*, F⁷ 3830.

indemnity was nothing like a year's salary, and recipients complained accordingly.[9]

The parliamentary assemblies met for the opening of the session on 21 February 1803 in an atmosphere of gloom and despondency. The clause in the Constitution of 1799 whereby parliament met as of right on 22 November had been rescinded by Article 75 of the senatus-consultum, allowing the government to convoke, adjourn, and prorogue the Legislative Body at pleasure. The government had delayed the session of the Year XI for three months beyond the usual date for no known reason, and speculation had inevitably arisen as to whether there was ever to be a meeting at all.[10] Even the members of the Legislative Body felt that Napoleon had treated them with scant respect in the senatus-consultum, although in fact they had lost only one of their former powers, the right to suggest a candidate for each vacant place on the Senate.[11] The members of the Tribunate were bound to feel worse. During the winter the three sections into which the Tribunate had previously been divided had remained in existence, and Napoleon had frequently summoned delegates from the legislative section to discuss parts of the Civil Code with the Council of State. Thibaudeau, who assisted at these sessions, thought that the system possessed advantages as far as getting through the work was concerned, but that the Tribunes, though perhaps achieving small amendments here and there, were at a permanent disadvantage as against the authors of the bills. Moreover the public knew nothing of what was being done in its interests. It was clear that if this practice continued during the session, bills would arrive in parliament already 'purified', and the Tribunes who had discussed them with the Council of State would be expected to explain them convincingly to their colleagues. Napoleon virtually told the members of the Tribunate that their future depended on their usefulness in this new role:

> The reputation of any official body rests on the services it renders to the country. The Tribunate, summoned to discuss bills proposed by the Council of State, forms, along with the Council, one of the most essential parts of the legislative organization. Equal in numbers, divided like it into sections, it will continue to show in discussions the spirit of wisdom, the zeal and the talents . . . of which it is now giving such a fine example in examination of the Civil Code.[12]

General meetings of the Tribunate continued to be held regularly during the two parliamentary sessions of the Life Consulate. Often there was no business, and the meeting would be adjourned after the reading of the minutes, which were of a very brief nature since there had

9 *Arch. nat.*, F⁷ 3831.
10 *Arch. nat.*, F⁷ 3831.
11 This was henceforward to be done by the departmental colleges (see chapter 8).
12 Thibaudeau, *Mémoires sur le Consulat*, p. 211; Napoleon, *Correspondance*, no. 6251.

probably been no business at the previous meeting either. Even when a bill arrived for discussion, normal procedure was to hear a report from the section concerned, and proceed at once to the vote. The police reported poor attendances on the part of the Tribunes – 20 or 30 for the purely formal sessions, and 50 or 60 for sessions devoted to the Civil Code. Carnot was described as looking very surly: on one occasion he paid no attention to the business in hand and devoted himself to reading a pamphlet. There was much grumbling about pay, which was said to be late in arriving. The galleries continued to attract a fair number of visitors, but most of them were foreigners. They were not impressed by the room, with its wooden benches covered with blue cloth: one visitor described it as 'small and mean'; another, more polite, thought it looked like a private chapel. A new hall had been in preparation for at least two years, but there had been inexplicable delays.[13]

In the Legislative Body the so-called debating of bills was even duller than before, since the government seldom bothered to send speakers, and a single delegate from the Tribunate either gave a précis of the report previously given to that body by a member of the relevant section, or announced that the Tribunate recommended the bill 'for the reasons given by the government when presenting it'. Meetings were given a certain amount of interest, however, by the arrival, two or three times a week, of important bills from the Council of State, to be given a preliminary reading. Attendance of members seldom rose much above 220, but this was due in large measure to the fact that the new electoral colleges were slow to produce the 80 members required for the renewal of Series 4. Often 30 or 40 members were noted as not wearing the official costume, but this was owing to genuine dislike of the garment prescribed, and negotiations were begun for a more comfortable outfit. The public galleries were frequently full, though it is a mystery how people can have known when to arrive, since meetings began at various times between noon and 1.30 p.m. Often the crowd was composed of people likely to be affected by a particular bill – financiers, especially directors of rival banks, followed with considerable anxiety the fortunes of the bill establishing the Bank of France; medical students turned up in large numbers to hear the government's proposals for putting an end to the 'anarchy' of the past ten years by confining the practice of medicine and surgery to qualified persons; and young men from all walks of life came away grumbling from the session in which conscription was adopted with fewer exemptions.[14]

Opposition speeches were rare, and the vast majority of bills passed both Tribunate and Legislative Body with only a few dissentient votes. The various sections of the Civil Code, for instance, received votes in

13 *Arch. nat.*, F⁷ 3831; Pictet, *Journal*, p. 104; Yorke, *France in 1802*, p. 207; Reichardt, *Lettres*, pp. 372–3; *Journal des Débats*, 25 Dec. 1801.
14 *Arch. nat.*, F⁷ 3831; *Arch. parl.*, 26 Feb., 3, 7, 10 Mar., 4, 5, 9, 12, 14, 16, 22, 29 Apr. 1803.

the Tribunate of 61 to 3, 54 to 2, 57 to 1, 54 to 3, and in the Legislative Body of 217 to 7, 215 to 3, 204 to 8, 216 to 6. The Tribunate advised the rejection of only one bill in two sessions (a proposal by the government to recover the use of national forest land let out to private individuals), and this created so unusual a situation that the Tribunate had to go into secret session to decide who should convey its recommendation to the Legislative Body. The task fell to Siméon, who made heavy weather of it in a speech to the Legislators, pointing out that the Tribunate had but used its constitutional right and that its temerity on this one occasion need not destroy the harmony which existed between the various branches of the government. He was hard put to it to explain just why so many Tribunes had voted against the bill, since the report from the relevant section had been favourable and there had been no general discussion to enlighten him. Improvising rapidly, he discoursed on the detrimental nature of the bill to the rights of private property. Defermon replied on behalf of the Council of State, and the Legislative Body passed the bill by 142 to 124.[15]

The paucity of opposition has sometimes led historians to describe the Legislative Body as a showpiece, by which Napoleon kept up an elaborate pretence at parliamentary government. He himself saw it, rather, as a means of communication between the government and the public. Councillors of State made increasingly elaborate speeches introducing bills to the Legislators, and presidents of sections performed the same function vis-à-vis the Tribunes. Speaking to the Legislative Body on the marriage clauses of the Civil Code, Siméon addressed himself to 'the whole of France', whose eyes, he said, were 'fixed on this tribune for the explanation of matters new to a great number of departments'.[16] The notion was no doubt false as far as ordinary members of the public were concerned: an English family, on leaving Paris, offered their ticket for a visit to the Legislative Body to the hotel porter, who asked them in all seriousness: 'What is the Legislative Body and what does it do?'[17] More interested persons such as lawyers, however, may well have regarded the proceedings of the parliamentary bodies as a source of information and comment on a mass of legislation pouring out of the Council of State. For posterity the proceedings are of interest for the reasoning by which the government saw fit to commend, and other politicians to accept, the measures characteristic of the Napoleonic régime.

The main legislative work of the Life Consulate was the passing of the Civil Code (later given the name of Code Napoléon), presented in thirty sections over a period of twelve months. There had been much talk by Napoleon and the Council of State about presenting the Code in larger sections than before in order to avoid the detailed scrutiny which was

15 *Arch. parl.*, 28, 31 Jan., 1 Feb. 1804.
16 *Arch. parl.*, 17 Mar. 1803.
17 Greatheed, *Journal*, p. 139.

believed to spoil the look of the whole, but this does not in fact appear to have been done. The first three sections were presented much as before, and government spokesmen were apparently anxious to avoid any appearance of having been influenced by previous opposition speeches. Portalis gave virtually the same opening address, and the articles concerning the promulgation of laws contained only the most minor verbal amendments. The section on civil rights still accorded only reciprocal treatment to foreigners and still prescribed civil death for certain criminal offences. By contrast the third bill, on the registration of births, deaths, and marriages, omitted one of the more enlightened clauses of the original version, by which the mother of an illegitimate child could name the father on the birth certificate. Siméon, reporting on the bill to the Tribunate, praised the authors for not being afraid to back down 'in the interests of justice and truth'.[18]

The only articulate opposition was to the provisions for divorce. During the Revolution divorce had been extremely easy to obtain, for instance by one party claiming incompatibility. In the ensuing reaction, Carrion Nisas may well have been correct in stating in the Tribunate that 90 per cent of the people of France were against divorce altogether and would rather revert to legal separation only. Napoleon, however, was determined to maintain divorce in certain circumstances, including incompatibility; and his spokesman Treilhard was sent to the Legislative Body with the difficult task of stressing all the safeguards that had been invented against abuse. Divorce for incompatibility was to be obtainable only by mutual consent of husband and wife, publicly proclaimed four times in the course of a year, and approved by the parents of both parties if alive. The husband must be over twenty-five, the wife over twenty-one and under forty-five, and the marriage must have lasted more than two years and less than twenty. The section of the Tribunate involved in preliminary discussion with the Council of State had been responsible for raising the requisite age of the husband from twenty-one to twenty-five, and had wanted the further stipulation that the marriage should be childless, but Treilhard believed that adequate provision could be made at law for any children that were involved. The bill passed, but with larger opposition votes than usual: 46 to 19 in the Tribunate and 188 to 31 in the Legislative Body.[19]

A noticeable feature both of the bill on divorce and the previous bill on marriage was the inferior status accorded to women. 'A husband owes protection to his wife: a wife owes obedience to her husband.' No law of the Revolutionary epoch could have made such a statement. A husband could divorce his wife for adultery; a wife could divorce her husband for the same cause only if he brought his mistress to live in the marital home. A husband who found his wife in adultery could put her in

18 Thibaudeau, *Mémoires sur le Consulat*, pp. 217, 220; Napoleon, *Correspondance*, no. 6087; *Arch. parl.*, 23, 25, 28 Feb., 3, 5, 7, 8 Mar. 1803.
19 *Arch. parl.*, 8, 9, 21 Mar. 1803; Durand, 'L'Exercice de la Fonction législative'.

a house of correction for a period lasting up to two years at his discretion; if he murdered her he could be acquitted at law. Neither of
these rules applied to women vis-à-vis their husbands. Portalis, presenting the marriage bill to the Legislative Body, explained the double
standard in terms of the peculiar nature of women, at once capable of
greater purity and greater wickedness than men: 'Women have received
from God that touching modesty which triumphs over all dangers, and
which they cannot lose without becoming more vicious than men.
Husbands and wives undoubtedly owe fidelity to the vow they have
made, but infidelity on the part of the wife supposes a greater degree of
corruption and has more dangerous effects than infidelity on the part of
her husband.' The subject passed without further comment.

Equally there was little comment on the bill establishing the authority
of the father over his children, to the extent of allowing him to obtain on
request a warrant for the detention of a son for a period up to six months
without judicial proceedings. Réal, who presented the bill to the Legislative Body, described fatherhood of a family and magistracy of a
people as institutions sanctified by nature, and Albisson, reporting the
views of the Tribunate, agreed that it was time both were fully restored.
Some members of the Tribunate wished to keep young men under the
authority of their fathers until they reached the age of twenty-five, but
the Council of State insisted on twenty-one, the age of majority established during the Revolution. A little enlightenment was shown in the
bill preserving the right to adopt children, a practice which had been
widespread during the Revolution; but, as with divorce, the provisions
were strictly limited, and presented in almost apologetic terms by government spokesmen. 'I see your attention focused upon the subject with
that anxiety which surrounds all new ventures in legislation,' said Councillor Berlier to the Legislators; they could rest assured, he continued,
that every precaution had been taken against injuring family life.[20]

Portalis opened the second session of the Life Consulate by presenting a lengthy section of the Civil Code establishing the rights of private
property-owners. His speech was derived almost entirely from the
writings of John Locke:

> There have been property-owners ever since there have been men.
> The savage was the owner of the fruits he gathered, and of all that
> served his needs. . . .Landed property began with agriculture and
> the arts, in other words with labour and industry. All that the
> labour of man's hands can add to the work of nature constitutes
> man's right to possession of the soil; it is by industry and labour that
> man has conquered the soil which he inhabits and cultivates. This
> conquest is in accordance with nature; it fulfils the great work of
> creation. . . .Property is not responsible for inequality among men:
> all individual inequalities are the work of nature and bring in their
> train those that we meet with in society.

20 *Arch. parl.*, 7, 12, 14, 17, 24, 26, 29 Mar. 1803.

Here Portalis might have had to part with Locke, had not the recent changes in the electoral system introduced a property qualification for members of electoral colleges. This enabled him to continue: 'You have seen the genius who governs France establishing upon property a sure foundation for the Republic. The men whose possessions guarantee their fidelity are henceforward called to choose those whose intelligence and zeal guarantee their deliberations. In sanctioning the new Civil Code, Citizen Legislators, you will strengthen all our national institutions.'[21]

Portalis was not the only politician to refer to 'the genius governing France'. Speech after speech contributed to the atmosphere of awe and wonder which Napoleon had thought appropriate to the passing of the Civil Code from the beginning. When the final bill was passed, and Jaubert cried out in the Legislative Body, 'Frenchmen! the code of your civil laws is finished!', members might have been excused for wondering if parliament was ever going to be summoned again. 'How sweet it will be for you to return to your homes blessed by your compratiots,' said Portalis, in a speech more appropriate to a school-leaving ceremony than the closing of a parliamentary session. It may have been as some sort of insurance for the future that the Legislative Body approved a suggestion by Marcorelle that a marble burst in honour of Bonaparte the lawgiver be placed in their midst at the beginning of the next session.[22]

In the financial sphere the parliaments of the Life Consulate saw the culmination of the efforts made by their predecessors to secure a single annual financial bill. On 12 March 1803 Cretet, on behalf of the Council of State, announced that the government had at last seen its way to abandoning the partial bills of previous years and to presenting a 'budget'. Henceforward the word *budget* was regularly used in government terminology in place of the former *aperçu des recettes et dépenses*. Something which at least looked like a budgetary law was placed before parliament annually, apart from 1812, till the fall of the Empire, and in spite of the increasing number of extraordinary expenses which Napoleon claimed for war purposes and which escaped the control of parliament, the legislative assemblies of the Consulate could claim to have laid a solid foundation for France's budgetary history.[23]

From a more immediate point of view it is was unfortunate that the same assemblies gave away with one hand what they have gained with the other, by encouraging Napoleon to rely heavily on a system of indirect taxation. The Constituent Assembly in 1791 had regarded the abolition of indirect taxes as one of the major achievements of the Revolution, yet it was not long before direct taxes became unpopular with articulate sections of the community. From the beginning of the Consulate, complaints were made in parliament of the unequal distri-

21 *Arch. parl.*, 17 Jan. 1804.
22 *Arch. parl.*, 19, 21, 24 Mar. 1804.
23 Bruguière, *La Première Restauration*, p. 3.

bution of the land tax, which varied from 10 to 50 centimes in different parts of the country; of the prying into people's private lives which was necessary to levy the personal property tax; and of the detrimental effect which direct taxes in general had upon producers. Consumer taxes were advocated as falling more fairly on all sections of the community. 'Though it may be true that all comes from the land and all must return to the land, it is not true that all must fall as direct taxes upon the land,' said Chassiron in a report to the Tribunate. Indirect taxes, it was argued, by raising the price of commodities would encourage people to work harder to obtain both necessities and luxuries.[24] Yet the government hesitated before the manifest unpopularity of commodity taxes among the poorer sections of the community. Instead, the unpopular land tax was reduced as much as possible; some particularly hard-pressed departments were exempted for a time and their quota levied upon the newly acquired departments near the Rhine. In 1802 the enormous task of making a new cadastral survey was put in hand.[25] Eventually, however, in February 1804, the government created taxes on tobacco and drinks, to be known as *droits réunis* and administered not by the old iniquitous farming system but by a *régie*, a branch of the civil service. Cretet, who presented the bill to parliament, congratulated the government on having avoided taxes on food, yet hit upon commodities which were so widely used that the taxes would fall lightly on a great many people. Neither tobacco nor drinks, he pointed out, were absolute necessities: only people who could afford to buy them did so. Napoleon had taken a personal interest in the whole question, summoning members of the financial section of the Tribunate to a meeting with the Council of State under his own chairmanship. The bill was received enthusiastically in the Tribunate and passed the Legislative Body by a vote of 198 to 7.[26]

To Napoleon the advantage of indirect taxes was that they constituted a supple source of revenue which could easily be manipulated by government officials, thus freeing him from control by parliament on the one hand and bankers on the other. There is no evidence that the members of parliament who encouraged him to adopt the policy realized its political implications: in the forefront of the campaign were such political opponents of Napoleon as Andrieux, Bailleul, and Bouteville. Nor is there reason to suppose that they were more than ordinarily influenced by selfish motives. Like most bourgeois Frenchmen they had doubtless invested money in land, but the majority were by profession lawyers and administrators, not landowners *per se*. The latter gradually increased in numbers in the Legislative Body as the new electoral laws

24 *Arch. parl.*, 12, 13 Mar. 1800, 8 Mar. 1801, 4 May 1802.
25 *Arch. parl.*, 13 Mar. 1800, 12 Mar., 3 May 1802, 17 Mar. 1803. The cadastre was only a third complete by 1814.
26 *Arch. parl.*, 14, 20, 23–5 Feb. 1804; Pictet, *Journal*, p. 128.

of 1802 took effect, but by then Napoleon was well on the way to the 24 per cent reliance on indirect tax receipts reached in 1813.

The return to indirect taxation was allied to another move – the imposition of more and more customs duties on both imports and exports. These, again, formed an easily manipulated source of revenue, particularly during wartime. It was during the Peace of Amiens, however, that they were first admitted to the ranks of public revenue, and they were defended by government supporters both as a source of ready money and as a necessary protection for French industry. The first major increases came in April 1803 and were defended on the grounds that without them France would become a 'tributary' of Britain. It was left to Pictet, a professor of political economy from Léman and one of the members recently appointed to the Tribunate, to point out the disadvantages of the policy. A quarter of the revenue anticipated from customs duties never reached the Treasury, Pictet said, because it was either drained away by smugglers or swallowed up by the cost of trying to suppress them. The loss of personal freedom was, moreover, considerable: already, Pictet pointed out, a wide belt of frontier land had been placed under patrol by armed police, and manufacturers had been subjected to inquisitorial investigations. The Tribunate was about to discuss a further measure to impose the death penalty on smugglers caught under arms. All this was unnecessary, in Pictet's view, for France could flourish, like her neighbour Switzerland, under a system of free trade. The sheer stylishness of this speech aroused a good deal of annoyance among Councillors of State and fellow Tribunes. Napoleon, who had always liked Pictet, continued to greet him affably at receptions, and even promised to read the speech one day; but the arguments it contained, though never effectively answered, simply ran into the sand. Apart from one more effort by Pictet in the following year, nothing more was heard in Napoleonic parliaments about free trade.[27]

While accepting protection against foreign industries, politicians were also prepared to accept a certain amount of government regulation at home. The factories bill of 31 March 1803 which set up consultative committees under government supervision, forbade coalitions of either employers or workers, and obliged workers to carry a work-book, was commended by the Tribunate as a just mean between the controls of the *ancien régime* and the laissez-faire of the Revolutionary period. The *livret* or work-book, regarded by historians as one of the more oppressive of Napoleonic devices, was not at this stage seen as an instrument of police control but simply as a device for preventing employers from stealing each others' employees by offering higher wages.[28]

During the early days of May 1803, crowds of people filled the galleries of the Legislative Body in expectation of news regarding the

27 *Arch. parl.*, 25 Mar., 18, 26–8 Apr. 1803, 12 Mar. 1804; Pictet, *Journal*, pp. 119–20, 127–8.
28 *Arch. parl.*, 31 Mar., 9 Apr. 1803.

outbreak of war against Britain. On one occasion they were sent away grumbling while the Legislators went into secret session to hear a member of the Council of State read out a letter from Talleyrand to the British ambassador.[29] The parliamentary bodies vied with each other in expressing their support of the First Consul. On 15 May the Tribunes sent a message to say how much they were struck by his moderation in negotiating with the British cabinet; on the 16th, the Legislative Body sent a deputation assuring him of their confidence; on the 20th, when Councillor Lacuée announced the departure of the British ambassador from France, more messages were sent. When war was declared, those members of parliament who had at any time seen military service toasted the First Consul after a dinner at the Tivoli and begged him to take them with him on the ship which carried him to England. Sophisticated members, like Pictet, may have been embarrassed by such proceedings, but they made no effective protest. All appear to have accepted the official reason for the outbreak of war, expounded to the Legislative Body by Regnault at the closing of the session – namely, Britain's jealousy at the revival of France's industry and commerce, a revival brought about by the wisdom and strength of her government.[30]

Words like the latter seemed to put a premium on the life of Napoleon. The police at once began reporting plots, or rather rumours of plots, many of them involving members of the parliamentary assemblies. Such rumours multiplied when on 15 February 1804 General Moreau, who had a brother in the Tribunate, was arrested and accused of complicity in a royalist conspiracy. On 10 March the Tribunate and Legislative Body made haste to pass in a single day a law prescribing the death penalty for anyone harbouring the notorious royalist conspirators Pichegru and Cadoudal. It was not long before the two men were arrested and duly found to have plotted violence against the person of the First Consul. The legislative session ended at this inopportune moment, but the Tribunate was still at hand to do what was expected of it.

On 20 April Napoleon put the proposition of an hereditary crown for himself to the Council of State. The Councillors, not without dissentient voices, agreed, and discussion ensued as to how to put the machinery in motion. Napoleon was in no doubt that the Senate, if called upon, would do the job at once by senatus-consultum. The Constitution of the Year X had officially recognized the Senate's power to supply further parts to the governmental machine, provided that a two-thirds majority was prepared to produce a *sénatus-consulte organique*. In January 1803, Napoleon had taken steps to bring the Senate to heel by creating a new kind of benefit, the *sénatorerie*, with which to endow favoured members. There were thirty-six *sénatoreries* in all, one for each area covered

29 *Arch. nat.*, F⁷ 3703, 3830; *Arch. parl.*, 14 May 1803.
30 *Arch. parl.*, 28 May 1803; *Journal de Paris*, 13, 14 June 1803; Pictet, *Journal*, p. 121.

by an assize court, and in return for overlooking public affairs, both administrative and judicial, in the area, the incumbent was given a stately residence and an annual income of 25,000 francs (over and above his salary) derived from national land. Senator Cornet referred in his memoirs to the *sénatoreries* as a divisive factor, and it is not unlikely that Napoleon created as many enemies among those who did not receive one of the new benefits as friends among those who did, but he was a great believer in the efficacy of dangling carrots in front of people, and was sure that the Senators were vying with each other to please him. However, in the matter of the crown it was important, as he told his brother Joseph, that the offer should be made to him by a body which the nation regarded as independent. In the Tribunate there were many men still known for their revolutionary origins. Some of these were genuinely afraid of a return of the Bourbons and might be persuaded to offer a crown to Napoleon as a means of keeping out the dreaded foe. Among them was one Jean-François Curée, who had sat in both the Legislative Assembly and the Convention and had recently been heard to welcome the news of the murder of the Duc d'Enghien. He was given a hint, and on 30 April he moved in the Tribunate that the Senate be asked to declare Napoleon Bonaparte emperor, charged in that quality with the government of the French Republic, the title becoming hereditary in his family. Such a step, Curée said, would be an eternal barrier against the return of the Bourbons.[31]

There was an immediate rush to the rostrum to support the proposal. Siméon, who had also been in the know about it, was the first to get his say, which consisted mainly of arguing that government by one man was the most suitable form for a large nation. Jaubert added that republican government led to chaos and that all great nations were ruled by hereditary monarchs; Gillet invited his colleagues to look at the great examples of the past. Duveyrier declared that it had been for three years the dearest wish of all their hearts to bestow hereditary power upon Napoleon, and that they had hesitated only because of the reluctance of the hero himself.

The President of the Tribunate, Fabre de l'Aude, with some difficulty established an order of priority among the many speakers for the next day. When the meeting opened he ruled that Carnot, as the only man inscribed to oppose the motion, should be given the chance to speak first. Carnot mounted the rostrum without any hope of affecting the issue, but content to make what he described as the one last cry of a free soul. He denied that the requests for hereditary power which had poured into Paris from army officers and government officials typified the wishes of the people. How was it possible to discover the opinion of the people when the press was muzzled? Napoleon Bonaparte had rendered a great service to France's liberty by giving her a code of laws:

31 Cornet, *Souvenirs*, p. 43; Pelet, *Opinions*, pp. 56–62; Miot, *Mémoires* II, pp. 187–8; Bourrienne, *Mémoires* V, pp. 249–59.

was it logical to reward him by offering up France's liberty as a sacrifice? Despotic government did not necessarily bring stability; the Roman Empire lasted no longer than the Roman Republic. A free government could be just as stable as an authoritarian one if its institutions were carefully thought out, witness the USA whose prosperity grew daily. After making the speech Carnot resigned from the Tribunate.

This episode caused no more than a momentary embarrassment. The rest of the Tribunes were so anxious to speak in favour of the motion that when the President closed the discussion on the grounds that the people of France were waiting for a resolution, those who had not spoken insisted on having their wish to do so reported in the minutes. In the general euphoria, Savoye-Rollin had had the good sense to secure the setting up of a commission to draft the resolution properly. An extra clause was added to the original motion, to the effect that the Senate, when modifying France's governmental institutions to accommodate an hereditary chief of state, should preserve the equality, liberty, and rights of the people in their entirety. Gallois wanted to make a speech stressing the importance of this clause, but colleagues shouted impatiently for the vote. Outside parliament, the proceedings of the Tribunate were in any case regarded as a complete farce, because it was well known that the decision to establish the hereditary empire had already been taken.[32]

The President of the Legislative Body sent a letter to the Senate on behalf of the members scattered up and down the country, supporting the motion. All the authorities of state hoped to get something out of the transaction. The Tribunes wanted more salary, the Legislators wanted the right to speak in debate, the Senators wanted their titles to be made hereditary. What Napoleon thought of these aspirations became clear when the constitutional amendments were published on 18 May 1804.[33]

32 *Arch. parl.*, 30 Apr., 1, 2, 3 May 1804; *Arch. nat.*, F⁷ 3705.
33 *Arch. parl.*, 10 May 1804; Pelet, *Opinions*, pp. 65–8.

8

The Electoral Colleges

The senatus-consultum which made Napoleon First Consul for life inaugurated a new electoral system. Its author, as to details, is unknown, but in general terms it can safely be attributed to Napoleon, who identified himself closely with it throughout the ensuing twelve years of its existence. On the day that the Senate passed the necessary 'organic' measure (4 August 1802), Napoleon took it upon himself to explain the whole project to the Council of State. The Constitution of 1799, he said, had left the governing bodies 'in the air'; the people, whose only duty was to draw up a vast list of names, could not possibly feel that they had any part in electing them. It was necessary to anchor the government to the people, and to make the latter feel that they were really represented. Those objectives would be attained by the formation of electoral colleges.[1]

Henceforward all male adults in enjoyment of civil rights were to meet for electoral purposes in an assembly of their canton. (The canton, of which there were several in an arrondissement, was the area forming the jurisdiction of a justice of the peace, and had long ago been suggested by Duchesne as offering a more suitable unit for electoral purposes than the enormous communal arrondissements.) Each cantonal assembly was to elect a required number of members to an arrondissement college and a required number to a departmental college; its nominees must be men resident within the arrondissement and the department respectively, and those for the departmental college must be chosen from a list of the 600 biggest taxpayers (*plus imposés*) in the department.[2] The arrondissement colleges were to have one member to every 500 inhabitants of the arrondissement, provided the number was not less than 120 and not more than 200; the departmental colleges were to have one member to every 1,000 inhabitants of the department, provided the number was not less than 200 and not more than 300. The

1 Thibaudeau, *Mémoires sur le Consulat*, pp. 288–9.
2 These stipulations are frequently misunderstood. For instance L. Bergeron in *L'Episode napoléonien*, p. 85, says that the cantonal assemblies elected the arrondissement colleges and the arrondissement colleges elected the departmental colleges.

First Consul could reward members of the Legion of Honour and other persons who had performed public service by nominating them to the arrondissement and departmental colleges to the number of 10 per college, and he could also add to the departmental colleges 10 members chosen from among the 30 biggest taxpayers in the department.

The members of all the colleges were to serve for life, unless they were removed for having lost their rights of citizenship or for having failed, without due cause, to attend at three successive meetings. When the membership of a college had become depleted by one third, the cantonal assemblies were to be reconvened to fill the gaps. The colleges were to meet once every five years, when elections were held for their particular series. At the meeting, each arrondissement college and each departmental college was to present the names of two candidates to form a list from which the department's deputies to the Legislative Body would be chosen – the choosing being done by the Senate as usual. The number of candidates resulting from the college elections must be at least three times the number of seats available to the department, so that the Senate had a wide enough choice. The arrondissement colleges, at each of their statutory meetings, were also to name two candidates for the list from which Tribunes were to be chosen, and the departmental colleges, similarly, two candidates for the list from which Senators were chosen. The First Consul was to appoint presidents to the cantonal assemblies to serve for five years, and to both types of electoral college to serve for one session.

Historians commenting on the system have fastened upon certain features – the opportunities for governmental control, the life membership of the colleges, the presentation of mere candidates rather than actual deputies – and assumed not only that the system was a farce but that Napoleon saw it as such. In fact, though the cantonal assemblies and arrondissement colleges hardly interested him at all, he was deeply involved in the functioning of the departmental colleges, which he saw as having a purpose quite outside their electoral role. They embodied the propertied elements in the nation and symbolized his especial care for those elements. They were his representatives before the people and his point of contact with the nation at large. Lucien Bonaparte, presiding over the initial convocation of the electoral college of the department of the Seine, pointed out to the members that they were a group, destined to stay together, welded together by a common interest, and connected with the government by mutual bonds of respect.[3] It was in order that the departmental colleges should exist as groups with a continuing influence in their localities that Napoleon insisted on membership being for life; colleges which were continually being re-elected would enjoy no respect in the neighbourhood, he told the Council of State.[4] Years later, Napoleon told a deputation from the electoral

3 *Journal de Paris*, 26 Mar. 1803.
4 Thibaudeau, *Mémoires sur le Consulat*, p. 294.

college of the department of the Seine-et-Oise: 'I take a special interest in the departmental colleges of my Empire. I created them so that they could be intermediaries, and make known to my people the love that I bear them.'[5]

Usually Napoleon bestowed upon deputations from the electoral colleges a few complimentary remarks concerning their department. Sometimes he took the opportunity to deliver a political message; a deputation from the Dordogne in 1810 was treated to the following harangue:

> My ally, the Emperor of Russia, and I have done everything we could to bring peace to the world, but we have not been able to succeed. The King of England, grown old in his hatred of France, wants war. His condition prevents him from realizing the evil to the world and from calculating the results for his family. However, the war will come to an end; and then we shall be greater, stronger and more powerful than we have ever been. The French Empire has the vitality of youth; it can only grow and consolidate itself. That of my enemies is in its latter years; everything presages its decline. Each year that they delay the peace of the world will only increase my power.[6]

Members of deputations themselves seldom spoke on general political subjects. They paid compliments to Napoleon, and expressed a wish that he would visit their department or asked permission to raise a statue to him in their public square.[7] Pressure of work sometimes obliged Napoleon to keep delegations waiting around in Paris for a few days, but in the end he received them graciously and did his best to bestow favours on them. 'I have just received deputations from the colleges of the Seine-Inférieure and the Seine-et-Oise,' he wrote to the Minister of the Interior on 10 January 1810. 'Let me know who the members are and what I can do for them.' Sometimes the prefect of the department wrote to the Minister beforehand informing him of the hopes and aspirations of the party: places were sometimes requested, but most often the members of deputations were sufficiently well-heeled not to require paid appointment, and honours and decorations were more in demand. Four out of the five members of a deputation from the Nord in 1811 were hoping to get the cross of the Legion of Honour. Not surprisingly, colleges were eager to submit the results of their deliberations by means of a deputation rather than by post, and there was keen competition to get on to one. At first the president of the college used to nominate the members of the deputation, choosing men whom he thought would impress Napoleon. 'I have named three members to present respects to the Emperor – all three rich proprietors,' wrote General Garnier-Laboissière from the Charente in 1807. In

5 *Journal de Paris*, 16 Jan. 1810.
6 *Journal de Paris*, 8 Feb. 1810.
7 e.g. *Journal de Paris*, 21 July, 9 Nov., 22 Nov. 1804.

1808, however, Napoleon decreed that all members of deputations, which were to number no more than five, were to be elected by the college.[8]

Pursuing further the idea of rapport between himself and the departmental colleges, Napoleon liked to appoint as presidents such of his marshals and high offices of state as were natives of the department concerned. For the elections in Series 5 in 1806, 13 marshals and 7 colonels-general were pressed into service, along with Cardinal Fesch, Talleyrand, Duroc, Caulaincourt and Ségur.[9] Appointees were not consulted beforehand: they read their names in an imperial decree, issued perhaps from Spain or Austria. Only Davout was ever known to demur. Appointed to preside at Dijon in 1810, he pleaded difficulty in leaving command of his troops; but Napoleon was so determined to have him that he put off the election for a year. All others seem to have regarded themselves as duty bound to accept the commission. The Cardinal-Archbishop of Paris presided for several strenuous days over the electoral college of the department of the Seine in 1807, although he was nearly a hundred years old. Mercy Argenteau, appointed by decree from Spain in 1808 to replace Soult at Liège, believed he had 'no choice in the matter' because 'great importance was attached, particularly by the Emperor, to the assembly of the electoral colleges.' He dutifully travelled to Liège in the depth of winter, though his young wife was about to face a difficult confinement in Paris, and a recent family bereavement made the festivities attached to the electoral proceedings distasteful to him. The president of a departmental college was expected to make a lavish display, with parades, ceremonial masses, banquets, balls and soirées. Cambacérès, who was a vain man as well as a gourmet, thoroughly enjoyed his visit to Bordeaux in 1807, and even Marshal Marmont, who was a simple soul, came away from the Côte-d'Or in 1805 believing that his compatriots really loved him.[10]

In spite of the appointment of illustrious personages as presidents of departmental colleges there seems to have been some scope for lesser men to obtain the post. In 1807 Napoleon decided that the job itself should confer rank: all presidents were to be given the title of baron. They could apply for permission to transmit the title to their heirs if they were able to set aside a considerable amount of property to form an entail. Members of departmental colleges were to be given the same title when they had honourably fulfilled their duties for six years, and they too could apply for the title to become hereditary. By 1814, 103 members and 7 presidents of colleges had become barons, and a further 12 members and 4 presidents, benefiting from Napoleon's discretionary

8 Napoleon, *Dernières Lettres* I, p. 992; *Arch. nat.*, F^{IC}III Nord (4), Charente (3); *Bulletin des Lois*, 26 Nov. 1808.
9 *Journal du Soir*, 16 Sept. 1806.
10 *Arch. nat.*, F^{IC}III Côte d'Or (4); Mercy-Argenteau, *Memoirs* I, pp. 108–15; Viallès, *Cambacérès*, pp. 309–10; Marmont, *Mémoires* II, pp. 204–5.

powers, had become counts.[11] There was no suggestion of according the same privilege to presidents and members of arrondissement colleges, although they fulfilled, officially at any rate, the same electoral functions vis-à-vis the Legislative Body. 'The electoral colleges of the departments today form the intermediary bodies in the state,' wrote Napoleon to Cambacérès. 'If the need should arise to dissolve the Legislative Body, it would be for them to elect the elements from which the new Legislative Body would be formed. It is true that they exercise this function along with the colleges of the arrondissments, but it is no less certain that if their choices were good the Senate could nominate their candidates, and it would be no matter if the choices made by the arrondissement colleges were bad.'[12]

No man could be a member of an arrondissement college and a departmental college at the same time, and there was no law to say that only the members of departmental colleges could be chosen from among the 600 *plus imposés*. Although members of arrondissement colleges were often petty officials such as small-town mayors or their deputies, whose 'personal fortune' was listed as 100 francs or so, it could, and frequently did happen that some members of arrondissement colleges were richer than some members of departmental colleges. Sometimes a man who was elected to both colleges opted for the arrondissement. The distinguishing feature of the departmental colleges was that they were composed *exclusively* of rich men. Since membership must total between 200 and 300, chosen from the 600 *plus imposés*, the choice open to the primary voters was a mere one in two, or at the most one in three, of the richest men in the department. The fact that the least populous departments had to have 200 members in their departmental colleges, and the most populous could have no more than 300, tended to favour rural over urban wealth, as did the nature of the tax system; but it is difficult to discover whether the numerous departmental electors who figured in lists as *propriétaires* were landowners pure and simple or whether they were men who had derived an income from other activities and invested it in land. Fiévée, writing when the new electoral system first came into operation, was under the impression that landowners were less eager to get themselves on to the lists of *plus imposés* than 'les hommes à l'argent', because the latter were 'the world's democrats' while the former were afraid there might be danger for the future in being known as rich; but the position may have changed a few years later. The prefect of the Ourthe (formerly Liège), writing in 1813, was certainly under the impression that the Minister of the Interior wanted landowners in the departmental college. He felt obliged to point out that in Liège power and influence had long been in the hands of bourgeois families, the 'noble' families being few and

11 A. Révérend, *Armorial du Premier Empire*.
12 Napoleon, *Correspondance*, no. 13020.

comparatively poor, their education neglected and their standing almost nil.[13]

In 1805 Napoleon addressed to the Minister of Finance a highly confidential letter. He required the Minister first of all to produce lists of the sixty richest and most important 'proprietors' in each department – 'important either on account of their fortune or on account of the consideration they enjoy or the influence they exercise'. Whether proprietors meant only landowners, and whether the second half of the sentence meant that they could be included if not actually rich, is not clear. They must have been born in the department, Napoleon continued, or their families must have lived in the department for some time.

> The intention of the Emperor is to include among the thirty *plus imposés* only those persons who belong to the families which are weightiest on account of their former or present existence, on account of their family connections in the department, their good conduct, and their virtues both public and private. Weightiest families does not mean those which enjoyed most consideration under the former régime by reason of their birth, although it is not intended that these former circumstances should exclude them; but it means especially the good families belonging to what used to be called the Third Estate, the soundest part of the population which is attached by the tightest and most numerous bonds to the government.

In the eighteenth century, 'proprietary' wealth had included such resources as annuities and venal offices, distinguished from capitalist investment in industry and commerce by their relatively low level of risk. Though official positions were no longer bought and sold, Napoleon's reference to the Third Estate suggests that he had in mind that governing élite which had developed in France in the eighteenth century, part noble and part bourgeois in origin, jointly concerned in landowning and in government office. Two thirds of the 60 persons on each list must be taken from such families, Napoleon said; the lists would then be reduced (by whom?) to the 30 *plus imposés*. Persons whose estates were encumbered with debt, and those who had acquired a fortune by dubious means, should be left off; and perhaps, also, returned émigrés. The lists of 600 and 30 *plus imposés* were never intended to be based purely on tax returns, Napoleon said. The intention was 'to bring to elections the influence which is attached to property'.[14]

Napoleon's personal interest in the new electoral system did not prevent the relevant sections of the senatus-consultum of the Year X from being drawn up in just as ambiguous and slipshod a manner as those of the Constitution of the Year VIII, and there was a similar

13 Fiévée, *Correspondance* I, p. 20; *Arch. nat.*, F^{IC}III Ourthe (2).
14 Napoleon, *Correspondance*, no. 8406.

muddle when attempts were first made to put them into practice. Article 4 was intended to suggest that, when departments first held elections under the new system, cantonal assemblies could use the registers of voters made not too long before by sub-prefects for use under the former system; but its obscure wording was interpreted by some cantons to mean that only the one tenth of adult males who had appeared on lists of communal notables could vote.[15] What was to happen if the candidates presented by the electoral colleges could not possibly add up to three times the number of seats available for the department, or if they amounted to more? Could out-going members of the Legislative Body be renominated? The Council of State, annoyed because the constitutional amendments had been produced by senatus-consultum, took it upon itself to publish 'decisions' in these matters, which were not approved by the Senate and were ignored by some of the colleges.[16] The question of re-eligibility was settled when Napoleon became Emperor: the senatus-consultum of the Year XII (18 May 1804) declared that out-going members of the Legislative Body could be re-elected without interval. The question of too few candidates was settled by a decree of 1806; in cases where the presentation of two candidates by each college did not produce a number at least three times that of the number of deputies allowed for the department, each college was to elect three candidates and if necessary four. The question of what to do if there were more than three times the number of candidates was left open.

A decree of 13 May 1806 laid down for the first time a form of procedure to be followed by the assemblies and colleges. The electoral session in each case was to begin at sunrise on the day of convocation. The electors present were to elect two polling clerks and a secretary, the latter to proceed at once to keep the minutes of the meeting in duplicate. The president was to declare the poll open, and to read out twice over a roll-call of the electors. Each elector, as he came to the table to vote, was to fill in, or allow to be filled in for him, a form stating his name, address and occupation, the forms being collected as soon as the poll was closed and attached to the minutes. Each elector was to deposit his voting slip, written out either by himself or by one of the polling clerks in the presence of the president, in a box upon the table, the box having two keys, one kept by the president and the other by the elder of the two polling clerks. There were to be, if necessary, three ballots, two by list and the third by simple majority between the candidates who had obtained the most votes in the previous ballot. At each ballot the poll was to remain open until at least half the members of the college had voted. Having read out once more the roll-call of electors, the president

15 *Arch. nat.*, F^{IC}III Côte d'Or (3). Some historians have also interpreted the article in this way.
16 Thibaudeau, *Mémoires sur le Consulat*, p. 301; Cambacérès, *Lettres inédites* I, pp. 62–7.

was to declare the poll closed and count the number of voting slips in the box. If it exceeded the number of name and address forms appended to the minutes, the voting slips were to be burnt without further investigation. If the numbers tallied, the president and polling clerks were to examine each voting slip and erase from each one the last names over and above the number it should contain, and any names which, for lack of forenames or qualifications, did not designate clearly the persons to whom they were meant to apply. At the counting of the votes, it was to be borne in mind that each arrondissement and each departmental college was supposed to elect one of its candidates from outside its own membership, though if a third ballot was necessary to secure any candidates at all the distinction could be waived. At the end of the proceedings, the president was to send one copy of the minutes with supporting documents to the prefect, and keep the other copy himself, to be handed on to his successor.

The proceedings were so complicated that irregularities were almost bound to occur. Cantonal assemblies were divided into as many as ten or twelve sections, and to synchronize three ballots, making sure that the required number had voted at each one, was beyond the wit of some presidents. Article 21 of the *règlement*, describing the third ballot, was intended to produce results at all costs, but its details were so formidable that they were very often misunderstood. Prefects, responsible for scrutinizing the minutes and sending the result to the Minister of the Interior, sometimes annulled irregular elections on their own initiative, especially if they were forceful characters like Imbert of the Vosges, a former member of the Tribunate. Others submitted queries, or happily dismissed minor irregularities. Thus the prefect of the Loiret, discovering in 1807 that two members of an arrondissement college had been improperly elected by a cantonal assembly four years previously, wondered whether it was incumbent upon him to declare the entire proceedings of the arrondissement college null and void; the prefect of the Apennins in 1808, on the other hand, simply added a name to the list of members of one of his colleges, having decided that it had been omitted by an oversight on the part of the president.[17]

The chief problem, however, was lack of attendance, particularly at the cantonal assemblies. Cambacérès regarded these assemblies as a great concession to democracy, but primary voters were more interested in attending meetings at which they elected two candidates for the position of justice of the peace than those at which they chose members of the electoral colleges. In both years when elections were held in the Côte-d'Or there were ballots which failed to poll a single elector, and many cantons which could not complete their proceedings because the statutory fortnight had run out and the number of voters had not reached a half of the number of registered electors. The prefect of Loiret netted a certain number of voters in 1808 by opening the polls

17 *Arch. nat.*, F^{IC}III Vosges (5), Loiret (2), Apennins (1).

in the churches immediately after mass on a Sunday, and other prefects may well have done the same since the church was often the only building large enough for the convocation of a cantonal assembly should all the qualified voters turn up. The prefect of the Loiret thought that most of the voters in the countryside had too little education to understand the importance of elections, but the president of one of the cantonal assemblies in the department of the Drôme thought that they were shrewd enought to realize that elections were of no importance at all, and that 'the government knew how to get on without needing votes from the people.' The prefect of the Vosges pointed out that formalities connected with conscription occupied the inhabitants of the countryside during the first three months of the year, after which they were intensively occupied in the fields for another couple of months: cantonal assemblies were likely to be deserted unless held in May or June. One of the presidents of a cantonal assembly in the Gironde thought that the government should give people an incentive to vote if it wanted to get them to the polls: he suggested that they should be debarred from petitioning against taxes unless they could prove attendance at an electoral assembly.[18]

At arrondissement and departmental colleges the poll was seldom much more than 50 per cent, but this may have been because presidents took a pride in being able to report that they had finished the business in four or five days, and hence closed the poll as quickly as possible. Sometimes their speed was attributed, rightly or wrongly, to nefarious motives: an anonymous writer to the Minister of the Interior on 8 April 1803 complained that the elections in the arrondissement of Bazas had lasted less than twenty-four hours, which did not allow time for all the electors to get there, and that the precipitation suggested a secret motive on the part of the officials. 'Everything was prepared in advance, and certain candidates for the Legislative Body had an interest in seeing that nothing was done with the coolness of reason.'[19]

Prefects continually complained of the amount of administrative work involved. The first time a department held elections under the new system, processing the results of the cantonal assemblies could take anything up to six weeks. The drawing up of lists of the 600 biggest taxpayers was an immense work, resulting in many complaints regarding inaccuracy and downright fraud. When the series came round a second time, matters were worse.[20] Prefects had to ascertain anew the population of each arrondissement, in order to work out if the college was entitled to a greater or smaller number of electors. They had to find out how many people had died or moved away, or been taken off the list

18 *Arch. nat.*, F^{IC}III Côte d'Or (3, 8), Loiret (2), Drôme (3), Vosges (5), Gironde (2).
19 *Arch. nat.*, F^{IC}III Gironde (2).
20 One fifth of the departments never had a second set of elections. There were no elections in 1810 owing to the lateness of the parliamentary session of the previous year, and none in 1812 or 1814. This meant that there were only nine years in which the system actually functioned.

of *plus imposés* because their fortune had declined or they had become bankrupt. If more than a third had disappeared and new cantonal elections were required, new registers had to be drawn up. At each stage the prefects had to send to the Minister of the Interior vast and detailed lists: each member of an arrondissement college, for instance, had to be listed according to his name, canton, date of birth, civil status, number of children, profession before 1789, profession since 1789, personal fortune, the number of votes he had obtained, and the number voting in the cantonal assembly. In addition to the minutes of electoral colleges, the Minister required a description of the 'spirit' prevailing at the elections. Some prefects wrote lengthy, impressionistic accounts: others were more perfunctory. The prefect of the Sarre, for instance, had a form which he filled in every three months, in which the inhabitants of his department always figured as 'docile', not interested in politics, entirely devoted to the Emperor, delighted at the birth of the King of Rome, and so on. The prefect of the Gironde had to be sent two 'hasteners' by the Minister, after which he replied that all elections in his department were carried out with scrupulous attention to legality, that all the members of the colleges were 'men worthy of esteem and respect', and that all the candidates were 'men worthy of praise: the most obvious evidence that one can quote being that they were all comfortably-off proprietors, commendable for their morality, their talents, and above all their attachment to the government'.[21]

The collection of all this information required co-operation from semi-literate mayors, reluctant polling clerks, and hard-pressed sub-prefects. Sometimes investigators had to be sent out. The cost was considerable, not least in printing and postage. From 1804 onward all electors, primary and upward, had to swear an oath of loyalty to Napoleon, and to expedite business at elections the oath was printed on a form and sent out through the post. All electors had to be supplied with identity cards to obtain entry to the assemblies: the prefect of the Gironde pointed out that for primary elections in his department this involved printing 58,956 cards at a cost of 3,000 francs, after which a scribe had to be employed six days a week for eight months to fill in all the names and addresses.[22]

One of the tasks all prefects had to carry out was that of suggesting to the Minister of the Interior the names of persons whom they regarded as suitable for the presidency of each cantonal assembly and electoral college. One nominee for each post was not enough: three had to be sent, to give a choice. The suggestions had to be motivated and accompanied by full details regarding the occupation and income of the candidate. The post of president, even of a cantonal assembly, was much sought after, and aspirants frequently sent testimonials to the prefect of their department, to the Minister of the Interior, and even to Napoleon.

21 *Arch. nat.*, F^{IC}III Sarre (2), Gironde (2).
22 *Arch. nat.*, F^{IC}III Gironde (2).

Former royalists were particularly given to writing to the higher authorities, perhaps because they felt that local opinion was not abreast of the more liberal policies of the government. Thus Lally-Tollendal wrote on 14 December 1802 to the Minister of the Interior supporting the request of Latour-du-Pin to be made president of a cantonal assembly in the Gironde: the mayor of the canton had recommended the former émigré to the prefect, but the prefect had left him off his list, 'which makes me think', wrote Lally-Tollendal, 'that the prefect has not appreciated the great and wise principles that I have had the happiness to hear confirmed by the mouth of the First Consul'. The position of president of a cantonal assembly was apparently considered one of honour and influence in the locality: an aspirant to one of the posts in the Pas-de-Calais thought it would give him more authority as a JP. Napoleon thought well enough of the presidents of the cantons to invite them all to the coronation: more than 1,500 turned up, from 108 departments, wearing the prescribed dress – 'Habit en velours de couleur; culotte pareille; veste de drap d'argent, brodée; chapeau à trois cornes; plumet blanc; l'épée'.[23]

The attraction of becoming president of an electoral college, though also an unpaid post, was greater, since it might lead to election as a candidate for the Legislative Body or, if one were president of a departmental college, for the Senate. There could be no denying that this frequently happened. Duplessis, president of the departmental college of Loiret, wrote candidly to the Minister of the Interior on 21 November 1808: 'I owe all to the goodness of Your Excellency. It has caused me to be nominated to this presidency, which has fulfilled all my desires, for the electoral college, almost unanimously, has nominated me as its leading candidate for the Senate.' On the other hand the sub-prefect at Belfort said he wanted to be made president of the college of the arrondissement solely for the sake of the honour. 'My aim is certainly not to influence the elections,' he wrote. 'I was named leading candidate for the Legislative Body at the last election without being president, and I shall be chosen again at the next election whether I am president or not: the confidence that I merit among my *administrés* as a result of the integrity of my conduct gives me this influence.'[24]

The position of deputy to the Legislative Body was still worth having, if only for the salary. Travelling expenses were not paid, but a fear expressed by a pamphleteer in 1800 that this would render the salary worthless seems not to have been widely shared.[25] There was certainly no shortage of men putting themselves forward as prospective candidates, a fact which increased the difficulty of getting majorities for any two of them in an arrondissement or departmental college. There were few open channels along which they could press their claims – no

23 *Arch. nat.*, F^{IC}III Gironde (2), Pas-de-Calais (4); Masson, *Le Sacre.*
24 *Arch. nat.*, F^{IC}III Loiret (2), Rhin, Haut (3).
25 Montyon, *Examen de la constitution*, p. 45.

independent local press, and no public meetings. Colleges were not allowed to assemble except when convened by the government, and the procedure on those occasions allowed for no speeches other than a formal opening address by the president. Canvassing was therefore a matter of personal approach to individuals, and bore an unfortunate resemblance to intrigue. In March 1803 the police reported several members of the electoral college of the department of the Seine to be grumbling that the nominations had all been agreed upon beforehand. At Falaise, in the department of Calvados, the outgoing member of the Legislative Body was said to have 'obtained, and even bought votes a long time beforehand'. The prefect of the Haut-Rhin reported that there were more 'cabals' in the arrondissement colleges, where members knew each other, than in the departmental college. In 1811 a former member of the Legislative Body for the Haut-Rhin, Metzger, actively solicited votes in two arrondissement colleges at once, relying, the prefect said, on his experience of revolutionary assemblies, his numerous family connections, and his influence with the Lutheran population: however, his greedy and vexatious conduct as director-general of *droits réunis* was remembered against him and he was defeated in both colleges. A more successful campaigner was Rosée, who had been a member of the Legislative Body for ten years. He too campaigned in more than one electoral college. He impressed strangers by boasting of his influential friends in Paris, but people who knew him realized that he never carried out any of his promises; and perhaps for this reason he only gained second place on the list. In a situation where there were no political parties, elections were bound to turn in large measure upon personalities. Some of the prefects and presidents found that the memory of former divisions died hard: in the departmental college of the Charente in 1805, for instance, the former royalists of Angoulême swayed the voters against any candidate who had played a part in the Revolution. Occasionally other factors were mentioned. The prefect of the Bouches-du-Rhône thought that public opinion had some effect: writing towards the end of 1805 he thought that if the elections had been held then instead of a year earlier the choices might have been less satisfactory to the government, for the war had hindered commerce and caused a lot of unemployment in Marseilles, which always had a formative effect on opinion in the department. Local interests were seen to have some importance in Finistère, whose prefect criticized the choice of candidates made at Brest, where most of the people 'lived as in a colony', without concern for anyone else.[26]

In territories recently acquired by France the system encountered peculiar difficulties. At Liège the prefect complained that the inhabitants, long accustomed to political assemblies, had acquired ingrained habits of opposition, and would oppose for the sake of opposing, out of a

26 *Arch. nat.*, F⁷3831; FᴵᶜIII Calvados (4), Rhin, Bas (1), (2), Rhin, Haut (3), Charente (3), Bouches-du-Rhône (2), Finistère (6).

sort of 'republican vanity'. From the department of Marengo, vicious and libellous complaints about successful candidates were continually descending upon the authorities in Paris from disappointed aspirants. In 1803 the general in charge of the 27th military division reported that all the ballot boxes from the cantonal assembly of Castelnova Scriva had been stolen from the town hall in the night. In 1805 all the electoral operations throughout the department were found by the Minister of the Interior to be irregular. In 1807 the prefect had to report that the arrondissement of Casale, which covered a third of the department and included, he said, eight or ten millionaires among the inhabitants of the town alone, had failed to produce a single candidate for the Legislative Body. The candidates produced by the remaining colleges he dismissed as nonentities. He blamed all upon the ineptitude of the presidents (whom he had recommended in glowing terms the previous year) and advised the government to send out men from Paris. In 1806, results from the department of the Po were many months late. In the department of the Apennins, one Maghella was said to have got himself elected by means of 'pratiques scandaleuses – orgies, séductions, corruptions et tous les intrigues'. The candidate eventually chosen by the Senate was not, in the event, willing to take up legislative duties: he declined the appointment on the grounds that he was seventy years old, broken in health, and incapable of carrying out the shortest journey.[27]

With the possible exception of these fringe departments, the presence of authority was pervasive throughout the electoral process. The prefects drew up the registers of electors in the cantons and decided where and when the meetings were to be held. Public officials had the right to attend and vote in cantonal assemblies, and to stand for membership of arrondissement and departmental colleges: it was not unusual for half or more of the members, particularly of arrondissement colleges, to be men who held government posts. The presidents of assemblies and colleges were not only appointed by the government but were made to look like government officials by the order to wear a uniform. The presidents of electoral colleges had full police powers during sessions, and could call out the gendarmerie and even the military. There was no appeal at law against electoral fraud.

At no stage in the proceedings were the opportunities for government pressure fully exploited, however. The key factor at the outset was the election, by the cantonal assemblies, of arrondissement and departmental colleges which were thereafter to become permanent, yet there is no evidence that the government realized the importance of controlling this crucial operation. It was in any case foolhardly of Napoleon to have allowed the senatus-consultum of 1802 to declare membership of the colleges permanent before he had seen how they turned out. Curiously enough, Napoleon was well aware of the risk, for when a member of the

27 *Arch. nat.*, F^{IC}III Ourthe (2), Marengo (1), Apennins (1); Cambacérès, *Lettres inédites* I, pp. 404, 450.

Council of State with democratic leanings objected to the life tenure of the electors, Napoleon pointed out to him that 'revolutionary' majorities were far more likely to be produced at that moment than in a few years time when the régime had consolidated itself.[28]

The number of members Napoleon could nominate to the colleges was increased in 1804, but the object in mind seems to have been not so much to increase government control as to advertise the government's recognition of 'merit'. In 1802 Napoleon had been allowed to nominate ten members of the Legion of Honour to each electoral college. The senatus-consultum of 18 May 1804, however, pronounced *all* legionaries members of the electoral college of their arrondissement and all officers members of the college of their department. The implications of this statement, as to numbers, had apparently not been considered. Nearly a year later, Napoleon asked the Minister of the Interior whether these appointments were to be included in the maximum membership of the colleges, or whether they were to be additional. Since the former course was impracticable, the latter was adopted. Napoleon then realized that he could not admit the whole lot, even as additional members, without swamping the elected members entirely: he thought that, 'although one could not make a positive restriction', it would be 'inopportune' to admit more than 20 legionaries to the arrondissement colleges and more than 30 officers to the departmental colleges. The matter was eventually decided by senatus-consultum, but not until another year had elapsed (22 February 1806), and then with different numbers – a maximum of 30 legionaries for the arrondissement colleges and 25 officers for the departmental colleges. Applications were received by the Minister of the Interior, with testimonials stressing war service and other meritorious activities. (The Bishop of Orleans applied, in his capacity as an officer of the Legion of Honour, to be nominated a member of his departmental college.) By the time they had been sorted out, another couple of years had passed. Few colleges ever received their full quota.[29]

When suggesting suitable persons to preside over electoral colleges, prefects were chiefly concerned to secure men who would understand the technicalities and were likely to get through the business efficiently. Since it was the prefects who had to report on elections to the Minister, they seemed to think that irregularities reflected on them. In their reports they liked to stress the orderliness of the assemblies above all other features: *la tranquillité la plus parfaite, le calme le plus imposant, la décence et le bon ordre* were the phrases most often reiterated. Officially inspired articles in the newspaper press contrasted the conduct of French elections favourably in this respect with proceedings in England, where 'tumultuous scenes' and 'general uproar' were said to be the rule, leading sometimes to 'bloody battles' in which as many as forty people

28 Thibaudeau, *Mémoires sur le Consulat*, p. 294.
29 Napoleon, *Correspondance*, no. 8403; *Arch. nat.* F^{IC}III Loiret (2).

might be killed in different parts of the kingdom. 'The roaring of tigers, the miaowing of cats, the howling of wolves convey only a feeble idea of the tumultuous cries which accompany the exercise of the finest privilege of the English people,' wrote the *Journal de Paris* in an article on the Westminster election of 1806.[30]

Senators and members of the Council of State, not to mention members of Napoleon's family, tried to get their protégés elected as candidates by the colleges, but for personal reasons rather than to promote the interests of the government. At the elections of 1808 at Marseilles, the Empress Josephine and Princess Pauline strongly supported the candidature of Lestang-Parade of Aix, for no better reason than that the Princess knew the gentleman's wife and would have liked the family to be transferred to Paris: the president of the departmental college, Senator Barthélemy, opposed the imperial candidate, but only because he wanted to get his nephew nominated instead.[31]

If authority failed to exert itself, however, it was doubtless because there was no real reason for it to do so. Political opposition hardly existed. Even in departments like the Charente and the Côte-d'Or, where former 'parties' ostensibly took the field, the rivalry was over personalities rather than principles, and ancient vendettas rather than current programmes. All were more or less loyal to the régime. 'The electoral colleges are in general composed of the richest individuals, and from all the parties which existed during the Revolution,' wrote the prefect of the Bouches-du-Rhône proudly on 5 December 1805. Mme de Chastenay afterwards claimed that men like her father, a former royalist, got themselves elected so as to be positioned ready for an attack on Napoleon when the opportunity came, but there is no evidence that they had anything of the kind in mind at the time.[32]

The last stage in the electoral process began when the recommendations from the colleges arrived in Paris. The Minister of the Interior collated the information on printed lists for each department, giving the name and age of each candidate, a list of the official positions he had held throughout his career, his present occupation and fortune (sometimes stated in figures and sometimes by the word *riche, considérable*, or *aisé*) and the number of votes he had obtained. The lists were sent to Napoleon, who pored over them eagerly: he insisted on having them sent to him even if he was in camp at Boulogne or on campaign in Poland or Austria. Sometimes he asked for further information before annotating the lists and indicating his preferences. He sent the lists to whoever was going to preside at the electoral sessions of the Senate, with urgent injunctions to get his wishes carried out. 'I beg you to use as

30 *Décade Philosophique*, 29 July 1802; *Journal de Paris*, 31 July 1802, 13 Nov. 1806, 1 Dec. 1807; *Gazette de France*, 15 Dec. 1806; *Gazette de Liège*, 22 Dec. 1806; *Journal du Soir*, 16 Dec. 1806, 30 Nov., 17 Dec. 1807.
31 Thibaudeau, *Mémoires*, pp. 251–2.
32 Chastenay, *Mémoires* II, p. 150.

much influence as you possibly can to keep out those with bad notes,' he wrote to Cambacérès from Boulogne in 1805. In the end, however, the decisions rested with the Senators, and while it seems unlikely that they would have nominated someone definitely blackballed by Napoleon, they used their discretion regarding other candidates.[33]

The Senate normally held a meeting lasting several hours at which the merits of the candidates were discussed, followed by further meetings at which votes were taken by ballot. In 1804 the Senators agreed that petitions from candidates requesting nomination could not be presented at the meetings, but it remained common for candidates to approach individual Senators, solliciting support. The cynical Cornet got a certain amount of amusement out of those who presented themselves at his house, curriculum vitae in hand; they formed, he thought, 'une galarie d'originaux assez curieuse'. Morellet, doubtless remembering that Joseph Bonaparte, King of Naples, was officially styled 'grand elector', even thought it worthwhile writing in 1807 to an acquaintance who was finance minister at Naples, asking for his good offices. Felix Faulcon, who had made something of a mark as president of the Legislative Body during the debates on the Civil Code and was anxious to make a come-back, dashed off an almost illegible note to the Minister of the Interior requesting his support in securing re-election in 1808, but he received the reply that the Minister had no influence over the choices made by the Senate. Godefrey de Waldner, one of the candidates at Colmar, actually sent a curriculum vitae to the Emperor in 1811, to which he got no reply at all (though he was ultimately elected). Cambacérès, who as Arch-Chancellor presided over all sessions of the Senate during the early years of the Empire, found himself besieged by suitors and was not altogether sorry when Napoleon in 1807 transferred to Senator Monge the duty of presiding at electoral meetings: 'For this year, almost all the individuals presented [by the colleges] have arrived in Paris,' he wrote to Napoleon, 'with the result that, the parties being face to face, intrigue arises, and can sometimes prevail over merit.'[34]

Nepotism and favouritism clearly played a part in decisions taken by the Senators, and seem to have been more important than devotion to the régime. Martin Léjéas of the Côte-d'Or owed his election in 1803 to the fact that he was father-in-law to Maret, the Secretary of State, and not to the fact that he was an ardent Bonapartist who celebrated the feast of Saint Napoleon in his chateau at Aiseray with banquets and fountains flowing with wine. Where there were no personal issues, the Senators judged on public service. In December 1803 the Senate discussed the candidates presented by the Côtes-du-Nord, and according to Cambacérès were most struck by two, Coupé and Boisléon. Both had

33 Cambacérès, *Lettres inédites* I, pp. 103–6, 285, 447, 658; Napoleon, *Correspondance*, no. 9165.
34 Cornet, *Souvenirs*, p. 5; Morellet, *Mémoires* I, pp. 231–9; Cambacérès, *Lettres inédites* I, p. 437; *Arch. nat.*, F^IC III Vienne (3), Rhin, Haut (3).

been magistrates under the old régime, and members of the Constituent Assembly in the early days of the Revolution. A few days later, Cambacérès reported to Napoleon that Coupé had been elected with 33 votes out of a possible 50, but that Boisléon had been defeated by Brelivet, a businessman, who had not sat in any previous parliament but was thought to deserve preferment on account of the service he had rendered in putting down the chouans and because of the consideration he enjoyed in the locality. In choosing among candidates from the Italian departments, the Senate relied heavily on advice from its Italian members.[35] There is no evidence that the Senators favoured candidates put up by departmental rather than arrondissement colleges, or that they favoured the most wealthy. When the Empire fell, quite a number of Napoleon's Legislators were unable to meet the tax qualifications of the next regime.

35 Viard, *Côte d'Or*, p. 286; Cambacérès, *Lettres inédites* I, pp. 118, 123, 179–80, 689.

9

Imperial Parliaments

Towards the end of the Life Consulate Napoleon let it be known, through a series of 'official rumours', that he intended to bestow 'greater distinction' upon the various state authorities.[1] The necessary senatus-consultum was passed on 20 December 1803. The Legislative Body was no longer to be left to elect its own president every month, but was to be given a president appointed by the First Consul to serve for a year. The Legislative Body was to produce the inevitable list of candidates for the post (one from each of the five series, elected by secret ballot) and the First Consul was to choose between them. The president would take up residence in the Palace of the Legislative Body (as the Palais Bourbon was now called) and act throughout the year as spokesman for the members, whether they were assembled in Paris or scattered throughout the departments. 'The Legislative Body will no longer be denuded of the majesty that its functions demand,' wrote Napoleon to the Senate. 'We shall no longer look for it in vain between sessions. . . . This body will at last have the dignity it could never have with mobile and indeterminate forms.'[2]

There was a slight hitch at the beginning, because the members of the Legislative Body thought they ought to have received special notice of the senatus-consultum and not simply have been left to read about it in the newspapers. Cambacérès wrote to Napoleon at Boulogne to warn him of their displeasure, but nothing had been done to rectify the omission when the new session opened on 6 January 1804. It was not until two days later that Councillors of State arrived to make the desired communication. Voting began at once for the five candidates and had already taken the better part of two days when Masséna, one of the successful candidates in the second ballot, pronounced himself unsuited for political duties and insisted on withdrawing, to the delight of his admirers who had been waiting for some gesture of independence from him ever since his nomination to the Legislative Body a year earlier. A further ballot had to be held, and a list was finally sent to Napoleon on

1 *Arch. nat.*, F⁷ 3832; *Journal du Soir*, 26 Nov. 1803; *Journal de Paris*, 27 Nov. 1803.
2 Napoleon, *Correspondance*, no. 7482.

11 January. From the candidates he chose Louis de Fontanes, one of the deputies for the department of Deux-Sèvres.[3]

Fontanes had been elected to the Legislative Body in 1801, when Grégoire was raised to the Senate. Perhaps it was true that he owed his good fortune to his connection with certain members of the Bonaparte family, as gossip said. He was believed to be the lover of Napoleon's sister Élisa, and to have been the real author of a timely pamphlet, attributed to Lucien Bonaparte, presaging the establishment of the life consulship. Certainly his appointment aroused a good deal of criticism, from some quarters because he was still suspected of the royalist views he had held before Fructidor, and from others because he seemed to bow too easily to the prevailing wind. He continued, nevertheless, to reappear during the next few years with far and away the largest number of votes among the candidates for the presidency of the Legislative Body, and Napoleon reappointed him without fail until 1810. Cambacérès thought him invaluable: in 1807, when there was likely to be a slight gap in Fontanes's tenure of office while he sought re-election as a deputy for his department, the Arch-Chancellor wrote off in something of a panic to Napoleon in Poland: 'Since the senatus-consultum of 20 December 1803, the Legislative Body had been ruled monarchically. It will fall back into anarchy if it is left for a month without a head.' A year later Cambacérès gave Fontanes a good deal of credit for the passing of the Criminal Code, which was not liked by the deputies.[4]

As a minor poet, Fontanes had the distinction of being a member of the Institute. He was a friend of Chateaubriand, who credited him with inspiring the *Génie du Christianisme* and whose precarious relationship with Napoleon he did much to save. With the public at large, however, Fontanes was chiefly noted for his flowery speeches on public occasions. Unable to utter a single sentence extempore, given a few minutes for preparation he could produce an apparently effortless flow of grandiloquent phrases. Many of them were in praise of Napoleon, as the occasion demanded; but it was not altogether true that he was 'the imperturbable adulator of everything Bonaparte did and desired', as Miot de Melito described him. In 1808, when Napoleon announced in his opening speech to the Legislative Body, 'I leave in a few days' time to put myself at the head of my army, and with God's aid to plant my eagles on the fortresses of Lisbon,' Fontanes had the courage to reply in his presence: 'Authority based on wise legislation and national institutions is more lasting than authority based on armed force. The Legislative Body must first and foremost celebrate peaceful triumphs, which can never bring other than blessings to mankind.' There is some evidence that Napoleon would have got rid of Fontanes for the following year if

3 Cambacérès, *Lettres inédites* I, p. 122; *Arch. nat.*, F[7] 3831; *Arch. parl.*, 7, 9, 10, 11 Jan. 1804.
4 Ménéval, *Mémoires* I, p. 354; Fiévée, *Correspondance* I, pp. 195–6; Miot, *Mémoires* II, pp. 123–4; Cambacérès, *Lettres inédites* I, p. 405; II, p. 623.

the other candidates presented by the deputies had been anything but nonentities. Fontanes was probably aware of it, for he deliberately prevented Montesquiou, who would have been a more considerable rival, from being named among the candidates.[5]

The Tribunate began the session of 1804 at long last in its new hall. The President and officers sat facing a tiered semi-circle, around which ionic pillars supported the public gallery. Simple and tasteful, it was rightly admired by visitors. The President, Carrion Nisas, whose flamboyant oratory was a source of embarrassment to his fellow Tribunes, was with difficulty dissuaded by them from making an inaugural speech. In spite of all that had been done to subdue the Tribunate it still had a certain amount of independence, as Siméon remembered, somewhat ruefully, when he was made a Councillor of State for his services in bringing about the hereditary empire. He would rather have been given the presidency of the Tribunate, he told his friend Thibaudeau. As a Tribune he had been able to carry on with his job as a barrister, which gave him something to fall back on and brought him in as much money as a salary from the Council of State.[6]

The outlook among the Tribunes was brighter at the beginning of the Empire than it had been at the beginning of the Life Consulate. Everybody knew that there would be changes in the constitution, and it was rumoured that the Tribunate would be merged with the Legislative Body to form a genuine lower house in relationship to the Senate. Napoleon had hinted to Thibaudeau a little while earlier that something of the kind might be done: 'Two chambers are the only thing. We already have the Senate.'[7] In the event, however, nothing of the kind happened. According to the senatus-consultum of 18 May 1804, bills were to continue to be discussed by the Tribunate, but not in public and not in a general assembly. The members were to be permanently divided into the now familiar three sections, and copies of bills were to be sent to all three sections meeting simultaneously. Each section was to choose two of its members to appear before the Legislative Body when the bill was 'debated' with the Councillors of State, but not all would speak. A single section could still be summoned for prior discussion with the appropriate section of the Council of State, as had been happening since 1802, the three sections being designated 'legislation', 'interior', and 'finance' for the purpose. The Legislative Body was specifically forbidden to set up committees, but was told that at the request of fifty of its members the whole body could form itself into a committee for (strictly private) discussion of a bill. The Senate, whose members did not receive the hereditary status they had hoped for, was given no

5 Chateaubriand, *Mémoires d'outre tombe* I, pp. 479–82, 487–90; Miot, *Mémoires* II, pp. 123–4; *Arch. parl.*, 25, 27 Oct. 1808; Napoleon, *Correspondance*, no. 15978; Hauterive, *La Police secrète* I, p. 524.

6 *Journal de Paris*, 7, 9 Jan. 1804; *Arch. nat.*, F⁷ 3832; Pictet, *Journal*, p. 123; Thibeaudeau, *Mémoires*, p. 134.

7 *Arch. nat.*, F⁷ 3832; Thibaudeau, *Mémoires sur le Consulat*, p. 315.

integral part in the formation of law, but merely the right to denounce a law as unconstitutional. The Emperor could ignore such denunciations if he saw fit, and promulgate laws regardless.

Fiévée, commenting on the rumours that there was to be a constitution *à l'anglaise*, thought how politically ignorant the French people were to have expected such a thing. 'An English-type constitution will never be formed with a ruler commanding three to four hundred thousand men,' he wrote. Far from seeing this as a veiled insult, Napoleon liked the idea, and adopted it as his own. 'Who, in France, would protect the power of the Chambers against a prince who has at his disposal an army of four hundred thousand men?' he asked the Council of State in one of his endless digressions.[8] His little son, he told Narbonne in 1813, would have a better chance of being a constitutional monarch. 'He will probably be an ordinary man, with moderate abilities, for you know the law of nature that genius is not handed down.' If so, Napoleon continued, he would find the basis for a parliamentary system already laid, in the Senate and the Legislative Body.[9]

There were some respects, however, chiefly ceremonial, in which Napoleon liked already to copy the English. On 27 December 1804 he opened the parliamentary session for the first time in person. There was a cavalcade, an oath-taking by the deputies, and a 'speech from the throne' into which Napoleon had taken care to insert references to 'my people' and 'my armies' in the manner of the king of England. He was delighted when Fontanes began his reply with the words, 'Sire, your faithful subjects'. Deputies who objected to the phrase were told that it was the mode adopted by the House of Commons, and Fabre de l'Aude, who had used no such words in his reply as President of the Tribunate, found them inserted in the report of his speech when it appeared in the *Moniteur*.[10]

Thereafter the opening ceremony took place each year, Napoleon refusing to allow parliament to meet without him. It was often preceded or followed by some other dazzling event with which Napoleon sought to impress the deputies and make them think it had been worth their while coming to Paris. The session of 1804–5 was a bumper year. It began with the Coronation, for which Tribunes and Legislators were not only invited to attend the ceremony at Notre Dame but were received by the Emperor and Empress afterwards. Inevitably a few grumbled at the expense of having to buy the special costume, but the majority were delighted, especially when they were told that they could wear a cloak, which put them on a par with Councillors of State.[11] The Coronation was followed, a few weeks later, by the unveiling of the statue com-

8 Fiévée, *Correspondance* II, p. 7; Pelet, *Opinions*, p. 64.
9 Villemain, *Souvenirs* I, pp. 287–8.
10 Miot, *Mémoires* II, pp. 248–51.
11 *Arch. nat.*, F^{IC}III Marengo (1); F⁷ 3833; Cambacérès, *Lettres inédites* I, pp. 122, 139, 141.

missioned the previous year – an evening occasion, with a chamber orchestra hidden in an ante-room to play magical music as Josephine ascended to her throne, and a banquet served afterwards by the restaurateur Robert. The statue itself, a plaster replica of the finished product, depicted Napoleon in the nude, larger than life, with a laurel wreath on his head and an imperial cloak flowing from his shoulders, clutching in his hand a copy of the Civil Code. The sculptor was Chaudet. Napoleon was always embarrassed at encountering statues of himself in the nude (though they were an occupational hazard in the heyday of neo-classicism), and was probably relieved when the replica was removed from the centre of the hall, where it obscured members' view of the rostrum, and the finished statue, in white marble, placed further to one side.[12]

1806 saw the first of many ceremonial presentations of flags taken from the enemy, Napoleon having, as Villemain pointed out, an incongruous liking 'for playing in full civilization the Conquering Legislator of barbarous times'. The new façade of the Legislative Palace, for which the foundation stone was laid in 1806, was designed to have a sculptured tympanum depicting Napoleon presenting to the Legislative Body the flags taken at Austerlitz. In 1807 came a magnificent *Te Deum* for the return to France of the victorious armies. 1808 was to have seen more flags, from Spain, Napoleon thinking it peculiarly fitting that the Legislative Body should receive the trophies of a battle fought within two weeks of the opening of the parliamentary session; but the young Colonel Ségur, who was bringing the flags from Madrid, fell ill on the journey of wounds received during the campaign, and the ceremony had to be put off till the following year.[13] One of the more unlikely members to be delighted by these grand occasions was Morellet, who always insisted on wearing a sword.[14]

The opening of parliament in 1804 was the first occasion on which Napoleon spoke in public, and critical members of the audience noticed some irritating faults of pronunciation such as the addition of the letter *s* to the ending of the first person singular of the future tense and of the letter *t* to the third person. The majority of people, however, were simply relieved to hear Napoleon promise that 'whatever may be the needs of an unjust war, he would require of his people no new [financial] sacrifice'. A renegade Englishman, quoted in the *Journal de Paris*, contrasted Napoleon's speech favourably with those of George III, whom he accused of annually mouthing meaningless platitudes as a preliminary to demanding large sums of money.[15] The statement that

12 *Journal du Soir*, 15, 17 Jan. 1805; *Journal de Paris*, 16, 17, 18 Jan. 1805, 3 Mar. 1806.
13 Villemain, *Souvenirs* II, p. 188; Napoleon, *Correspondance*, no. 14463; Ségur, *Mémoires* III, pp. 296–8.
14 Burney, *Journals* VI, p. 620
15 Miot, *Mémoires* II, pp. 248–51; *Arch. nat.*, AF[IV] 1429; *Journal de Paris*, 30 Dec. 1804. The English writer, Lewis Goldsmith, signed himself 'Argus'.

there would be no new taxes was a constant feature of Napoleon's addresses to parliament up to 1813. In other repects they became more and more the speeches of a war lord. In 1804 Napoleon assured the members: 'I have no ambition to exercise a greater influence over the states of Europe,' and in 1807 he described France's links with Germany, Holland, Spain, Switzerland and Italy as forming 'a federative system'; but by 1809 he was referring callously to the 'subjugation' of Aragon and Castile. In 1804 he professed reluctance to go to war, but by 1809 he was talking of planting yet more eagles on ramparts (this time around Vienna) and boasting to the deputies: 'All who try to oppose you will be vanquished and conquered.' The speech of 1811 exceeded all bounds of decency in its references to the war in Spain: 'When England is exhausted; when she has at last felt the effects of the suffering she has so cruelly imposed upon the continent for twenty years; when half of her families are in mourning; a thunderbolt will put an end to the business of the Peninsula and the destiny of her armies.'[16]

Ceremonies and speeches apart, however, the work of the legislature was prosaic enough. Both bodies spent a good deal of time balloting to produce names for various lists. The Tribunate had to name 3 candidates from which the Emperor chose the President, and 6 candidates from which he chose 3 quaestors. Each section had to produce a list of 3 of its members from which the president chose the chairman of the section. The Legislative Body, in addition to electing 5 candidates for the presidency, had to elect 4 vice-presidents and 4 secretaries each month, and 12 candidates from which the Emperor chose 4 quaestors each year. Whole afternoons went by in which nothing was done but balloting. When the session finally got under way, a great many local bills had to be dealt with. Any commune which wanted to sell part of its land to individuals, or alternatively to buy land from individuals for some public purpose such as opening a cemetery, building a town hall or providing a presbytery, had to have an act of parliament. Since there were no private members' bills, communes petitioned the government, which drew up the necessary bills and presented them as official measures. At first they were presented separately, and each one given the full treatment by the Tribunate and Legislative Body: Bourrienne said that it gave Napoleon cynical pleasure to send these scraps to parliament, describing them as 'bones for the dogs to gnaw at'.[17] By 1801, however, the Legislators had found a method of dealing with them five at a time, at least as far as voting on them was concerned. By 1802 they were actually being presented ten or twelve at a time, with one motivating speech. By 1803 the government had begun to merge vast numbers of them into one bill, but this method proved to have its drawbacks, for on 5 April 1803 the Tribunate advised rejection of a bill dealing with 148 local transactions on the grounds that one of them was unacceptable.

16 *Arch. parl.*, 27 Dec. 1804, 25 Oct. 1808, 3 Dec. 1809, 16 June 1811.
17 Bourrienne, *Mémoires* IV, p. 299.

The government continued to present omnibus bills, however, some of them requiring hundreds and even thousands of supporting documents. Tedium was unavoidable, but any irritation the deputies might have felt was smoothed away by Regnault de St Jean d'Angély, who as chairman of the 'interior' section of the Council of State usually had the unenviable duty of presenting these bills to parliament. A prodigious worker and a fluent and persuasive speaker, Regnault managed to make light of a burdensome task. Most of the memorialists of the period mention him with respect, and many were of the opinion that Napoleon would have made him Minister of the Interior if his way of life had been more acceptable (he was, it seems, a notorious womanizer).[18] In 1805 Regnault admitted that the Council of State had had its doubts as to whether legislation was necessary for local matters, but had come to the conclusion that the Legislative Body should continue to be involved because its members were men with experience from all over France. Napoleon himself clearly thought that local legislation was the one function above all others that the deputies were eminently suited for. Better preparation helped to avoid bills foundering because of some minor technical defect, but it did not prevent two or three men from casting negative votes every time local bills came before the Legislative Body.[19]

The first three years of the Empire witnessed a deliberate attempt by the Tribunate to co-operate with the régime. The sections into which it was divided were apparently so much at one in their acceptance of the government's bills that they frequently sent only one spokesman to expound their opinion to the Legislative Body. Their speeches were adulatory in the extreme. Sahuc, reporting in favour of a conscription bill, spoke of the beneficent influence conscription had had on the destinies of France, producing some of the finest armies in the world; Pictet, speaking on a minor bill to authorize repairs to a bridge across the Lac du Bourget, took the opportunity to praise the government's entire policy of public works as a happy combination of central initiative and private enterprise; Faure expressed the Tribunate's gratitude at being allowed to take part in the production of so great a work as the Code of Civil Procedure; Villot-Fréville, in the debate on the bill setting up the University, described the 'enthusiasm' with which the Tribunate had greeted the proposal of a state teaching corps.[20] Napoleon, for his part, made use of the Tribunate on a number of occasions as an organ of communication when the Legislative Body was not in session. On 24 September 1805 he sent Councillors of State to the Tribunate to explain why the war against England had developed into a war against Austria

18 Bourrienne, v, p. 255; Gohier, *Mémoires* ii, pp. 106–8; Pasquier, *Mémoires* i, p. 264; Molé, *Mémoires* i, pp. 73–4; Broglie, *Souvenirs* i, pp. 122–8.
19 *Arch. parl.*, 9 Jan., 28 Feb. 1805, 18 Jan. 1810; Pelet, *Opinions*, p. 150; Cambacérès, *Lettres inédites* ii, p. 618.
20 *Arch. parl.*, 17 Jan. 1805, 21 Mar., 14 Apr., 11 May 1806.

and Russia. 'Vainly the Emperor offered peace to England. The British ministry, far from accepting the offer, has just seduced by its gold and its intrigues two governments whose interests are remote from its quarrels.' Three months later a deputation went from the Tribunate to Austria to congratulate Napoleon on his victory at Austerlitz, and came back with fifty-four flags to divide between itself and the Senate. There was a rush to the rostrum to propose triumphal columns, national holidays, and renaming of public squares.[21] None of this rapport saved the Tribunate from extinction in 1807, however.

The reason for the abolition of the Tribunate was probably that the Tribunes, for all their eloquence, failed to secure a satisfactory degree of co-operation from the Legislators. Bills again and again received what were to Napoleon sizable opposition votes in the Legislative Body. In the session of 1805 a bill to cut down expenses incurred by the state in trying criminal cases was opposed by 56 voters out of 250; a bill to allow the orphanage of St Cyr to sell some of its property and invest the proceeds in government bonds was opposed by 67 voters out of 237; and a bill attributing cases of violence against the police to special courts was opposed by 53 voters out of 248. In the session of 1806, during the debate on a bill to allow offences against forest law to be tried by administrative tribunals, Toulongeon created a sensation by trying, albeit unsuccessfully, to get 50 members to support a demand for a secret committee. A bill allowing the Emperor to nominate the governor of the Bank of France got a majority of only 186 votes to 70, and the University bill was opposed by 42 voters out of 252. The session of 1807 was mainly occupied with a commercial code which the public had been awaiting for several years, but in the last few days a bill to enable the government to enforce the draining of pestilential swamps got an opposition vote of 79 out of 243, and another to allow the Council of State to adjudicate in civil cases after three abortive interventions by the Court of Cassation was opposed by 60 voters out of 226.[22]

It was in keeping with Napoleon's whole attitude to parliament to think that if he could involve the Legislators in intimate discussion of bills at an early stage, opposition would be avoided. He realized that if he gave the task of preliminary discussion to the Legislators he would make the Tribunate redundant, but this did not worry him unduly. Successive depletions had left only a few members remaining in the Tribunate, and these could easily be accommodated in the Legislative Body. On 12 August 1807 he wrote to Regnault de St Jean d'Angély asking him to prepare 'a little decree, not forgetting to mention the services rendered by the Tribunate'.[23]

The required senatus-consultum was duly passed on 19 August 1807.

21 *Arch. parl.*, 30 Dec. 1805.
22 *Arch. parl.*, 15, 25, 28 Jan., 8 Feb. 1805, 22 Mar., 22 Apr., 10 May 1806, 16 Sept. 1807.
23 Napoleon, *Correspondance*, no. 13021.

It stated that bills were no longer to be sent to the three sections of the Tribunate for discussion but to three commissions of the Legislative Body. The three commissions were to be devoted to legislation, interior and finance respectively, and a later clause in the senatus-consultum revealed that bills were to be sent not to all three simultaneously, as had been the case with the Tribunate, but to the appropriate one only. Each commission was to have seven members elected by the Legislative Body, and a chairman appointed either from among the seven or from the remaining ranks of the deputies by the Emperor. If the competent commission of the Legislative Body disagreed with any aspect of a bill, the Arch-Chancellor or the Arch-Treasurer was to summon the members to a conference with the relevant section of the Council of State. If agreement was reached, the chairman of the commission was to report to the Legislative Body; in the event (unlikely) of no agreement being reached, all seven members of the commission were to have the right to speak. The Tribunate would no longer exist; the remaining Tribunes would be given places in the Legislative Body till their term of office expired.

Boulay de la Meurthe, who was given the task of explaining the senatus-consultum to the Legislative Body, said that it inaugurated 'not a change but an improvement' – the combination, at last, of both assemblies into one chamber. The Tribunes pretended, at least, to accept it as a compliment; they decided to draw up an address expressing 'neither regret on their own part nor anxiety for the country', and their president assured Napoleon that 'they believed they had arrived not at the end of their political career but at the object of all their endeavours.' It was a plausible line, but its effect was spoiled by all that was known of the previous relationship between Napoleon and the Tribunate. Few people could regard the senatus-consultum as anything but the final blow in a continuous campaign to destroy the Tribunate, which had never been looked upon as anything more than an 'hors d'oeuvre', Pasquier said. According to Méneval, Napoleon's secretary, the public applauded the closure of the Tribunate as yet another smart move on the part of Napoleon, and the story got about that Napoleon had gone himself one morning to the hall of the Tribunate, locked the door, and put the key in his pocket. Again, Napoleon seems to have liked the idea: 'In the Tribunate they did nothing but make revolution, so I put them in order,' he told Metternich. 'I had only to take the key from the door of the assembly hall and put it in my pocket.'[24]

At the moment of dissolution the Tribunate had fewer than 50 members. In addition to successive depletions, a number of members had from time to time left to take up posts as prefects or Councillors of State, and they had never been replaced since there was no machinery for by-elections. Another 25 were due to go during the Year XVI

24 *Journal du Soir*, 27 Sept. 1807; *Arch. parl.*, 18 Sept. 1807; Pasquier, *Mémoires* I, p. 146; Méneval, *Mémoires* II, pp. 123–4; Metternich, *Memoirs* I, p. 151.

(1807–8). The remaining group had been intended at the time of the Life Consulate to remain until the Year XIX (1810–11), but their term of office had been extended at the beginning of the Empire to the Year XXI (1812–13). Some of these accepted office in the newly founded Cour des Comptes, leaving only 14 to be found seats in the Legislative Body.

There was the usual muddle about dates. Carrion Nisas, who was one of those due to retire during the Year XVI (1807–8), managed to claim another year's salary when he found himself redundant in August 1807, but none of the others got on to this.[25] Napoleon was continually rearranging lengths of service both for Tribunes and Legislators, a practice which gave an air of improvisation and uncertainty to the whole parliamentary system. Originally the parliamentary year began on 1 Frimaire by the Republican calendar (22 November). In 1804 the date was changed to 1 Vendémiaire (23 September). In 1806 France reverted to the Gregorian calendar and the parliamentary year was declared to end on 31 December. In 1809 the session was so late in starting that it overlapped into the following year, so the deputies of Series 5, due to retire in December 1809, were given an extension. In 1812 there were no elections, so the deputies of Series 4 had to be given an extension for the parliament which met early in 1813. Deputies from annexed territories frequently had to be given special dispensation to bring them into line with one of the series. On no occasion were these changes announced until the last minute, regardless of the anxiety this might create for men dependent on a salary.

Napoleon was always hoping that his legislators would be men of independent means. Among other things, he needed men who could travel to Paris and stay there for an indefinite number of weeks at the drop of a hat. From 1803, when the obligation to open parliament on 1 Frimaire ended, the actual date on which parliament would meet was always uncertain. On 10 March 1807, when Napoleon had been away from France for six months and seemed to be lingering in Poland with no obvious intention of returning, Cambacérès wrote to him: 'Now that the Senate has finished, or almost finished, the elections, people are thinking of the next session of the Legislative Body. Some go so far as to fix on the 1st of May for the opening.' Napoleon ignored the hint and replied from Finkenstein on 19 April: 'It is my intention to convoke the Legislative Body for the 1st of June. . . . It is necessary to arrange everything as if the Legislative Body were in fact going to meet on the 1st of June. It could be, however, that I shall not convoke it till the 10th.' On 6 May the *Journal du Soir* informed its readers: 'We are assured that the Legislative Body will be opened sometime between June 1st and June 15th.' Nothing more was heard on the subject until 13 July, when Cambacérès received the news via Maret that Napoleon had fixed the opening for 16 August: the decree had in fact been made at Tilsit. The year 1807 was in

25　Napoleon, *Lettres inédites* (Brotonne), p. 9.

no way unusual in respect of its uncertainties, for in 1808 parliament opened on 25 October, in 1809 on 3 December, in 1810 on 1 February, and in 1811 on 16 June, and no one knew the dates much beforehand.[26]

These fluctuations were due to the fact that while in some respects Napoleon failed to take parliament seriously, in others he gave too much personal attention to it. He insisted on receiving full information about all bills that were to be submitted, and would send back detailed comments on such technical matters as the budget. The delay to the opening of parliament in 1807 was due in part to the fact that Napoleon thought the Commercial Code should be presented *in toto* whereas Cambacérès had hoped to make a start by presenting the first two sections, which were the only ones finished by the Council of State. Napoleon himself nominated the Councillors who were to present the various bills to the Legislative Body. He required full details concerning persons nominated to sit on commissions, and even those nominated for the pettifogging duties of quaestor: 'Send me notes on the six candidates proposed for quaestor of the Legislative Body – their fortune, the role they played in the Revolution, and their talents,' he wrote to Fouché in 1807. He liked to add 'finishing touches' to the annual *Exposé de la situation de l'Empire*, delivered by one of the Councillors of State at the beginning of the parliamentary session. It was no doubt because of the Emperor's personal interest that the task of presenting the *Exposé* was regarded as an honour and that quaestors were regarded as persons of influence, but delays were inevitably caused by efforts to communicate with Napoleon on his campaigns. Some correspondence was actually lost.[27]

In spite of Napoleon's efforts the session of 1808, the first without a Tribunate, was a source of disappointment to him. The major work of the session was the passing of the Code of Criminal Procedure. Presented to the Legislative Body in nine parts, the various bills passed with majorities of only 178 to 85, 164 to 100, 181 to 96, 190 to 72, 199 to 62, 194 to 41, 197 to 56, 150 to 105, and 199 to 58. Hearing these results while he was in Spain, Napoleon wrote angrily to Talleyrand:

> The Legislative Body is full of individuals who want to make themselves important, who are offended because they haven't got titles, and who, having lived through the Revolution, think they are still in the National Assembly.[28] No law is perfect: the Code Napoléon, which nevertheless produces so much good, is far from being so. Why, instead of voting by ballot against the law, didn't they ask for a secret committee, in which each could have given his opinion? One would have known then, by the minutes, whether

26 Napoleon, *Correspondance*, no. 12409; Cambacérès, *Lettres inédites* I, pp. 450, 503, 537.
27 *Cambacérès*, I, pp. 532, 535–7; II, pp. 619, 627, 635; Napoleon, *Correspondance*, no. 12583, 12776; Napoleon, *Dernières lettres*, pp. 264, 390; Thibaudeau, *Mémoires*, p. 55; Duchâtel, *Correspondance inédite*, pp. 29–30.
28 Titles had been created by Napoleon earlier in the year, and granted to Councillors of State but not to members of the Legislative Body.

they had a case or not. But to reject a law without giving their reasons is to show little zeal, little love of good, and little consideration for me. They find serious drawbacks to this law, do they? Yet the commission of the Legislative Body, which is composed of serious-minded men, found it good. But if they are right it seems to me that instead of giving an adverse vote they should have asked to discuss it in a secret committee, as is allowed by our constitutions, and made known what they found wrong with it.[29]

Cambacérès believed, or said he believed, that opposition was due to dislike of the jury system, which the Code proposed to retain, although in a modified form. Perhaps Cambacérès thought that by attributing such a motive to the deputies he would exonerate them in the eyes of Napoleon, who had himself wished to abolish the jury system but had been overruled by a vote of 14 to 10 in the Council of State. Certainly Riboud, reporting for the commission of legislation, defended the bill before his fellow deputies as though he knew them to be hostile to juries. A police reporter, on the other hand, found quite different reasons for the opposition, the main one being the presentation of the Code piecemeal and in a hurriedly finished state. Three weeks before parliament opened, only two of the nine bills were ready. Something of this situation had leaked out to the deputies, presumably via members of the Council of State. Many of the latter were annoyed at having to await instructions from Napoleon before they could proceed with the bills, and in consequence they tended to deny responsibility for the contents. Cambacérès himself, the police reporter said, made no secret of the fact that he disliked the Code, though he told the deputies that they must pass the bills or Napoleon would blame him for their failure. The reporter felt obliged to mention self-interest motives, also. The Code abolished the criminal tribunals established by the Constitution of the Year VIII, in which many of the deputies held positions as presidents, judges, and barristers, and replaced them with a single appeal court in each department. He believed too, however, that there was genuine disquiet over the judicial power given by the Code to uneducated mayors in rural communes, and over the increased power of public prosecutors. Deputies hoped, he said, that opposition votes of 85 and 100 would be enough to persuade the government to withdraw the bills. The government did no such thing, however. On the contrary, the Emperor's annoyance with the opposition became so well known that a rumour got around that he would have destroyed the Legislative Body but for the intervention of the Arch-Chancellor. Not until elections for 1809 were made by the Senate did the deputies feel quite safe.[30]

Napoleon learnt something by his mistakes, if not quite the lesson his

29 Napoleon, *Correspondance*, no. 14516.
30 Cambacérès, *Lettres inédites* II, pp. 614, 619, 622, 628, 649; *Arch. parl.*, 7 Nov., 9 Dec. 1808; Pelet, *Opinions*, p. 75; Pasquier, *Mémoires* I, pp. 208–9; *Arch. nat.*, AF[IV] 1504; Hauterive, *La Police secrète* I, p. 524.

opponents wanted him to learn. During 1808 the Council of State had experienced considerable difficulty in framing a new penal code. The Council felt obliged to accept several emendations proposed by a commission of the Legislative Body, and Cambacérès told Napoleon that more time would have to be spent on the measure if it was to avoid the rough passage accorded the Code of Criminal Procedure.[31] No bills of importance were presented during the brief session of 1809, which took place in the last month of the year. Not until 1 February 1810 did Treilhard introduce the long awaited Penal Code. Its harsh provisions met with little opposition, the sections restoring perpetual hard labour, branding, and confiscation of property as penalities for certain offences of a public nature arousing no more than 40 opposition votes on average.[32] A bill to reorganize the law courts was less popular, though its main provisions had been foreshadowed by the Code of 1808. Its outstanding feature was the power given in each judicial area to the *procureur-général*, described by Noaille in his report for the commission of legislation as 'the government's man, its immediate agent, the mainspring of the whole machine'; but whether it was this which produced an opposition vote of 55 against a majority of 188 it is impossible to tell. Cambacérès thought that the deputies were still afraid of losing their jobs in the criminal courts if there was too much reorganization. Mme de Chastenay noted a general feeling of insecurity around this time, owing to the fact that Napoleon was no longer carrying out reforms left over by the Revolution but was altering laws and systems he had made himself.[33]

Treilhard described the Penal Code as the work of Napoleon, and told the deputies how honoured they were to have been allowed a share in it. In fact Napoleon, for some unknown reason, was less interested in either of the judicial measures of 1810 than in a bill regulating the property rights concerned in mining enterprises. When this measure was first discussed in the Council of State in 1808, Napoleon hit on the idea of describing newly discovered mines as 'new properties' which did not belong, as of right, to the owners of the surface area; and it was perhaps because of this that he looked upon the measure as particularly his own. It was, of course, a tricky subject whose complexities could hardly be encompassed in a few slick words, and there were powerful interests involved, especially in the Belgian departments. The Council of State had to hold several conferences with commissions of the Legislative Body over a period of two years before the bill finally passed on 21 April 1810.[34]

31 Durand, 'L'Exercice de la fonction législative'.
32 Cambacérès, *Lettres inédites* II, p. 619; *Arch. parl.*, 12, 13, 15, 16, 17, 19, 20 Feb. 1810.
33 Cambacérès, *Lettres inédites* II, p. 776; *Arch. parl.*, 12, 20 Apr. 1810; Chastenay, *Mémoires* II, p. 199.
34 *Arch. parl.*, 1 Feb., 13, 21 Apr. 1810; Cambacérès, *Lettres inédites* II, pp. 619, 754, 756, 759; Broglie, *Souvenirs* I, pp. 67–8.

The combined sessions of 1809 and 1810 lasted less than four months, yet according to Cambacérès the deputies were beginning to grumble towards the end at being kept in Paris too long. More than twelve months elapsed before they were summoned again, and on arrival in the capital they found a notice pinned up outside their assembly hall to the effect that a preliminary meeting, planned for 1 June 1811, was postponed indefinitely. Members would be summoned individually, by letter. The delay was caused by the fantastically elaborate arrangements for the baptism of the King of Rome, which Napoleon particularly wished the deputies to attend. The official opening of parliament took place a week after the ceremony, the actual working session lasted a mere seventeen days. Apart from the budget (consisting of fifteen laconic articles) and a few local bills, there was nothing requiring attention. Such matters as the reduction of the press to one newspaper per department, the appointment of censors, and the requirement of all printers to be licensed had been dealt with by imperial decree during the previous winter. The territories whose annexation Napoleon announced in his speech from the throne were provided with governments by senatus-consultum. Even without the Moscow campaign there might well have been no meeting of parliament during 1812.[35] Under these circumstances Mme de Chastenay can be forgiven for having thought that the Legislative Body was of no importance. She changed her mind when her father was elected to it and travelled to Paris early in 1813 for the delayed session of 1812.[36]

35 Cambacérès, *Lettres inédites* II, pp. 776, 807–9; Pasquier, *Mémoires* I, p. 471; *Journal du Soir*, 31 May, 9, 12 June 1811; *Arch. parl.*, 16, 29 June, 8–25 July 1811.
36 Chastenay, *Mémoires* II, p. 150.

10

The Two Sessions of 1813

Napoleon arrived back in Paris from the disastrous Moscow campaign on 19 December 1812. When the shattered remnants of his army regrouped behind the Niemen they numbered less than 40,000 men; but the Russians had scarcely more, and Napoleon was convinced he could raise enough new forces to beat them off. The Prussian and Austrian contingents that had been fighting on his side deserted the field on the initiative of their commanders, and the French were thereby obliged to withdraw to the Vistula, but still Napoleon believed that by the spring of 1813 he would be able to outnumber the enemy in a fight for Germany. The half million new recruits he envisaged would need to be paid for, however, and existing sources of money were exhausted for new expedients it was necessary to summon the legislature.

The elections that had been held during 1811 to replace the deputies of Series 1 had never been finalized. The lists sent in by the electoral colleges were now hastily referred to the Senate, which made the necessary nominations on 6 January 1813. No elections at all had been held during 1812, and the term of office of the deputies of Series 4 ran out at the end of that year. A senatus-consultum of 9 January 1813 obligingly prolonged their term for the whole of the session about to take place. At that time, parliament was said to be opening on 1 February, but on 30 January, when the deputies were already assembled in Paris, the session was for some unknown reason put off, officially for a week but actually for two weeks. It eventually opened on 14 February. The crowd that gathered to see the inaugural ceremony was expected to be so great that even ticket holders were advised to turn up two hours before the commencement if they wished to secure their seat in the hall.[1]

The Legislative Body which confronted Napoleon at this crisis in his career officially numbered 376 members. The list had been lengthened considerably since the early years of the Napoleonic régime by the annexation of more and more departments to the Grand Empire: Dutch and North German representatives had been added as late as 1811, not

1 Duchâtel, *Correspondance inédite*, p. 29.

by holding elections but by the Emperor nominating deputies from lists sent in by the prefects, bringing the number of foreign-born representatives in the Legislative Body to 116 by 1813. Not all were strangers, by any manner of means. Belgium had been represented in French assemblies since its annexation by the Directory; Bassenge, Gendebien, Van Cutsem and Lahure were men whose connection with French politics and ideas had begun during the Belgian revolution of 1789–90 and who had sat in the Legislative Body since the days of the Consulate. Botta, who had represented one of the Piedmontese departments since 1803, felt himself so much a Frenchman that when Piedmont separated from France in 1815 he applied for naturalization. So did Paroletti, who had represented the department of Pô since 1807 and whose brother was a brigadier in the French army. Paroletti and Poggi, the member for Taro, had been among the 'patriots' who supported Napoleon when he first invaded Italy in 1796; Poggi had lived most of his life in Paris since that time and was to continue to do so after 1815, when Marie Louise employed him as chargé d'affaires for her duchy of Parma. Pictet Diodati, though officially the member for Léman, had sat in the Legislative Body since 1800, long before members were allotted to particular departments, and was to use this argument as a claim to continue sitting in the French parliament after the collapse of the Grand Empire.[2] Of the members newly drafted into the Legislative Body from Holland and North Germany, one at least was an old friend of France. Karel Henrik Verhuell was an ambitious man, who had risen by a combination of talented seamanship and cynical statesmanship to high rank in the Dutch navy and high office in the Batavian Republic. While serving as ambassador to France after the Peace of Amiens he had become a passionate devotee of Napoleon, whom he recognized as an opportunist after his own heart. At the outbreak of war he had entered enthusiastically into the 'Grand Design' of invading England; in 1806 he had headed a deputation which offered the crown of Holland to Louis Bonaparte; in 1809 he had defended the coast of Holland against the British at Walcheren. When Holland separated from France in 1814 he was to write a letter to the President of the Chamber of Deputies regretting having to part from his former collegues. It was on a ship commanded by Verhuell that Napoleon hoped to sail to America after his defeat at Waterloo.[3]

Not all the new members were so loyal, however. Abendroth, who as mayor of Hambourg was nominated to the Legislative Body in 1812, when his city became the *chef-lieu* of the new department of the Bouches-de-l'Elbe, did not appear in Paris for the February session because he was negotiating for the surrender of Hambourg to the

2 This is not the Pictet who attracted attention to himself in the Tribunate by his free trade speeches. They were cousins, differentiated by the names of their wives – Pictet Diodati and Pictet Turrettini.
3 Schama, *Patriots and Liberators*, pp. 480–81.

advancing Russians. His colleague Meding was a similar case. Limburg-Stirum, on the other hand, sat for the Yssel-Supérieur in February, but shortly afterwards headed an insurrection at The Hague.[4] A dozen or so of the 'foreign' members applied for leave of absence on account of illness; two others, more credibly, were said to be absent on public duty.

The 260 men who represented metropolitan France were predominantly elderly. Of 252 whose age is known, 116 were in their fifties. Of the rest, 51 were in their forties, and 85 were over sixty. Three of them, Maine de Biran, Morellet, and Sylvestre de Sacy, are known to posterity for their scholarly works. The others, though not distinguished, are for the most part not contemptible as far as experience is concerned. The vast majority had held posts in local administration. Only 34 of them were entirely new to parliament, and to balance their inexperience there were 21 members who had sat in either the Tribunate or the Legislative Body for the whole of the time since Brumaire, and another 38 who had come in at some time during the Consulate. Thirty-four had sat in parliaments before the fall of Robespierre, 13 of them in the Convention. There was even one regicide left, the amazing Bonnet de Trieches. The fact that members were not allowed to speak in debate in the Legislative Body does not mean that they were men who would have been incapable of doing so: a dozen or more became prominent members of the left in Restoration parliaments, and Dupont de l'Eure gained such fame as a liberal politician that he was chosen to head the Provisional Government after the Revolution of February 1848. A handful emerged as vigorous ultra-royalists.

Napoleon had only once before, in a speech to parliament, been obliged to admit a defeat in war, and he had done so with an ill grace. The occasion was on 2 March 1806, when amid mock-modest announcements of victories at Ulm and Austerlitz he had skirted over defeat at Trafalgar in two short sentences: 'Tempests caused us to lose several ships following on an imprudent engagement. This loss will be repaired.' He did his best, now, to explain away the Russian disaster. His speech began with claims of success in Spain, where Wellington had retreated for the third time into winter quarters at Torres Vedras: 'The renewal of war in northern Europe offered a favourable opportunity for the plans of the English in the Peninsula. They made great efforts, but all their hopes have been crushed. Their army fell before the citadel of Burgos, and after sustaining great losses was obliged to evacuate the entire territory of Spain.' He continued:

> I myself entered Russia. French arms were constantly victorious on the fields of Ostrovna, Polotsk, Mohilev, Smolensk, the Moscova, Malo-Yaroslavetz. Nowhere were Russian armies able to hold out against our eagles. Moscow fell into our hands. When the frontiers of Russia had been forced and the powerlessness of her armies recognized, a swarm of Tartars turned their parricidal hands

4 Schama, *Patriots and Liberators*, pp. 641–2.

against the most beautiful provinces of this vast empire which they had been summoned to defend. In a few weeks, despite the tears and despair of the unfortunate Muscovites, they burnt more than four thousand of their most beautiful villages and more than fifty of their most beautiful towns, thus gratifying their ancient hatred and surrounding us with a desert, under the pretext of retarding our advance. We triumphed over all these obstacles. Even the burning of Moscow, by which they destroyed in four days the fruit of the toil and sacrifice of forty generations, brought no change in the prosperous state of my affairs. But the premature and excessive rigour of the winter brought down upon my army a frightful calamity. In a few nights I saw everything change. I sustained great losses; they would have broken my spirit if, in these grave circumstances, I had been capable of thinking of anything but the interests, the glory and the future of my people.

The English, Napoleon said, had tried to tempt the member-states of his Empire to rise against him with offers of territorial reward, but all in vain. 'With lively satisfaction we have seen our peoples of the Kingdom of Italy, of the former Holland, and of the annexed departments rivalling the native French and realizing that there was no hope, no future, no well-being for them other than in the consolidation and triumph of the Grand Empire.' All would soon be well, he promised. 'The French dynasty reigns and will continue to reign in Spain. I am satisfied with the conduct of my allies; I shall not abandon any of them; I shall maintain the integrity of their states. The Russians will retreat within their frightful climate.' He desired peace, he said, but he would make peace only if it conformed to the 'interests and greatness' of his Empire. Compromise over the maritime war was unthinkable.

So much for foreign affairs. Home affairs, he said, were flourishing. 'My Minister of the Interior will make known to you, in his *exposé* of the condition of the Empire, the prosperous state of our agriculture, industry, and internal trade, as well as the constant growth in our population. In no century has agriculture and industry reached in France a greater degree of prosperity.'

Curiously enough, Mme de Chastenay was favourably impressed by this speech, in spite of her growing dislike of Napoleon. He seemed disposed to renounce wars of conquest, she wrote, and spoke only of sending the Russians back to their 'frightful climate'.[5] Molé, on the other hand, attending the ceremony as a member of the Council of State, professed afterwards to have found the whole situation pathetic in every sense of the word. A great man was on the brink of a tragic downfall, and his speech was

> nothing but a long and unfortunate attempt to convince people of things he no longer believed himself, and to appease resentments whose irresistible force he recognized too late. Thus he represented

5 Chastenay, *Mémoires* II, p. 223.

the desert . . . by which the French army had been surrounded as the work of Tartars revenging themselves upon their former conquerors, and his affairs as flourishing and prosperous until the rigours of a premature winter. He praised the fidelity of the conquered provinces, which he knew were near to escaping him, and he declared that a Napoleonic dynasty would never cease to reign in Spain. He finally protested his sincere desire to make peace while affirming all the excuses which made it impossible. At the end he fell back on his favourite theme, that in no century had French agriculture and industry been more prosperous, and that warfare, far from being disastrous to the growth of population, had favoured it.[6]

Molé's reminiscenses owed something to the speech made on 25 February by Montalivet, the Minister of the Interior, under the heading *Exposé de la situation de l'Empire*. It was Montalivet, and not Napoleon, who connected warfare with the growth of population. The increase in fertility among the rural population Montalivet attributed mainly to the prosperity produced by 'the liberal laws which govern this great empire; to the suppression of feudalism, *dîmes, mainmorte*, monastic orders'. 'And why not admit', he added, 'that conscription itself has contributed to this growth, by multiplying the number of marriages?' It was a desperate argument, since young men could claim exemption from military service on the ground that they had recently married, and the number making such claims had nearly doubled in the past year.

Molé's recollection of impending disaster probably owed something too, to hindsight. It was not until 28 February that the Prussian king signed an agreement with Tsar Alexander, and not until the beginning of March that Eugène Beauharnais, commanding his step-father's troops, withdrew behind the Elbe, making it clear that Napoleon would have to fight a major campaign if he wished to regain control of Germany. Prior to that time there were probably many people, like Mme de Chastenay, who believed that it was enough for Napoleon to renounce further ambitions. The first week of the parliamentary session was spent by the deputies in the ordinary way, listening to obituaries of deceased members, receiving books donated to the library, and balloting for places on the three commissions. It was considered an honour to be elected to one of the latter, and Maine de Biran, who failed to secure a place on the commission of the interior, confessed to feeling cast down by the disgrace. A *grand dîner* for the deputies, given by the Arch-Chancellor, and a couple of *soirées brillantes* at the house of the President of the Legislative Body, doubtless did something to console him.[7]

On 28 February Cambacérès wrote to Napoleon at St Cloud, listing the deputies who had been elected to commissions and indicating those who might suitably be appointed to preside. Though not neglecting to

6 Molé, *Mémoires* I, pp. 165–8.
7 Maine de Biran, *Journal intime* I, pp. 73–4.

supply details relevant to all three commissions he ended his letter: 'Your Majesty will please note that of these three commissions only the Financial is important. The report on the budget needs great care, and a man can have merit and still be little suited to a task which requires not only knowledge but even more the facility to speak out before a large gathering.' The support of the Legislative Body was not, after all, a foregone conclusion. Of the seven members who had been elected to the commission, Cambacérès felt he could not recommend the Italian Paroletti, because he had insufficient knowledge of finance, nor Blanquart de Bailleul, who was a sound man and had been a quaestor but was not good enough at speaking in public. He passed over Septenville and the ambitious Félix Faulcon without comment, recommending that the Emperor choose between Dumolard, who had been a facile speaker in parliamentary assemblies ever since 1792 and now expressed 'an extreme desire to be employed usefully by Napoleon', Adet, the former Tribune, and Lezurier de la Martel, a businessman of Rouen, 'advantageously known in respect of fortune and integrity'. Napoleon's choice fell upon the last-named.[8]

The Emperor was already aware of the skill that would be needed on the financial front. In his speech at the opening of parliament he had once more told his hearers that he would levy no new taxes. He doubtless knew that the existing levels, especially of indirect taxes, were already too unpopular to admit of an increase; yet they were not enough. As an expedient, Napoleon had hit upon the idea of confiscating the property (land, houses and workshops) owned by municipalities throughout France in return for government bonds to the value of the net revenue. To put forward this unusual proposal he discarded the regular financial experts on the Council of State – Defermon, who had presented every major finance bill since 1800, Bérenger, a well known economist of the 'English' school, Baron Louis, whose reputation among financiers was unrivalled – in favour of a man whose political adroitness he more greatly admired, the thirty-one-year old Molé. 'Don't tell me you are not a financier,' he said when Molé obeyed his summons to appear at St Cloud. 'The circumstances are serious; it is a political speech you have to make.' He then began dictating, very fast, the things he wanted Molé to say. Asked to slow down so that the hearer could make notes, he did so for a brief moment but was soon talking again as rapidly as ever.[9]

By the time Molé presented the budget on 11 March the military position had deteriorated considerably. Hambourg had rebelled against French control and the Russians were advancing towards the city; Davout was preparing to evacuate Dresden. The deputies were looking grave and anxious, Molé said. In his introductory speech he referred vaguely to 'unforeseen events', and asked rhetorically whether any

8 Cambacérès, *Lettres inédites* II, pp. 885–6.
9 Molé, *Mémoires* I, p. 169.

nation had ever been able to sustain a maritime war and two continental wars at the same time without huge sacrifices. He then made out that the sacrifices he was asking for were really very small – no loans, except as a last resort; no further taxes, though the land tax and the salt tax could have been increased to bring in another 100 million francs. A better solution, he said, had been found – the confiscation of municipal property. It could be argued that the proposal had positive advantages, since some economists had long regarded it as a mistake to leave extensive properties in mortmain; and as a result of the confiscation France could remain the least heavily taxed nation in Europe.

Molé claimed afterwards that the Emperor had wanted him to make clear to the deputies that he would 'finish with them' if they did not give him what he asked for, and that he had evaded this unpleasant suggestion by neglecting to show the Emperor the draft of his speech beforehand. To his anger, however, he found, he said, when he read the report of the speech in the *Moniteur* next day, that several of Napoleon's offensive phrases had been inserted without his approval.[10] In fact, the version in the *Moniteur* seems harmless enough; there was no hint of a threat to the existence of parliament. However, many of the deputies undoubtedly got the impression that Molé was their enemy, with the result that ugly rumours about him grew up later in the year. Molé was destined throughout life to arouse hostility in other politicians. The reason for his unpopularity at this early stage could well have been jealousy, for in a mere nine years he had risen from Tribune to auditor, to prefect, to Councillor of State. Everybody agreed that Molé had talent, but not that much talent. Fouché thought that the young man's rise was due to the influence of his friend Fontanes. Broglie thought that it was entirely due to Napoleon, who was a great talker and liked Molé because he was the perfect listener, his big eyes visibly absorbing every thought that was put across to him, his fine figure expressing appreciation in every gesture.[11]

On 20 March Lezurier de la Martel presented the report of the commission of finances on the budget. The proposal with regard to communal property received favourable comment, both as benefiting the municipalities themselves and as binding them more closely to the national cause. Napoleon was thanked for the paternal solicitude which had caused him to refrain from raising taxation. Regret was expressed at finding that he had not actually been able to lower the commodity taxes, and it was hoped that these would be made easier to bear by greater efforts to eliminate arbitrary practices on the part of tax officials. This slight note of criticism was followed by an appeal to the deputies to rally round the Emperor in the unaccustomed hour of defeat, 'the inclemency of the weather having this time reversed the plans of genius'. The vote was taken at once and the bill passed by 303 to 26.

10 Molé, I, pp. 169–74.
11 Fouché, *Mémoires*, p. 205; Broglie, *Souvenirs* I, pp. 110–11.

On 25 March Regnault de St Jean d'Angély announced the closure of the session, which had lasted thirty-nine days. Apart from a few local matters, no business other than the financial bill had been presented. The President, however, stressed the importance of so imposing a body of proprietors having met to hear about the activities of the government, which it could then explain to people throughout the provinces. 'Such is, in fact, gentlemen, the most constant occupation of the Legislative Body – to pinpoint the benefits bestowed by the government and publish its merits. Its work is not confined to its fleeting sessions.' Napoleon was delighted with this speech and delighted with the deputies for granting him all that he had asked for. At a farewell reception for the members of the Legislative Body he moved among the guests full of smiles and charm, 'using plenty of those seductions and of that kind of coquetry at which he excelled', wrote Molé, promising the deputies that as soon as the war permitted he would recall them to Paris to attend the coronation of the Empress Marie Louise and the King of Rome. When Molé, who was feeling sore about his own unpopularity, pointed out to Napoleon that the deputies would not be so pleased with life if the war went badly, the Emperor's mood changed, and he privately described the Legislative Body as a gathering of obscure and poverty stricken mediocrities which he would have to change if he didn't dispense with it altogether.[12]

On 15 April Napoleon left Paris for the campaign of Germany. During the summer, while he fought and negotiated and fought again, the electoral process began in France for the replacement of the deputies of Series 3, who were due to retire at the end of the year. Letters ordering the prefects to collect information before the convocation of cantonal assemblies had gone out in December. In spite of heavy duties connected with the call-up of successive levies for the army, most of the prefects concerned managed to produce their lists of voters, lists of *plus imposés*, and lists of candidates for presidencies. There was no falling off in ambition for posts: Thibaudeau, who had been prefect of the Vienne since 1802, applied at this late stage to be made president of the departmental college.[13] The colleges had not yet assembled, however, when Napoleon was defeated at Leipzig on 18–19 October. On 2 November he recrossed the Rhine with only 60,000 men left from the half million who had fought with him in Germany.

He was already thinking of more money for another army. On 25 October 1813 he wrote from Gotha to tell Cambacérès that he had convoked the Legislative Body for 2 December, and that meanwhile he was contemplating an increase of something like 25 or even 50 centimes on all taxes. The land tax, he said, had been depressed far too much, and all the rest were susceptible of a considerable increase. He was waiting to hear the views of the Minister of Finance, after which he would expect the Council of State to order the taxes by decree. Cambacérès replied

12 Molé, *Mémoires* I, pp. 182–5.
13 *Arch. nat.*, F^{1C}III Vienne (3).

that it was a good move to summon the Legislative Body, as this was the one thing that would make for a truly national effort, but that in his view emergency measures should be confined to an increase in indirect taxes, and there should be a strict undertaking to put them to the Legislative Body for ratificiation when it met. He also advised Napoleon to let the Council of State gather together such legislative projects as were at all ready for submission to parliament. 'The deputies, I do not doubt, will arrive in Paris with good intentions,' he wrote. 'It is necessary to treat them well, and not seek to humiliate them with the burden of their idleness. If it should turn out that Your Majesty cannot make the opening yourself, and that it should be necessary to refer back to you some observations on the financial projects, it would be useful, in the interval, to occupy the Legislative Body with some matters of civil, criminal, or administrative legislation.'[14]

Napoleon took no notice of this advice. In spite of adverse comments from the Finance Minister, Gaudin, to the effect that an increase in taxation would bring nothing like the yield that he envisaged, he went ahead with increases in several of the direct taxes and held back only over the land tax, which he hoped would be increased for him by the Legislative Body. He made no effort to employ the deputies on any other projects. A draft of a rural code had been referred to consultative commissions as long ago as 1808, and its chief author, De Verneilh-Puyrasseau, one of the deputies for the Dordogne, had hopefully submitted a written report to the Legislative Body in March 1813, but nothing more was heard on the subject. During the Consulate, the Legislative Body had voted the contingents for the armed forces and allotted the numbers to the various departments; but since 1805 the size of contingents had been fixed by senatus-consultum and the apportioning left to administrative officials. Thus it was to the Senate that Regnault de St Jean d'Angély appealed on 14 October 1813 for 300,000 men to be put at the disposal of the Minister for War, the Legislative Body being given no part in the proceedings.[15]

Napoleon arrived back in Paris on 9 November. On the 26th he held a meeting of the Council of State to fix the budget for 1814. This was ready for presentation to the Legislative Body when, on 29 November, an imperial decree was issued deferring the opening of parliament from 2 December to 19 December. It came too late to prevent the deputies from starting out from home. Many of them found themselves kicking their heels in Paris for more than a fortnight, and men who had met each other only briefly before were thus presented with an opportunity to exchange opinions.[16]

Cambacérès had also reminded Napoleon, well in advance, of the

14 Napoleon, *Correspondance*, no. 20833; Cambacérès, *Lettres inédites* II, pp. 1107, 1117; Bruguière, *La Première Restauration*, pp. 21–4.
15 *Arch. parl.*, 16 March, 14 Oct. 1813.
16 Rovigo, *Memoirs* III, p. 169.

need for a senatus-consultum prolonging the term of office of the two series of deputies who were due to retire. The Arch-Chancellor was referring to the deputies of Series 4, whose term had already been extended to cover the February session but no more, and to those of Series 3, whose term would run out if the forthcoming session lasted beyond 31 December. With his characteristic hand-to-mouth attitude in such matters, Napoleon provided only for Series 4, prolonging their term for 'the whole of the ensuing session'.[17]

Meanwhile the Emperor, as was his wont, gave much more attention to the question of the presidency of the Legislative Body. As long ago as 1809 he had been worried because the five candidates presented by the deputies had included men whom he regarded as nonentities – Tupinier was one whom he mentioned with contempt; and even at that point he had had the idea of altering the constitution so as to allow himself to nominate one of the Grand Dignitaries of the Empire. Nothing had come of the notion, perhaps because when Fontanes withdrew from the lists in 1810 on account of being made Grand Master of the University an admirable successor to the presidency was found in the Comte de Montesquiou-Fézensac. Cambacérès thought well of Montesquiou for his work previously on the financial commission, and Napoleon was delighted with the speech he made at the end of the February session.[18] Montesquiou had already been named again by the deputies as their candidate from Series 1 for the presidency, and there was no earthly reason why he should not have been appointed once more; but perhaps Napoleon was alarmed at the thought that in some unforeseen circumstance he might have to choose between the candidates from Series 2 and Series 5; Deurbroucq of the Loire Inférieure, about whom no information has survived except that he was a businessman of Nantes and had never sat in parliament until 1810, and Van der Goes van Dixland, a Dutch diplomat with whom Napoleon had had many irritating dealings before drafting him into the Legislative Body in 1811. He may simply have disliked their names. The Swiss Pictet was under the impression that Napoleon set great store by the sound of people's names; and certainly he once dismissed all Dutch names as 'too barbarous' for him.[19] Whatever the reason, he now got Molé to present to the Senate a proposal drafted in precisely the terms he had had in mind four years earlier. Hitherto, said Molé, the Emperor had chosen the President from the five candidates presented to him by the Legislative Body. It might happen, however, that the men on the list were not known to him and could not therefore be suitably appointed to a position in which they would have direct access to him. For one thing, they might not be able to cope with the etiquette surrounding the Emperor, and this would result

17 Cambacérès, *Lettres inédites* II, pp. 1107, 1115, 1116, 1121, 1122; *Bulletin des Lois*, 15 Nov. 1813.
18 See above, p. 128.
19 Pictet, *Journal*, p. 124; Schama, *Patriots and Liberators*, p. 616.

in delays which might be misinterpreted by the waiting deputies. There was also the question of economy. (Molé did not enlarge on this point, but he presumably referred to the salary of the President, which could be saved if a Grand Dignitary did the job.) The Privy Council, continued Molé, had refrained from saying that a Grand Dignitary should *always* preside over the Legislative Body, because this would deprive deputies of the chance of competing for the post, but the Councillors were of the opinion that His Majesty should be allowed to appoint either a Grand Dignitary, or a Grand Officer, or a Minister of State instead of one of the candidates presented by the Legislative Body if it should seem desirable to him to do so. Chaptal reported favourably on the proposal, and the necessary senatus-consultum was passed on 15 November. A week later the Emperor appointed president His Excellency Claude Régnier, Duc de Massa, Minister of State.[20]

The senatus-consultum did not pass without opposition in the Senate, but criticism was aroused not so much by the proposal concerning the presidency as by the second clause, which allowed the Senate and the Council of State to attend imperial sessions of parliament in a body. Hitherto 'imperial sessions' had been confined to opening ceremonies, and the Senate and Council of State had been represented by deputations. Senator Cornet regarded the proposed change as unwise, for in the serious circumstances of 1813 he envisaged a situation in which a regency council might summon an imperial session of parliament and take advantage of all three state authorities meeting together to carry out a *coup d'état.* Cornet tells us in his memoirs that his colleagues on the Senate were astounded at his temerity in mentioning such a thing, and were sure it would be the end of him. Nothing untoward happened to him, however. Garnier replied to his objection, and a vote produced a favourable majority of 65 to 18, which as Cambacérès pointed out to Napoleon was a little more than two thirds majority required for constitutional amendments but only just.[21] The reasons for making the change are not clear. Mme de Chastenay, travelling to Paris with her father to attend the meeting of the Legislative Body, heard rumours to the effect that Napoleon himself was going to seize the opportunity afforded by an imperial session to establish a despotism, and that recalcitrant Senators (not Cornet but Lanjuinais was mentioned) had already been imprisoned in Vincennes; but none of this happened. Perhaps Napoleon was merely trying to reward the Senate and Council for their co-operation in the crisis. He always though that people like attending ceremonies.[22]

Napoleon seemed to be aware at last that France wanted peace at any price. Though not prepared for such extremities himself, he apparently

20 Napoleon, *Correspondance*, no. 15978; *Arch. parl.*, pp. 16 Jan., 1 Feb. 1810, 16 Mar., 1813; Cambacérès, *Lettres inédites* ii, pp. 618, 621, 627.
21 Cornet, *Souvenirs*, p. 62; Cambacérès, *Lettres inédites* ii, pp. 1121–2.
22 Chastenay, *Mémoires* ii, p. 223.

thought that his conduct during recent peace negotiations would at least bear investigation, and he delayed the opening of parliament in the hope of being able to report progress.[23] The Allies, however, were moving cautiously: having employed Baron St Aignan to let it be known unofficially in the Paris salons during November that they were offering peace on a basis of the natural frontiers, they issued on 4 December a 'Declaration' at Frankfurt whose language was evasive. By this time Holland had fallen, and the British were unlikely to honour any promise to allow France to keep Belgium. Unfortunately Napoleon had not replied categorically to the St Aignan proposals, though he had replaced Maret by the more diplomatic Caulaincourt as Foreign Minister and given him *carte blanche* to negotiate. Whether Napoleon had really made every effort to secure peace was a matter for dispute.

The opening of parliament on 19 December took place during a violent storm, the ceremonial booming of cannon alternating with rolls of thunder as Napoleon drove in state from the Tuileries across the Place de la Concorde and over the bridge. He had chosen this shorter route in preference to a tour of the *quais* because he was afraid of meeting with a hostile reception from the crowd, whether silent or abusive. Pasquier, who as prefect of police was in charge of security, traversed the route on horseback an hour beforehand and found a single slogan painted on the first pillar of the Pont de la Concorde, *A bas le tyran!*: he managed to get it cleaned off just in time. A solitary cry of 'What, will no one deliver us from this scoundrel?' greeted Napoleon as he emerged from the Tuileries into the gardens; the culprit, hustled in front of the police, turned out to be Bassompierre, the representative of an old and respected family, and Pasquier persuaded Napoleon that it would be wisest to overlook the incident.[24]

Some of the people who peered through the torrents of rain streaming down the carriage windows thought that Napoleon's air of stony calm was a sign of mental derangement: his mind had become unhinged, it was said, on the retreat from Moscow. Mme de Reinhard's little boy was chiefly interested in the pageboys clinging to the straps of the carriage as though in flight, and would have liked to have tried it out at home if he had dared; his sister, who had never seen Napoleon before, thought he looked fat and old. Paris was full of officials and their families recently returned from years of residence in distant parts of the Grand Empire; they were saddened to see Napoleon changed from the days of the Consulate, and a certain amount of sympathy softened their fears and criticisms.[25]

The Emperor's speech, which was short, was variously reported. Méneval described it as 'calm and touching'; Pasquier thought it was extremely well written and that it made a profound impression on the

23 Rovigo, *Memoirs* II, p. 167; Pasquier, *Mémoires* II, p. 117.
24 Pasquier, *Mémoires* II, pp. 118–19.
25 Chastenay, *Mémoires* II, p. 244; Reinhard, *Lettres*, pp. 378–9.

audience. Savary thought that Napoleon did not describe in sufficient detail the events which had brought about the existing crisis. Miot said that the speech made a bad impression because it contained no promise of peace and was all about men and money, money and men; but then Miot, by his own admission, was not present at the ceremony.[26] Addressing himself to all three authorities of state, the Emperor began:

> Resounding victories have brought fame to French arms in this campaign, but defections without example have rendered these victories useless.[27] Everything has turned against us. France herself would be in danger but for the energy and unity of Frenchmen. In these grave circumstances my first thought has been to call you to my side. My heart has need of the presence and affection of my subjects. I have never been dazzled by prosperity; adversity will find me unassailable.
>
> I have several times given peace to nations which have lost everything. From a part of my conquests I raised up thrones for kings who have abandoned me. I have conceived and executed great plans for the prosperity of the world. Monarch and father, I know what peace adds to the security of thrones and families. Negotiations have been opened with the allied powers. I have accepted the preliminary bases which they have offered. I had therefore hoped that before the opening of this session the Congress of Mannheim would have met, but new delays which are not attributable to France have deferred this moment which all the world desires.
>
> I have ordered you to be shown all the documents in the files of my department of Foreign Affairs. You will study them by means of a commission. Orators from my Council of State will make known to you my wishes on the subject.
>
> Nothing on my part is opposed to the re-establishment of peace. I know and share all the sentiments of the French people. I say the French people, because there is not one of you who would desire peace at the price of honour.
>
> It is with regret that I ask of this generous people further sacrifices, but they are demanded by their noblest and dearest interests. I have been obliged to reinforce my armies by numerous levies: nations negotiate with security only when they deploy all their forces. An increase in income has become indispensable. What my Minister of Finance will propose to you conforms to the system of finances that I have established. We shall meet everything without borrowing, which eats into the future, and without paper money, which is the greatest enemy of the social order.
>
> I am satisfied with the sentiments that my people of Italy have

26 Ménéval, *Mémoires* III, p. 182; Pasquier, *Mémoires* II, p. 119; Rovigo, *Memoirs* II, pp. 167–8; Miot, *Mémoires* III, p. 312.
27 He referred to the defection of Bavaria and Saxony to the Allies.

shown me in this situation. Denmark and Naples alone have remained faithful to my alliance. The Republic of the USA continues successfully its war against England. I have recognized the neutrality of the nineteen Swiss cantons.

Senators, Councillors of State, Deputies of the Departments to the Legislative Body: you are the natural organs of the throne; it is for you to give the example of an energy which will commend our generation to the generations to come. Let them not say of us, they sacrificed the chief interests of the country! they recognized the laws that England tried in vain for four centuries to impose on France!

My people need not fear that the policy of their Emperor will ever betray the nation's glory. For my part, I have confidence that Frenchmen will always be worthy of themselves and me.

The deputies who heard this speech were the same that had met earlier in the year, with a few more absences on account of 'legitimate causes'. (By 21 December, thirty-three had sent their apologies.)[28] They had been elected, or re-elected, during the years 1807–11, when the Empire had seemed stable and flourishing. They were not, perhaps, the men that France would have chosen to represent her in a crisis, but they rose fairly well to the occasion. Mme de Chastenay says they were annoyed from the start by the appointment of Massa as President instead of their own leading nominee, Montesquiou. Claude Régnier, Duc de Massa, had been for several years Minister of Justice. Respected as a man of integrity, he was nevertheless slow, broken in health, and generally incapable of conciliating an assembly to whom his presence was an affront. Invited by the Emperor to elect a commission to examine the papers relating to negotiations with the Allies, the deputies chose five men who had never received any sign of imperial favour – Lainé, Maine de Biran, Flauguergues, Raynouard and Gallois. No information has survived to indicate just how these men emerged. They were elected the day after Regnault de St Jean d'Angély had communicated the Emperor's invitation, and six ballots were necessary to secure five men with a majority.[29]

Joseph Lainé was a forty-six-year-old lawyer from Bordeaux. Of moderate but tenacious liberal opinions, he had been worried about continuing in his role as deputy when his mandate was due to run out at the end of 1813, and had wondered whether he should take his seat. Seeing Napoleon at last brought to the stage of consulting parliament, Lainé believed that the time had come to secure more genuine participation in government. Napoleon later accused him of negotiating with

28 *Arch. parl.*, 21 Dec. 1813. Mattei of Leghorn visited his prefect and pleaded 'a secret illness', but with 'a countenance so glowing with health' that the prefect was incensed, and denounced Mattei to the Minister of the Interior as a worthless creature, lacking both intelligence and character, never seen in good company but constantly surrounded by *canaille*. *Arch. nat.*, F^{IC}III, Méditerranée (1).
29 *Arch. parl.*, 21, 22 Dec. 1813.

royalist agents from the start, but the accusation seems unlikely to have been true. Pasquier, who interviewed all the members of the commission when they ran into trouble, was convinced that Lainé had never had any intention of overthrowing the imperial régime.

Maine de Biran had been expelled from the Council of Five Hundred for royalist opinions, but since then he had devoted himself mainly to philosophical studies, and among his fellow deputies he was generally regarded as a scholarly, detached, and upright man. Flaugergues was a more passionate individual. As a member of his local council in 1793 he had protested against the execution of Louis XVI and against the expulsion of the Girondins from the Convention, with the result that he had had to hide in the woods of Aveyron for some time to avoid arrest. For the first ten years of the Napoleonic régime he had held a post as sub-prefect at Villefranche, but finding the work tedious he had got himself presented as candidate for he Legislative Body by the college of his arrondissement. He seems to have passed without notice at his first parliamentary session in February 1813, but attracted attention on the very first day of the second session by denouncing Massa's installation as unconstitutional. François-Just Raynouard, at fifty-two, was a few years older than the three already mentioned, and the only one of the five who had a personal grudge against the régime. A tragic playwright of some renown, he had carried on a running battle with the censors ever since 1802, when his play *Les Templiers* was put into cold storage for several years. He held Napoleon personally responsible for the banning of his *États de Blois* after a single performance at St Cloud. Jean-Antoine Gallois, on the other hand, had no reason to bear grudges. Elected to the Tribunate with the Auteuil group in 1800 he had survived all purges and changes, and was among the few men transferred to the Legislative Body in 1807. He was now fifty-two. Reputed to be an honest man as well as a clever one, his knowledge of England, which he had visited in 1798 on a mission to secure an exchange of prisoners, and his friendship with Talleyrand were perhaps thought to make him particularly well qualified for an investigation into diplomatic affairs.[30]

The commission, joined by Massa, met for several successive days under the chairmanship of Cambacérès, the Arch-Chancellor.[31] Regnault de St Jean d'Angély and d'Hauterive attended on behalf of the Council of State. Its brief, according to the speech made by Regnault on 21 December, was to examine the papers put before it by the Minister for Foreign Affairs in order to be able to assess Napoleon's claim that he had done all he could to secure peace. Though the discussions were confidential, information was almost bound to leak out. Miot de Melito afterwards claimed to have heard what had happened from his friend Regnault. His account differs only in minor detail

30 Chastenay, *Mémoires* II, pp. 250–51; Pasquier, *Mémoires* II, p. 124; Rémusat, *Mémoires* I, p. 58.
31 *Arch. parl.*, 23–7 Dec. 1813.

from others.[32] Lainé, who had proved to be the toughest member of the commission, was chosen to draw up its report, which he did in three parts; the first accusing Napoleon of having failed to accept the Allied terms soon enough, the second urging him to join with the French people in asking for peace at any price short of enemy occupation and the third pointing out that if war became necessary to repel invaders, Napoleon could only secure a truly national effort by respecting the institutions which secured the people's rights. Regnault and his colleague were shocked when Lainé read out this report at the Arch-Chancellor's, and persuaded him, or so they thought, to modify it considerably; but Lainé read it out unrevised to the Legislative Body on 29 December, when it made a great sensation. The deputies had gone into general committee for the purpose of hearing the report, which meant not only that the vast crowd of would-be listeners had been cleared out of the galleries but that Napoleon, too, had been made to rely on hearsay.

Late that night the Emperor held a private council to decide what to do. The desirability of dissolving the Legislative Body was discussed. According to Rovigo, the Minister of Police, the Emperor asked if there were not reason to fear that if the enemy approached the capital the Legislative Body would declare itself in permanent session and seize the reins of government. Rumour had it that Molé advised shooting the members of the commission and arresting their supporters, but Pasquier denied that this was so. By all accounts Cambacérès, and by his own account Boulay, spoke out strongly in favour of negotiation, and Boulay was employed to draft a speech assuring the Legislative Body of the Emperor's desire to co-operate with their wishes. He was engaged in doing this when, during the afternoon of 30 December, the Legislative Body in public session voted by a majority of 223 to 31 that the report of the commission should be published. Napoleon hastily held another conference at which it was decided that Rovigo should obtain the report from the printer's to discover precisely what it said. At a police conclave that night Pasquier, supported by Réal, arrived at the conclusion that the report contained nothing culpable and that the Emperor, however much he disliked it, ought to take it in good part in order to win the co-operation of the Legislative Body for the war effort. Rovigo and Réal attended the Emperor's levée the next morning to give him this advice, but they were told that Napoleon had irrevocably decided to dissolve the Legislative Body and that the police must seize the whole issue of the report at the printer's.

What caused Napoleon to make this sudden decision is uncertain. Pasquier believed that he was particularly upset when the five members of the special commission were elected on to the finance commission as

32 Miot, *Mémoires* III, pp. 316–24; Pasquier, *Mémoires* II, pp. 124–9; Boulay, *Boulay*, pp. 214–18; Chastenay, *Mémoires* II, pp. 251–9; Rovigo, *Memoirs* II, pp. 172–80; Pontécoulant, *Souvenirs* III, pp. 176–82.

well; but this was not a new development on the morning of 31 December. Lainé, Flaugergues and Gallois had been elected along with Blanquart de Bailleul on 28 December, and Maine de Biran and Raynouard had been added, along with Pictet Diodati, on 30 December. Miot said that the Emperor had believed that the report of the special commission was going to be modified, and that when he saw certain objectionable phrases in the copy brought from the printer's he thought he had been tricked. There is also the possibility that he had suddenly hit upon what seemed to him a cunning way of getting rid of his opponents. The decree dissolving the Legislative Body gave as the reason for the dissolution the fact that the term of office of the deputies of Series 3 expired on that day, and the electoral colleges would have to meet to make new nominations.

On 30 December the President had read out to the deputies an invitation from the Emperor to attend a New Year's reception at the Tuileries. They were ordered to wear full dress uniform and to proceed, not in a body but privately to the throne room for 12 noon on 1 January. As things had turned out, some thought it best not to go. Others said that the reception was a mere formality and that there was nothing to be afraid of. In the end, large numbers went. Seeing them gathered together, Napoleon got very excited, and descending from the throne he stalked about in front of them, hurling disjointed accusations at them.

> Your address is inflammatory. . . . Most of the members of the Legislative Body are good citizens, but one in twelve are traitors. . . . You have let yourselves be led astray by five trouble makers. . . . Lainé is a traitor, in correspondence with the Prince Regent – I have proof of it. . . . Your report has done me a lot of harm; I would rather have lost a couple of battles. Is it in the presence of the foreigner that one should make remonstrances? . . . You are not the representatives of the nation; you are deputies of the departments. I alone am the representative of the people. . . . Even if you think me at fault you should not reproach me publicly; one does not wash one's dirty linen in public.[33]

A few days earlier a commission of the Senate, represented by Fontanes, had reported favourably on the Foreign Office evidence. The defection of the German princes had brought disaster to the French armies, Fontanes said; the Emperor had realized that he must withdraw his troops, and he had done so at once, fighting with them all the way. 'Since returning to his capital he has turned his eyes away from those battlefields on which the world has admired him for fifteen years; he has even turned his thoughts from the grand designs he had conceived. . . . He has desired peace, and ever since the hope of negotiation has appeared possible he has seized it eagerly.' The Allies, however, were equivocating; they spoke of peace, yet were invading the frontiers. 'Let

---

33 This is the version given by Pontécoulant (*Souvenirs* III, pp. 180–81) who was present as a member of the Senate. Other reports differ only in small details.

us rally round this diadem, whence the lustre of fifty victories shines across a passing cloud. Fortune does not long fail those nations which do not fail themselves.'[34] On 30 December Lacépède had read out to the Emperor an address composed in Fontanes' sonorous terms: 'The enemy has invaded our territory. The French people, united in heart and interest under a leader such as you, will not let its energy falter. . . . We shall fight for our beloved country between the tombs of our fathers and the cradles of our children.' Napoleon was pleased with this, though when he thought about it afterwards he was not so pleased with the next bit: 'Sire, obtain peace by a last effort worthy of you and of the French people, and let your hand, so many times victorious, lay down its weapons after signing the peace of the world.' Seeing a group of Senators standing near him at the reception on New Year's Day he gave them their share of criticism. 'It was when I was at the head of my victorious armies that you should have talked to me like that. Do you think I would have rejected the truth? The Council of State never feared to speak out.'

Back in his own apartment, the Emperor sent for Cambacérès and Rovigo. To their surprise he seemed to show no particular displeasure with the Legislative Body. He complained in general terms of the difficulty of getting any assembly to support the government, which was always seen as an enemy. It would be dangerous, he said, to have such an assembly in existence while foreign armies were invading the country, and he himself would have enough to do without having to control such a body. Cambacérès ventured to put in a word for the departing deputies, saying that although he did not agree with the line they had taken they should have been treated differently; but Napoleon had decided that they were a worthless set of men. They only came to Paris for the purpose of obtaining personal favours, he said. When they were invited to dinner (Cambacérès had always prided himself on the importance of his dinners for the deputies) they felt nothing but envy at seeing the opulence of the tables, and went back to their departments full of stories of how the government plundered France to enrich its favourites.[35]

On 25 January Napoleon left Paris to face the invading armies. There seemed to be no point in the deputies waiting about, and most of them drifted off home. Lainé was afraid he might be arrested as a Bourbon agent, and rushed round to the Minister of Police in an attempt to clear himself of suspicion, but the Minister couldn't be bothered with him and told him that Napoleon would have forgotten the whole thing by the next day. The famous report was subsequently published in England and a few copies smuggled into France, where former members of the Legislative Body took a pride in their show of courage at the last. The

---

34 *Arch. parl.*, 27 Dec. 1813.
35 Rovigo, *Memoirs* III, pp. 179–80. Bourrienne claimed to have heard the same story from Cambacérès: *Mémoires* IX, pp. 176–7.

Emperor could not hope to make the war into a national effort, they read, 'unless the French people are persuaded that the government no longer desires any glory but that of peace, [and that] their blood will not be shed except to defend the homeland and its independence. But these consoling words of peace and homeland will resound in vain unless there is a guarantee of the institutions which promise the benefits of both. It seems indispensable, therefore, that His Majesty should be begged to maintain wholly and constantly in operation the laws which guarantee to Frenchmen the rights of liberty, security and property, and to the nation the free exercise of its political rights.' If, as Pontécoulant said, the deputies had spoken such words when Napoleon was at the height of his triumph, the nation might have honoured them. As it was, Fontanes' more diplomatic language ensured that the Senate, not the Legislative Body, was at hand to play a significant role when Napoleon fell.

11

The Legislators

About 1,100 men are known to have been members of Napoleon's parliaments at one time or another between 1800 and 1814. Of these, some 200 sat only fleetingly. In the early years, especially, it was not uncommon for a man to make his mark in the first weeks of a session and find that he was offered more tempting employment: Belleville resigned after a few weeks to become chargé d'affaires in Tuscany, Cacault became minister to Rome, Frégeville was made head of an army division, Miot was appointed to the Council of State, Dédelay d'Agier and Boissy d'Anglas became Senators. Some (though by no means all) resigned if they were made prefects. Death and ill-health took away a few newly elected men each year. The parliaments of 1811 and 1813 brought in over a hundred men who had never sat before and whose maximum parliamentary experience was therefore twelve to thirteen weeks.

Of the remaining 900, about 380 sat for three or four of the early sessions of the Consulate, when a great deal of legislative work was done. By 1807 all but 40 of these uniquely experienced men had disappeared from parliament, never to return until, perhaps, the Hundred Days. With the reorganization of the Legislative Body in 1802 the general pattern was for men to serve their five years and go; some were presented again by their electoral college but few were chosen for a second term by the Senate. There is a temptation to suppose that this was because deputies were being chosen from higher strata of society as time went by, but this is not necessarily the correct explanation. Under the electoral system of 1803 it was very difficult to get re-elected, since a man who was popular with his local college might not have had the necessary influence in the Senate and vice versa.

As parliamentary sessions became shorter and shorter, a man who sat for only five of them can hardly be said to have had a great deal of parliamentary experience. In some years, sessions were so short that members might be absent from them for the whole time owing to some quite ordinary illness, as were, for example, Van der Leyen and Poujard, both of whom wrote at the beginning of the session of 1806 saying that they would not be able to appear at all.[1] There were, however, 177 men who sat for seven or more sessions out of a possible fifteen, and may perhaps be looked upon as providing a model of the Napoleonic legislator.[2]

Of these 'long-term' members, 97 entered parliament during the first two sessions – 71 into the Legislative Body and 26 into the Tribunate. Of 88 whose background is known, 57 began their careers as lawyers and achieved during the Revolution a position (varying according to age) in the legal or administrative affairs of their locality before entering parliament. Ten started their adult life in the army; 6 were businessmen (two from Belgium) and one a designer and engraver; 5 were doctors; 3 were employed in the diplomatic service; one was a financier employed in the central administration; one was a Protestant minister in Vaucluse, one had been a member of a religious order before entering local administration, and another was constitutional bishop of Mayenne; two were known simply as landowners. Only Chassiron, the son of a former treasurer of France, belonged to the near-noble class; at the other end of the social scale, only one, Louvet, was the son of a *laboureur* or peasant proprietor.[3] In some cases their unusually long service in parliament was due to chance. In 1802 lots were drawn to determine the order in which the various series of departments were to renew their deputations: 16 of the men now under consideration stayed until 1805 because they happened to belong to the second series, and 24 until 1806 because they belonged to the even luckier first series. Only 27 of the 71 Legislators achieved the difficult task of getting themselves elected for a second term. Six of the 26 Tribunes survived all eliminations and were transferred to the Legislative Body in 1807; another 6 were subsequently elected to the Legislative Body.

The remaining 80 of the 'long-term' parliamentarians came in after the purge of 1802. Two owed their length of service to the fact that they were transferred from the Tribunate to the Legislative Body in 1807; the others were re-elected to the Legislative Body after an initial period of five years. Of 74 whose backgrounds are known, 41 began their careers as lawyers, 13 were army men, 7 businessmen, 3 doctors, 3 academics, one a diplomat, one a member of a religious order who had entered local administration, and 4 landowners. The lawyers, like those belonging to the earliest group, had secured a variety of legal and administrative posts in their localities during the Revolutionary years. They were distinguished from the previous group in that this sort of

1 *Journal de Paris*, 5 Mar. 1806.
2 The ordinary and supplementary sessions of 1802 have been counted as two sessions since they came before and after the purge; the sessions of 1809 and 1810 have been counted as one because they ran almost consecutively and involved the same personnel; the two sessions of 1813 have been counted as two because there was a gap of eight months between them.
3 *Arch. nat.*, CC28–49 (results of elections) yields data on occupation and tax payments. Brief biographies in Bourleton *et al.*, *Dictionnaire*.

career had already led to employment under the Napoleon régime; at least a dozen of them, for instance, were sub-prefects. Eight are known to have been of the noble or near-noble class, one of these coming originally from Hesse-Nassau and sitting for the Rhineland department of the Rhin-et-Moselle.

Napoleon was continually being pestered for jobs for men leaving parliament. 'I take the liberty of reminding Your Majesty of Colonel Bord, who goes out of the Legislative Body without fortune, and with a numerous family' wrote Cambacérès on 20 April 1807. Many of the men who entered parliament with lowly jobs in local administration had obtained much better ones by the time they left. Since many parliamentarians kept on with their jobs in the long intervals between sessions, however, it is difficult to know whether their advancement was due to the influential contacts they had made in parliament or whether promotion would have followed in the ordinary course of events. The army officers who continued to fight in campaigns – Sahuc, for instance, who fought with distinction throughout the Revolutionary and Napoleonic wars and rose from lieutenant in 1792 to general of division by 1806 – can hardly be said to have owed their military advancement to their parliamentary careers.

Napoleon would have liked all his parliamentarians to have been men of independent means. He told the Council of State in 1806:

> The Legislative Body should be composed of individuals who, after their time has expired, are able to live off their fortunes without needing to be given places. There are now, each year, sixty Legislators going out that one doesn't know what to do with; those who are not given jobs are going to carry their grudges with them into their departments. I would like to have elderly property owners, wedded to the state, as it were, through their family or their profession – attached by some bond to public life. These men would come every year to Paris, speak to the Emperor at a reception, and be happy with this little bit of glory thrown into the monotony of their lives.[4]

He perhaps succeeded to a small extent in getting the type of person he wanted. The number of landowners who had no other identifiable form of income rose from 4 per cent of the total membership in 1800 to 29 per cent by 1811. (The proportion of titled nobility from the old régime also rose from one per cent to 10 per cent, but former noblemen were not necessarily either rich or lacking in ambition.)[5] A rise in the average age of deputies probably brought in more men who had already succeeded in their career ambitions: in 1811, 28 per cent of the members were over sixty. Napoleon himself was a young man when he came to power (thirty-one at the time of the *coup d'état*) but his Corsican instincts as well as his classical education gave him a respect for elder statesmen.

4 Pelet, *Opinions*, p. 151.
5 Percentages from Beck, *French Legislators*, chapter 4 and appendix C, table 5.

The fact that men who paid enough taxes to sit in departmental assemblies were likely to be elderly struck him as an advantage.[6] In 1807 he increased the minimum age of entry into the Legislative Body from thirty to forty, because he thought that men were more likely to appreciate his measures if they had an adult recollection of the troubles of the Revolution. As time went on he grew less enamoured of politicians who had actually taken part in the Revolution, and it probably pleased him that the number of men selected to sit in the Legislative Body who had sat in Revolutionary assemblies between 1789 and 1794 decreased from 38 per cent in 1800 to 13 per cent in 1811–13, with a particularly sharp decline (16 per cent to 2 per cent) in men who had sat in the Convention.

There were very few parliamentary families. Two brothers Girardin sat, one in the Tribunate from 1800 to 1803, the other in the Legislative Body from 1804 to 1814, and two brothers Faure, one in the Tribunate from 1800 to 1806, the other in the Legislative Body from 1811 to 1813. A father and son Villot-Fréville sat in the Legislative Body and the Tribunate respectively, their periods of service overlapping and their identity becoming confused even in official records. Montesquieu, President of the Legislative Body from 1810 to 1813, was succeeded as representative of the department of the Seine-et-Marne by his brother Henri. Three other pairs came from annexed territories. Two brothers Bassenge came from Liège, one being eliminated from the Legislative Body in 1802 and the other elected to it in 1806; two brothers Sturtz sat for the department of Mont Tonnerre, one from 1802 to 1811 and the other in 1813 only; and two rather more famous cousins Pictet came from Léman, one as a Tribune from 1802 to 1806 and the other as a Legislator for two spells of time, 1800 to 1803 and 1811 to 1813. A few younger relatives of previous members appeared in the parliament of the Hundred Days, but this was in many respects a different assembly from earlier ones.

Out of the 1,100 members sitting between 1800 and 1814, 203 received titles from Napoleon in the later years of the Empire.[7] One hundred and one became chevaliers, 80 barons, 21 counts and one a duke. By no means all of these received their titles while serving as members of parliament, however, and of those who did it cannot be assumed that they received their titles because of their parliamentary service. Indeed, as far as the higher ranks were concerned it was theoretically impossible for them to have done so, unless they had obtained the position of President of the Legislative Body, which carried the title of count. The decree of 1 March 1808 creating titles specified that Ministers, Senators, and Councillors of State were to become counts; that the presidents and members of departmental colleges, along with

6 Napoleon, *Correspondance*, no. 13020.
7 Figures collected from Révérend, *Armorial*. Napoleon awarded 3,600 titles altogether.

presidents and *procureurs-généraux* of the leading law courts, bishops, and mayors of large cities could, under certain circumstances, become barons; that officers of the Legion of Honour should become chevaliers of the Empire; and that titles could be awarded by the Emperor at his discretion to prefects, generals, and other civilian and military officials. Of the 80 members of parliament who became barons, 16 received the titles ascribed to the office of prefect and 14 to military service; 13 were judges or *procureurs-généraux*, 2 were attached to the Cour des Comptes and 2 to the Council of State; 2 were mayors, one (Jaubert) a bishop, one a minister, and one attached to the imperial household; 2 (Nougarède and Silvestre de Sacy) were designated *barons tirés des corps savants*; and the remaining 24 were either *barons propriétaires* or *barons membres de collège électoral*. Those who became counts were for the most part men who had been transferred from the Legislative Body to the Senate. Only Joseph-François Salm-Dyck, a descendant of the illustrious counts of Salm, who sat in the Legislative Body from 1805 to 1810 as representative of the department of the Röer, became a *comte membre de collège électoral*. The duke was Masséna.

More honours were awarded to men elected after 1803 than to those who had sat in the early days of the Consulate. Of the members of the first Legislative Body, only 17 per cent were later admitted to the Legion of Honour and only 10 per cent were given imperial titles. For those who sat in 1803 the percentages were 34 and 20, and for those elected in the years 1811–13, 58 and 33.[8] This would seem to indicate that the members of later parliaments were of a higher status, but how much their parliamentary careers had to do with it is impossible to determine.

8 Beck, *French Legislators*, pp. 30–32.

12

Abdication and Restoration

On 16 February 1814 Castlereagh reported from Châtillon-sur-Seine that Tsar Alexander was determined to consult the French nation on the form of régime to be established, or re-established, when the Allies entered Paris. His intention was 'that the corps legislative and other leading bodies of the State, with such persons *marquantes* as might be deemed proper, should be invited to assemble and declare the national will'. Castlereagh, who regarded the suggestion as dangerous, tried to persuade Alexander that 'if the constituted bodies were looked to for an opinion they would probably be gone.' The Legislative Body had indeed dispersed at the beginning of the year, brusquely adjourned by Napoleon, but the Senate had continued to hold regular sessions after Napoleon left for the war, and was still registering letters patent creating imperial counts, barons, and chevaliers when the Allied armies advanced upon Paris.[1]

Many people had realized towards the end of 1813 that the Senate, as the body which officially presided over changes in the constitution, would be in a position to play a crucial role should the Empire totter; and to prevent the Senators from making premature terms with the enemy, Napoleon had sent instructions to his brother Joseph that, if the capital seemed likely to fall, the Senators were to accompany the Empress Regent and other Grand Dignitaries to a new rallying point on the Loire. The Senators had no stomach for a last stand, however. They formed an unwieldy body, which had increased gradually from the orginal 60 to 144 members, the majority distinctly elderly. When Marie Louise eventually departed for Blois on 28 March, very few went with her. The Senators had every reason to fear the fall of the Empire, and one of their number, Lanjuinais, afterwards gave the opinion that if the Empress had remained in Paris they would have worked with her to secure a regency for her little son. Her departure, however, left them at the mercy of Talleyrand, who had been intriguing among them for at least the preceding six weeks for a restoration of the Bourbons. Be-

1 Bury, 'The End of the Napoleonic Senate', is authoritative on the role of the Senate in 1814.

tween 28 and 31 March, when Tsar Alexander entered Paris with the victorious armies sufficient numbers of Senators were won over to the idea that if they agreed to a monarchical restoration they would be able to dictate the terms on which it was to take place.

Alexander's actions on entering Paris gave them a good deal of encouragement. Announcing that the Allies would not treat with Napoleon or with any member of the Bonaparte family, the Tsar invited the Senate to nominate a provisional government which would carry on with immediate administrative tasks and 'prepare the constitution which will be suitable for the French people'. A declaration to this effect, posted on the walls of the city during the evening of 31 March, assured the French people that the Allies would 'recognize and guarantee the constitution with which the French nation was about to endow itself'.[2] Castlereagh was not a little surprised to find that the Allies had been pledged to guarantee a constitution they had not yet seen. Moreover, it was not at all clear whether the constitution was to be drawn up by the Provisional Government and handed straight to the Allied leaders, or whether some kind of consultation with 'the nation' was about to be arranged, using either the Senate, or the Legislative Body, or newly elected representatives. That Alexander intended at least the Senate to be involved seemed clear from his speech to those members who attended his reception on 2 April: they had been entrusted, he said, 'with one of the most honourable missions which generous men could fulfil, namely to ensure the happiness of a great people by endowing France with the strong and liberal institutions which she could not do without in her existing state of civilization and enlightenment'.[3] A statement from him which appeared in the *Moniteur* on the same day gave the impression that consultation might spread wider than the Senate: informing all soldiers in Paris that they need not regard themselves as fugitives, the Tsar told them that they were free men, 'called upon like all other Frenchmen to join in the measures which must decide the great question about to be judged for the happiness of France and all the world'.[4]

On 1 April a meeting of sixty-four Senators duly set up a provisional government headed by Talleyrand, who had already discussed the membership with the Tsar. Talleyrand promised the Senators that when the Provisional Government began on the task of drawing up a constitution it would keep them fully informed. This was not enough for the Senators, however; they insisted that certain principles, including preservation of the Senate and the Legislative Body as 'integral parts' of the new constitution, should be agreed upon at once by the Provisional Government and announced to the French people.[5] This having been

2 *Moniteur*, 2 Apr. 1814.
3 Bury, 'The End of the Napoleonic Senate'.
4 *Moniteur*, 2 Apr. 1814.
5 Supplement to *Moniteur*, 2 Apr. 1814.

done they were prepared to strengthen the hand of the Provisional Government by deposing Napoleon, who had not yet laid down arms or surrendered his claim to rule France. On 3 April the Senate formally approved a text drawn up by one of its members, Lambrechts, whereby Napoleon was said to have 'torn up the compact which united him with the French people, notably by raising duties and establishing taxes other than by law', and to have 'committed this assault on the rights of the people when he had just needlessly adjourned the Legislative Body and caused to be suppressed as criminal a report of this body, whose position and function in the representation of the nation he contested'. There followed a list of Napoleon's offences, including that of 'undertaking a series of wars in violation of Article 50 of the constitutional act of 22 Frimaire of the Year VIII, which required that declarations of war should be proposed, discussed, decreed and promulgated as law'. Napoleon was therefore dethroned and the nation and army absolved from its allegiance to him.[6]

When Napoleon came to reflect on these events at St Helena, he was chiefly annoyed by the clause about the wars. He argued, probably quite rightly, that the Senators would have made no difficulty about declaring war on Russia by decree if he had asked them to do so.[7] The Senate had, of course, acquiesced in all Napoleon's unconstitutional acts at the time, and it was ironic that the Senators should now have cited them as an assault upon the contract between ruler and nation. The idea that such a contract existed, however, possessed important implications for the future, and the Provisional Government decided to seek further support for it by summoning such members of the Legislative Body as could be found in Paris to a meeting at which they could associate themselves with the declaration of the Senate.

Under the presidency of Félix Faulcon, 76 deputies met and signed a statement to the effect that: 'The Legislative Body, considering that Napoleon Bonaparte has nullified the constitutional compact, recognizes and declares the deposition of Napoleon Bonaparte and the members of his family.'[8] Another 13 deputies added their signatures the following day. Altogether they were a mixed set of men. Only a handful could be described as Parisians, either because they had been born in Paris or had lived there for a long time. Eighteen were 'foreigners', representing German, Dutch, Italian and Swiss departments; the rest were men who had come up to Paris from the provinces. There is no clear evidence as to why they had stayed in Paris after the dissolution of the Legislative Body in January, though it may be assumed that some were cut off from their homes by the fortunes of war. Twelve had sat in all Napoleon's parliaments since the Year VIII; 52 had sat since the early days of the Empire; only 26 had been recently elected to the

6 *Arch. parl.*, 3 Apr. 1814.
7 Bertrand, *Cahiers, 1816–17*, p. 258.
8 *Arch. parl.*, 3 Apr. 1814.

parliaments of 1813. There were 3 counts, 8 barons and 18 chevaliers of the Empire among them, and 58 who had been admitted either to the order of the Réunion or to the Legion of Honour. A few (Flaugergues, Gallois, Raynouard) had shown themselves to be hostile to Napoleon's growing despotism, but this was no proof that they were enamoured of the Bourbons. Out of the whole 90, only 2 emerged as ultra-royalists after the Restoration. Sixteen sat in the Napoleonic Chamber of the Hundred Days.[9]

No mention had been made of the deputies joining in the work of constitution-making, though the enterprising Félix Faulcon was probably hoping to convey a hint when he thanked the members of the Provisional Government for summoning the deputies and added that: 'It was in the nature both of their rights and of their duties to take part in this great work of political regeneration.' Royalists such as Vitrolles, who had returned to France in the wake of the Allies, were angry that the Senate, let alone the Legislative Body, should be presuming to play a part. They had managed to get a spokesman, the Abbé de Montesquiou, appointed a member of the Provisional Government, and they were hoping that Alexander's declaration of 31 March could be interpreted to mean that the Provisional Government alone could frame a draft and hand it on to the Allies without more ado. When a first meeting of the Government was held at Talleyrand's house on 3 April, however, Montesquiou discovered that a miscellaneous collection of people, including a dozen or more Senators, had been invited. At this meeting the idea of restoring a Bourbon king to the throne was openly mentioned by Talleyrand for the first time. It seems to have been accepted as a foregone conclusion, and the meeting concentrated on the more controversial business of a constitution. In spite of Montesquiou's opposition it was decided that the Senators who were present at the meeting should consult their colleagues informally. They returned the following day with numerous proposals. By then, however, speed was of the essence, since it had been discovered that the Tsar was still toying with the idea of a Napoleonic regency. A constitutional draft was agreed upon and put to a formal meeting of the Senate on 6 April; the Legislative Body gave its approval on the 7th; and Talleyrand sent a copy to the Comte d'Artois, who was on his way to Paris to act as lieutenant general of the kingdom until his elder brother Louis arrived to take up the crown. At this point Napoleon, who would not accept the right of the Senate and Legislative Body to depose him, was obliged to realize that the army would no longer fight for him, and to everybody's relief he abdicated the throne.[10]

The 'senatorial constitution', as it came to be known, assigned to

9 During the next few days, many more deputies sent letters approving of the act of deposition, but since it was by then a fait accompli little significance can be attached to their compliance.
10 Thiry, *La Première Abdication*, pp. 181–213.

Louis XVIII a position similar to that later occupied by Louis Philippe. The French people were said to have 'freely' called Louis to the throne. He was to be proclaimed 'King of the French' after he had sworn to accept and observe the Constitution. He was to be head of the executive power, but his ministers were to sit in parliament. All laws, including an annual budget, were to be passed by parliament before being sanctioned by the king. Parliament was to consist of two houses, a Senate and a Legislative Body, both of which were to have the right of discussion. The Legislative Body was to meet on 1 October each year; the king could prorogue or dissolve it, but if he did the latter, elections must be held within three months. The electoral colleges were to remain in existence, but instead of producing candidates only they were to elect actual deputies. Various personal guarantees were scattered about the document (liberty of worship, no reprisals, no confiscation of property, maintenance of existing law courts, army personnel to keep their ranks and pensions) and the whole was greeted in the English press as 'a monument of political wisdom'.[11]

The future king, like Napoleon fifteen years earlier, could not afford to ignore the opinion of the constituted bodies, and he seems at first to have thought that he would have to accept the Senate's constitution as it stood. However, he soon learnt that the document had aroused considerable opposition in France. The Senators had naturally been anxious to provide for their own future within the new régime, but in doing so they had shown too detailed a regard for their own material gains. Article 6, which dealt with this matter, was far more explicit than any of the clauses dealing with the rights and liberties of the people. According to its terms the existing Senators, with the exception of those who had lost their French citizenship, were to move at once into the new Senate, keeping their dignities for life and handing them on to their successors by primogeniture in the male line; the *sénatoreries* were to remain in the hands of their present owners; the revenues currently at the disposal of the Senate were to be enjoyed exclusively by existing Senators, any new men whom the king appointed being specifically denied a share. Vitrolles was able to criticize the Constitution as 'determined by private interests rather than by a concern for the welfare of the State', and demonstrations against the Senate and its constitution broke out in royalist areas of the south and west.[12] The Tsar remained solidly behind the Senate, whose constitution he saw as the only means of holding the Bourbons to liberal practices, but by the time Louis XVIII landed on French soil Talleyrand had come to think that compromise was necessary. On 2 May at Saint-Ouen Louis issued a declaration saying that the basis of the Senate's constitution was 'sound' but that it bore the marks of hasty composition and could not therefore be accepted as an instrument of government. He undertook to work with commissions chosen

11 *The Times*, 14 Apr. 1814.
12 Vitrolles, *Mémoires*, pp. 372–3.

from the Senate and the Legislative Body to produce a new constitution and to place it before a gathering of these two bodies on 10 June. Among the principles which the King guaranteed to embody in the Constitution was 'the maintenance of representative government as it exists today, divided into two bodies, namely the Senate and the Chamber composed of deputies of the departments'.[13]

Louis had thus firmly taken the initiative into his own hands. He had undertaken to work with commissions 'chosen from' the Senate and the Legislative Body but had not said who was to choose them. He had promised that the Constitution would be 'placed before' the two parliamentary bodies, but had not said that they would be able to discuss or amend it. No complaints seem to have been voiced at the time, however; perhaps because neither the Senators nor the Deputies realized to what extent they were going to be ignored. More anxiety was aroused by the vagueness of the phrase 'representative government as it exists today'. This gave no specific guarantee that existing Senators would be allowed to sit in the new Senate, that their titles and endowments would be hereditary, or that existing members of the Legislative Body would continue to serve as a lower chamber with salaries intact.

In the event the King nominated and summoned two commissions by private invitation: no formal decree was issued, no announcement was made in the *Moniteur*, and Talleyrand, whom the King perhaps erroneously regarded as an ardent supporter of senatorial pretensions, was deliberately kept in the dark.[14] The nine Senators (Barbé-Marbois, Barthélemy, Boissy d'Anglas, Fontanes, Garnier, Pastoret, Sémonville, Serrurier and Vimar) did not include Lambrechts, who had taken the lead in promoting the senatorial constitution, or Lanjuinais, Garat, Grégoire, Sieyès, Destutt de Tracy and other possible constitutionalists. Of the nine Deputies (Lainé, Blanquart de Bailleul, Chabaud Latour, Dubois-Savary, Duhamel, Gillevoisin, Faget de Baure, Félix Faulcon and Clausel de Coussergues) only Lainé could be regarded as liberal. The King also appointed three royal agents, Beugnot (to act as secretary), Ferrand and Montesquiou. The latter appeared at the first meeting armed with a draft, which all three proceeded to commend to the assembled company. Though differing greatly from the senatorial constitution in origin, it was not very different in its terms. Louis's title was assumed to be that enjoyed by former kings of France, and the Constitution became a grant from the king rather than a condition imposed upon him. Parliamentary government, of a kind envisaged by the Senate, was nevertheless promised to the nations.[15]

The upper house, it is true, emerged not as a revival of Napoleon's Senate transformed into a House of Lords but as a chamber of peers nominated by the king on an hereditary basis or for life, as he saw fit.

13 Text in Duguit and Monnier, *Les Constitutions*.
14 Beugnot, *Mémoires*, pp. 169–70.
15 For an account of the proceedings of the commissions, see Beugnot, pp. 171–264.

The lower house, too, was to be ultimately rather different from Napoleon's Legislative Body, for a tax qualification of 300 francs was to be imposed on electors and of 1,000 francs on Deputies. The latter proposal was criticized by Félix Faulcon on behalf of men who, like himself, had played an active part in parliamentary politics since the Revolution and would henceforward find themselves disqualified, but no one supported him. Indeed there was a feeling not only that a tax qualification was desirable but that the relevant taxes should be those paid on land. Chabaud Latour thought that other forms of real estate ought also to be relevant, and to accommodate his point the term 'direct taxes' was employed; but nobody, according to Beugnot, wanted business incomes to qualify men for political rights, and none of the members remembered that the patents tax was one of direct taxes.

The ceremonial reading of the Constitution to the assembled parliamentary bodies had been fixed for 10 June to allow the commissions time to complete their work. On 2 June, however, Beugnot was informed that the Allied leaders planned to depart on 5 June and that they would like to see the Constitution proclaimed before they left. The ceremony was therefore brought back to 4 June, and a few outstanding points were hastily dealt with. The name Charter was adopted for the constitutional act, as being suitably reminiscent of the liberties granted to municipalities by former kings. Fontanes, the composer of so many fine orations in the past, was asked to write an introduction, but when he produced his manuscript Beugnot decided that it contained too much rhetoric and too little substance, so he himself wrote the famous 'preamble' ascribing the restoration of the king to divine providence. Louis was asked to decide what date to give to the constitutional enactment: having no views on the matter himself he accepted the advice of friends and dated it in the nineteenth year of his reign.

Chancellor Dambray urged Montesquiou to clarify the position of existing Senators and Deputies before the ceremony of 4 June but he failed to do so. Perhaps he simply forgot. Grave anxiety was aroused among the Senators by the fact that the ordinance convening the ceremony mentioned only the Legislative Body and forgot the Senate. When private summonses were sent out, 57 Senators were omitted. A general purge was feared, and the Senators could do nothing to defend themselves because they had forfeited public sympathy by their demands earlier in the year.[16] In fact no further purge was carried out. The remaining 87 Senators became Peers, forming the numerical majority in a chamber of 155 members. Their endowments were confiscated by the state, but they retained an annual pension of 36,000 francs. Of the 57 who were excluded, 26 had ceased to be Frenchmen as a result of territorial changes, 6 were members of the Bonaparte family, and 9 were either regicides or (in the case of Grégoire and Garat) closely associated with them. The remaining 16 were mostly men like Chaptal,

16 *Arch. nat.*, AB XIX, 341; Anglès, *Rapports inédits*, pp. 28–9.

Curée, Roederer and Caulaincourt, who had played very prominent parts in the Napoleonic régime: only Lambrechts seems to have suffered on account of the senatorial constitution. All 16 were subsequently granted pensions, the king remembering that Napoleon had admitted them to the Senate as a form of retirement from public life.[17]

Members of the Legislative Body, other than those representing departments no longer belonging to France, were invited without further discrimination to the ceremony. Rumour might have told them that the final clauses of the Charter had arranged for them to remain in the Chamber of Deputies until they had finished their five years, but they had been told nothing about salaries. Police reported meetings at which disgruntled Deputies threatened that at the public reading of the Charter they would protest against the secretive manner in which it had been devised, and demand that it be sent before primary assemblies for their opinion. The king assured, however, that the vast majority of the Deputies were on his side and that confirmation of their salaries would cure all complaints. The long-awaited announcement was made immediately after the reading of the Charter on 4 June.

The ceremony followed the pattern laid down by Napoleon for the opening of parliament. For the third time in sixteen months a throne was erected in the Palais Bourbon, and the politicians seated in tiers on either side. As Louis XVIII entered, dragging his feet slowly along the carpet, Charles de Rémusat remembered how Napoleon, whom he had seen for the first time in Februrary 1813, had seemed to devour the distance between the door and the platform, and had scaled the steps to the throne with impatient strides. The King's voice, however, was loud and clear, if somewhat tuneless, and it made a better impression on the critical young hearer than the foreign accent and grating tones in which Napoleon had pronounced the words *Anglais* and *Péninsule* The subsequent speech by Dambray, referring to the Charter as a 'reforming edict', and the unfortunate terms of Beugnot's preamble, aroused such indignation in Mme de Stael that she accidentally struck Pozzo di Borgo, who was sitting in front of her in the visitors' gallery, a sharp blow between the shoulder blades with a large key she was carrying in her hand. The Charter itself, however, was favourably received.[18]

Beugnot insisted in his memoirs that constitutional developments had undergone a hiatus with the advent of Napoleon, and that the Charter of 1814 belonged to a tradition which had been lost to view. The proposed parliamentary monarchy in fact owed many of its features to the Napoleonic régime. The king, like Napoleon, demanded the sole initiative in legislation as one of the most important prerogatives of the crown. The only concession he would make to the Chambers was the right to appeal to him to introduce a bill, a device reminiscent of the 'wishes' expressed by the Tribunate. Amendments to bills, also, could only be

17 Brotonne, *Les Sénateurs*, pp. 56–7, 69–101.
18 Rémusat, *Mémoires* I, pp. 165–6.

secured by application to the king. Louis, like Napoleon, was to nominate the President of the Chamber of Deputies from a list of five
candidates. After toying with the idea of integral renewal of the
Chamber, the commissions which drew up the Charter eventually
decided to stick to the system of renewal by fifths annually, with the
departments arranged in series (Lainé commended this system to his
fellow members on the grounds that it would prolong the life of the
popular Legislative Body of 1813). The collegiate system was to
remain, with Louis, like Napoleon, appointing presidents: when
Napoleon, on the voyage to St Helena, read in a newspaper the list of
presidents appointed by the king for the elections of 1815 he remarked
that they were the very men he would have chosen himself.[19] During the
discussions by the commissions, Montesquiou had actually proposed
that the departmental colleges should elect only candidates, and that the
king should choose the deputies as the Senate had formerly done.
Boissy d'Anglas had opposed the suggestion, but no decision had been
reached in the matter: apart from the tax qualification the Charter left
all aspects of the electoral system to be arranged by future legislation.[20]

No elections were to take place until 1816, and meanwhile the
members of the Legislative Body were to compose the Chamber of
Deputies. During the parliamentary session which now began, the five
men who had criticized Napoleon in December 1813 were prominent.
Four of them, Lainé, Gallois, Raynouard and Flaugergues, appeared
among the five candidates nominated by the Chamber for the post of
President; the fifth, Maine de Biran, was elected quaestor. As President
the King chose Lainé, amid general approval. The session opened with
a skirmish reminiscent of the Tribunate at the opening of the Consular
régime: a bill drawn up by the Privy Council to regulate parliamentary
procedure was criticized in the Chamber of Deputies as detrimental to
the dignity of the Chamber and Dumolard challenged the government
to define the role of the legislative in the new régime.

> We are neither those Estates General from which the king received
> at his pleasure the humble complaints of his subjects, divided into
> orders which no longer exist; nor those revolutionary assemblies in
> which the magic of an ill-conceived equality led the speakers into
> every kind of paradox and the people into every kind of excess; nor,
> indeed, that Senate, hapless accomplice of the recent tyranny, and
> that Legislative Body, dumb and repressed, which was denied even
> the right to complain.

They deserved, he said, a new name; and suggested the name of 'parliament'.

19 Cockburn, *Diary*, p. 37.
20 The required law, passed in 1816, abolished the arrondissement colleges and
allowed the departmental colleges to elect deputies. A law of 1820, however, revived
the arrondissement colleges and allowed them, as well as the departmental colleges, to
elect deputies. This was not unlike the Napoleonic system, except that both had then
elected only candidates.

The first major debate of the session took place over a press bill designed to subject pamphlets to a preliminary censorship and news-papers to control by the police. Raynouard, spokesman for the commit-tee which reviewed the bill, delivered an adverse report condemning censorship as contrary to the liberty of the press promised in the Charter: he thus emerged as one of a group of left-wing speakers which included Gallois, Flaugergues, Dumolard, Souques, Bedoch, Louvet, and above all Durbach of the Isère. A right wing, expressing fear and dislike of liberty of the press, also appeared. This was not yet, however, the ultra-royalism of the second Restoration, though it was supported by men of innately royalist opinion such as Tuault and Prunelé: it was, rather, the attitude of Napoleonic officialdom, expressed by such men as Challan, who had sat in Napoleonic parliaments since 1800 and supported every stage of Napoleonic despotism. Lainé proved to be a moderating influence and persuaded the government to accept several amendments. The bill was nevertheless vigorously attacked in the Chamber of Peers by Boissy d'Anglas, Lanjuinais, and Dédelay d'Agier, to the extent that the Duke of Wellington feared it was going to founder. More amendments were conceded, and the bill went back to the Chamber of Deputies, where a dispute broke out concerning pro-cedure, revealing a certain amount of hostility towards the Peers on the part of left-wing Deputies. The bill eventually passed as a temporary measure.[21]

Financial affairs occupied a large part of the summer. In the Chamber of Peers a commission consisting of Jaucourt, Boissy d'Anglas, Fon-tanes, and Lanjuinais rebuked the government for attributing nothing but economic ruin to the Revolution and Empire: the abolition of feudalism, the creation of administrative unity, the codification of laws, and the encouragement of new products, they pointed out, had laid a foundation for future prosperity which the king could best build upon by showing a firm adherence to the Charter. Baron Louis, when presenting the budget, showed that he had a more advanced view of the constitu-tional powers of the Chambers than some of the Deputies, who spoke as though the ministers were entitled to spend what they liked from a total sum and the main function of the Chambers was to provide ways and means; but the baron also showed that he was willing to transfer to his royal master the independence Napoleon had acquired as a result of relying on indirect taxation. Not only were the taxes on drinks, tobacco and salt to be maintained, but the customs duties on British manu-factured goods and American raw materials were to be revived in spite of the ending of the wars. The only thorough-going free trade speech was made by Bérenger. The constitutional significance of indirect taxa-tion seems to have escaped the Deputies now as earlier, except on a relatively minor point: Flaugergues and Gallois, supported by a hitherto

21 *Arch. parl.*, 1, 5–11 Aug. 1814; Duvergier de Hauranne, *Histoire* II, p. 263.

silent member Lehic, protested against a clause allowing the king to alter the customs tariff provisionally between sessions of the Chambers.

A 'party of the *ancien régime*' raised its head during September, when the government proposed to restore to the original owners such areas of national land, mainly woodland, as remained unsold in the hands of the state. The terms of the bill were seen by one and all as sensible and conciliatory. The speech in which Ferrand introduced it to the Chamber of Deputies, however, was calculated to arouse all the latent hostility and suspicion between the old and new France by describing the émigrés as the only Frenchmen who had never deviated from the path of honour. An equally tactless speech in the opposite direction was made by Bedoch, as reporter on the bill. Battle lines were drawn, with Prunelé, Cardonnel and Chilhaud de la Rigauderie leading the right, and Durbach and Dumolard prominent on the left. Again Lainé acted as mediator, and the bill passed without prejudicing the possibility of indemnity to the émigrés in the future.

The session ended with a debate on the familiar subject of the Court of Cassation. Though the Court was no more popular than it had ever been, an attempt by the government to reorganize it was once more, as in 1800, seen as an attempt to bring the whole of the judicial power into subservience under the executive. Flaugergues, reporting on the bill, made the most impressive speech of his brief parliamentary career and succeeded in getting the measure rejected in the Chamber of Deputies by 91 votes to 83.[22]

When Duvergier de Hauranne began, some forty years later, to write what he had hoped would be a complete history of France's parliamentary government, he gave a modest but honourable place to the parliament of 1814. He thought that 'men of outstanding talent were lacking', and that 'there was something timid and uncertain in its attitude and general behaviour which prevented it from exerting the influence it might have had on the proceedings of the government.' Nevertheless, it was 'honest, moderate, full of good intentions. . . . On a number of political questions it proved that the Charter was not, in its opinion, a dead letter, and that it took more seriously than the government the new institutions of France. Liberal without being factious, royalist without being counter-revolutionary, the Chamber of 1814 genuinely wished to accomplish the union of the old monarchy and the new institutions.' He was prepared to make excuses for a body of men elected to sit in a silent legislature and vote on a few remaining Napoleonic measures. 'If one considers the sudden and complete transformation events forced it to undergo, one is bound to admit that the Imperial Legislative Body did better than could have been expected.'[23]

The members were destined as a body never to meet again. The

22 Flaugergues was one of the men forced out of parliamentary life by the tax qualification.
23 Duvergier de Hauranne, *Histoire* II, pp. 319–21.

session was closed on 31 December 1814, the intention being that the Chambers should reassemble on 1 May 1815. On 5 March, however, news arrived in Paris that Napoleon had escaped from Elba and was marching northward from Fréjus. On 6 March Louis XVIII hastily summoned the Chambers in the hope of stopping the defection which had set in as Napoleon advanced from garrison to garrison. A skeleton group actually met for a few days, but Napoleon entered the Tuileries on 20 March and dismissed the lot as traitors. Louis XVIII made other arrangements when he was restored for the second time in 1815.

Epilogue: The Hundred Days

During the first part of his triumphal march from the south coast to Paris in March 1815, Napoleon had appealed as a simple soldier and patriot to the garrisons of the town and the peasants of the villages he passed along the route. By the time he reached Lyon he had been persuaded, perhaps by the facile Fleury de Chaboulon, a former sub-prefect who had been instrumental in plans for his escape from Elba, that it was necessary to appeal also to the more politically minded elements in the nation, and that these were determined to be consulted on the subject of a constitution.[1] The idea presumably derived from the opposition which had manifested itself, somewhat belatedly, in June 1814, when disgust at the pretensions of the Senate had eventually given way to annoyance at Louis's high-handed method of 'granting' the Charter. From the same source may have come the idea that the proper bodies to consult were the electoral colleges. Durbach, in a pamphlet published shortly after the ceremony of 4 June, was one of several publicists who had advocated discussion by 'primary assemblies'.[2]

It was at Lyon, in the presence of the municipal authorities, that Napoleon adopted his new stance. 'I do not wish, like Louis XVIII, to bestow upon you a constitution which I could then take away,' he said. 'I wish to give you an inviolable constitution, which will be the joint work of the people and myself.'[3] Like the Bourbons, however, he could not bring himself to abandon his antecedents. The new constitution was somehow to be connected with those of the Consulate and Empire: moreover the people to be consulted were to be none other than the old favourites, the members of the departmental electoral colleges. A decree dated from Lyon on 13 March announced: 'The electoral colleges of the departments of the Empire will meet in Paris in the course of the month of May next, in a special Assembly of the Champ de Mai, in order to take the measures necessary to correct and modify our constitutions in accordance with the interests and wishes of the nation.'

1 Chaboulon, *Mémoires* I, pp. 141, 160–61.
2 Thiry, *La Première Restauration*, pp. 59–60.
3 Chaboulon, *Mémoires* I, p. 167.

Attendance at the Assembly was to be recompensed in the old Napoleonic style, with an invitation to be present at the coronation of the Empress Marie Louise and the King of Rome.

Some historians have seen the announcement at Lyon as an attempt by Napoleon to escape from reliance upon the common people, whom he both feared and despised, by appealing to the bourgeoisie with an offer of constitutional government.[4] During the Hundred Days it became clear that Napoleon had two possible courses of action open to him: to rouse the spirit of revolution with appeals to popular sovereignty, or to take over the liberal movement which had begun in the parliament of 1813 and reappeared in the Senate at the approach of the Bourbons. In the early days at Lyon it is doubtful whether he saw the alternatives clearly. His pronouncements were nothing if not ambiguous. The decree of 13 March began with an appeal to a host of revolutionary discontents. Louis XVIII's Chamber of Peers was declared dissolved because it had been 'composed in part of persons who have borne arms against France, and who have an interest in the re-establishment of feudal dues, in the destruction of equality between the different classes, in the annulment of sales of national land, and in depriving the people of rights acquired by twenty-five years of fighting against the enemies of the nation's glory'. The Chamber of Deputies was dissolved because 'a part of the Chamber rendered itself unworthy of the confidence of the nation by agreeing to the re-establishment of the feudal nobility abolished by the constitutions accepted by the people; by causing France to have to pay the debts contracted abroad for producing and supporting armies to fight against the French people; by giving the Bourbons the title of legitimate kings and thus declaring the French people and armies to be rebels and the émigrés the only true Frenchmen.' The reference to the Champ de Mai could have been calculated to revive memories of the Frankish monarchy which Napoleon had studied in his youth and which was supposed to have rested on spontaneous election by a warrior nation; or it could simply have been an attempt to embarrass the supporters of Louis XVIII, who had never tried to revive the Champ de Mai though his Charter was described in the preamble as similar to the grants of liberty made by kings to their people on such occasions. It was anybody's guess whether Napoleon had in mind a constitutional monarchy run by the propertied classes or a popular dictatorship like that of the Jacobins.

In Paris the King on 6 March hastily convoked the Chambers. During the next few days groups of Deputies met informally to discuss possible action. They apparently felt a need for wider support, for Lainé suggested co-opting distinguished members of the parliament of 1789 along with publicists noted for liberal opinions. At a royal session on 16 March, the Bourbon princes swore fidelity to the Charter in the presence of a sparse gathering of Peers and Deputies. Lainé described the

4 Notably Le Gallo, *Les Cent-Jours*, p. 79.

Bourbons as offering the best hope of constitutional government, and forecast despotism and war if Napoleon regained the capital. At a further meeting on 18 March, Augier proposed that the Chambers should counter Napoleon's libellous attack on them by threatening to banish anyone who questioned the sanctity of sales of national land. None of these histrionics halted the advance of Napoleon.[5] Plans were discussed for the withdrawal of the King, with or without the Chambers, to a safer centre in the provinces. Blacas thought that Louis should ride in an open carriage, flanked by Peers and Deputies on horseback, in a cavalcade to confront the Corsican and ask him to his face what he was about. The King eventually left the Tuileries during the night of 19 March with the Household Guards en route for Lille. Finding insufficient support there he retired into temporary exile at Ghent. Lainé returned to his native Bordeaux in the hope of rallying resistance under the Duchesse d'Angoulême. Napoleon entered the Tuileries at 9 p.m. on 20 March.[6]

One of Napoleon's first actions was to ask the Council of State to draw up a declaration which would convince the French people that he and not Louis XVIII was their rightful ruler, entitled to their loyalty and obedience. The Council of State replied with an address which either wittingly or unwittingly mingled Jacobin and liberal propositions. Sovereignty, it said, resided with the people; Napoleon must rule with a constitution which had been reviewed in a grand assembly of the nation. At the same time, Napoleon must become the defender of liberal principles, ruling with an elected assembly. Thibaudeau, who drew up the address, described it as an attempt to rally both the lower and the middle classes to the government. If Napoleon ever made a deliberate choice between Jacobinism and liberalism it was probably at this point, for he told the presidents of the various sections of the Council of State that their address gave too much importance to the principle of sovereignty of the people, and he boasted to Molé that he knew how to master the Jacobins. He rejected a suggestion from Carnot, his new Minister of the Interior, that he should make a direct appeal to the people with a view to maintaining a dictatorship until peace was assured. He had already set up a committee consisting of Defermon, Boulay de la Meurthe, Carnot, Cambacérès, and Regnault de St Jean d'Angély to draw up a constitution. On 14 April he fell in with a suggestion originally made by his brother Joseph that Benjamin Constant should be called in to draft a constitution acceptable to liberal opinion. Constant could not resist the temptation, and the work was completed within ten days.[7]

5 Constant, *Mémoires* I, pp. 55, 100; Lafayette, *Mémoires* V, pp. 372–3; *Moniteur*, 17, 19 Mar. 1815.
6 Vitrolles, *Mémoires* II, pp. 320–21; Bourrienne, *Mémoires* X, pp. 269–70; Le Gallo, *Les Cent-Jours*, pp. 150–59.
7 *Moniteur*, 27 Mar. 1815; Thibaudeau, *Mémoires*, pp. 463–4, 475; Miot, *Mémoires* III, pp. 379–80; Houssaye, *1815*, p. 539; Le Gallo, *Les Cent-Jours*, pp. 206–11.

It was at Napoleon's insistence that the new constitution was called an *Acte Additionnel aux Constitutions de l'Empire*. Benjamin Constant thought that any connection with the former Napoleonic régime would impair the popularity of the new venture, but the Emperor was adamant. The preamble to the *Acte* also owed a great deal to Napoleon, and may actually have been written by him. It ascribed the new liberal institutions to the need to rally the nation to defend the frontiers against foreign powers, and encouraged the inevitable suspicion that Napoleon would revert to despotism if he returned victorious from war.

In other respects there seems to have been a genuine exchange of ideas between Napoleon and Constant, with some contributions also from other members of the committee. This was particularly the case on the subject of franchise and representation. Benjamin Constant was a well-known admirer of the British political system, in which a curiously mixed set of franchises (in some constituencies open to the greater part of the male population and in others restricted to one or two large property owners) created an atmosphere of liberty while producing a House of Commons mainly composed of landowners. Unable to reproduce either the archaic franchises or the system of patronage which went with them, Constant believed it would be possible to produce the same kind of lower chamber by restricting the franchise to property owners. Among the latter he had the greatest respect for landowners, and wished these to compose the majority of deputies, but he also realized that competence in commercial and industrial affairs was an essential asset to a modern parliament, and he was prepared to incorporate a modest number of experts from these fields. Napoleon, however, insisted on keeping the old system whereby cantonal assemblies in the first instance elected arrondissement and departmental colleges. There was no property qualification in the cantonal assemblies and the arrondissement colleges, and this, he said, added a democratic element which counterbalanced the oligarchic nature of the departmental colleges. He agreed that in future the cantonal assemblies should fill gaps in the membership of the colleges every year and that the colleges should elect deputies instead of merely candidates. It is arguable that the 100,000 members of arrondissement and departmental colleges who were thereby given a direct vote in the elections of May 1815 formed a more numerous electorate than any that would have emerged from Benjamin Constant's qualified franchise, and undeniable that they were more varied.[8]

Meanwhile a certain amount of special representation was given to industry and commerce. Vague suggestions along these lines had come from various quarters during the preceding year: for instance Vitrolles when the Charter was being drawn up had suggested to Louis XVIII that the businessmen of France's largest towns should be allowed to

8 Le Gallo, *Les Cent-Jours*, pp. 205–21. The 300 franc tax qualification established by the Charter produced 90,000 voters in 1817.

elect members to parliament, and Lainé, at the puerile meeting of the Chamber of Deputies held on 11 March 1815, had told the members that the government had long been meditating upon a scheme to extend representation to commerce. It seems likely that Carnot, very anxious in his new capacity as Minister of the Interior to stimulate the economy, was won over to the idea, and that Napoleon favoured it as a recompense for the rapturous welcome he had received at Lyon.[9] It was a deviation from the principle of population as the sole criterion of representation which had been accepted by constitution-makers since 1793, though tempered by the fact that the choice of commercial and industrial representatives was to be made by the departmental colleges. France was divided into thirteen regions, each centred upon a large industrial or commercial complex. The Paris region was to furnish four representatives; Lille, Rouen, Nantes, Marseilles, Nîmes, Lyon and Bordeaux were to produce two each, and Toulouse, Troyes, Strasbourg, Orleans and Tours one each. The chambers of commerce in each region were to send in long lists of candidates, amounting in all to 840 candidates for 23 seats. As in all Napoleonic legislation there was a good deal of ambiguity and muddle. The chambers of commerce were told that their candidates must be 'businessmen who were the most distinguished in character and talent, who paid the most taxes, whose operations were the most extensive in France or abroad, or who employed the most workpeople', but they were not told how to operate these criteria; Article 33 of the *Acte* said that the departmental colleges were to make the choice of deputies from the lists but did not make it clear whether all the departmental colleges in a region were to co-operate in the task or whether it was to be left to the college of the department in which the relevant town was situated. Nevertheless, twenty-three representatives were elected in time to take their place in the Chamber.

Benjamin Constant's particular ideas were most apparent in the creation of a chamber of hereditary peers which he hoped would turn out to be like the British House of Lords. Napoleon, in spite of his penchant for the nobility, was shrewd enough to forsee the difficulties which the scheme involved. 'The peerage is out of tune with the present state of feeling,' he told Constant.

> It hurts the pride of the army, it goes against the wishes of the partisans of equality, and it will arouse a thousand pretensions against me. Where do you expect me to find the aristocratic elements that a peerage demands? The older wealthy families are my enemies; several of the new are discreditable. Five or six illustrious names are not enough. Without traditions, without historical renown, without extensive property, on what will my peerage be

9 Warlomont, 'La Representation économique dans L'Acte Additionnel'. Mention was also made, by both Vitrolles and Lainé, of possible representation for scholarly institutions, on the lines of the British university representation, but this idea was not taken up.

founded? That of England is another matter; it is above the people but has never been against them. It was the nobles who gave them Magna Carta. They have grown with the constitution; but for the next thirty years from now my mushroom peers will be nothing but soldiers or chamberlains; they will be looked upon as no more than a camp or anti-chamber.

Since he was not prepared to abolish aristocratic titles altogether, however, there was something to be said for the argument put forward by Benjamin Constant that an aristocracy without political occupation was useless, dangerous, and a source of resentment, whereas if it supplied representatives to a Chamber of Peers it would support the monarchy, counterbalance the lower house, and defend the Constitution. In discarding the life peerages which had been an alternative to hereditary peerages in Louis XVIII's upper chamber, Constant claimed afterwards that he was trying to make the new Chamber of Peers more independent of Napoleon.[10]

The lower house envisaged by the *Acte Additionnel* was no longer, like the old Legislative Body, to invite the suggestion that its members were mere deputies of the departments. It was given a new name, the Chamber of Representatives, and its members were described at several points in the document as representing the nation. Though elected by local colleges they were not required to have lived in the locality which elected them but could be chosen 'from the whole of France' (Article 32). There were to be 629 members; they were not required to fulfil a property qualification and they need only be twenty-five years old, whereas the Charter had stipulated a minimum age of forty for deputies. The Chamber was to elect its own President, subject only to the approval of the Emperor, and membership was to be renewed *in toto* once every five years. In these and in many other respects Napoleon seems to have been anxious to go one better than the Bourbons. 'Public discussions, free elections, responsible ministers, liberty of the press, I want all that,' he told Benjamin Constant. 'Liberty of the press especially: it is absurd to silence it.' 'What a man!' was all that the former Tribune could find to comment.[11]

Censorship had been abolished by decree on 24 March, and liberty of the press was now confirmed by Article 64 of the *Acte*. Other personal liberties were at least as wide as those guaranteed by the Charter. The legislative rights given to the Chambers were similar in that bills must be passed by both Chambers before they could be ratified by the Emperor, and debate in both was unfettered and open to the public; neither Chamber could initiate legislation, but there was a slight advance on the Charter in that bills were described as initiated by the government instead of by the monarch, and the Chambers as having the right to 'invite the government' rather than 'appeal to the monarch' to introduce

10　Constant, *Mémoires* II, pp. 56–63; Le Gallo, *Les Cent-Jours*, pp. 218–22.
11　Constant, *Mémoires* II, pp. 19, 22–6.

a bill. The right to suggest (though still not to make) amendments were more clearly defined. The financial powers of the Chambers were again basically the same as those allowed by the Charter (direct taxes voted for one year, indirect taxes for several years), but the barriers to governmental power were spelt out in greater detail in Article 35 of the *Acte*: 'No direct or indirect tax may be levied in money or in kind, no loan may be raised, no increase may be made in the public debt, no land may be alienated or exchanged, no levies of men for the armies may be ordered, no piece of territory may be exchanged by virtue of a law.' The responsibility of ministers, as in the Charter, was taken to mean chiefly the right of the lower chamber to impeach ministers before the Peers, but the *Acte* sought to improve relationships between government and parliament by introducing a few ministers and councillors of state permanently into the two Chambers, allowing them to take part in debate and to answer questions but not to vote.[12]

Napoleon's sincerity has always been open to question. Some people at the time thought that his constitutionalism was a show designed to deter the Allies from renewing war against France. When the *Acte* had been drafted, however, he did not put it into cold storage, although war was by this time clearly inevitable. How to put it into effect was his immediate concern. His previous constitutional acts had been placed before the nation in the form of a plebiscite, and he decided that the same thing should be done again, though Benjamin Constant deplored the 'caesarism' which such a process implied. By a decree of 22 April, registers were opened in all prefectoral and municipal offices, all law courts, and all offices of solicitors and justices of the peace to receive the votes of citizens over the age of twenty-one and in enjoyment of civil rights. From the publication of the decree, twenty-five days were allowed for the final figures to reach the Minister of the Interior. On analogy with former plebiscites, a favourable result would allow the Emperor to promulgate the constitution as law. What, then, was to be the function of the Assembly of the Champ de Mai, to which departmental electors were expecting to be summoned as a constituent body? This problem was dealt with in another decree of 22 April. Members of all colleges, both of arrondissements and departments, were invited to the Champ de Mai, where their function was to be that of ratifying the results of the plebiscite. Five members from each department were to form a central committee under the chairmanship of Cambacérès to add up the votes, and the result was to be announced to the general assembly in a grand ceremony at which the Emperor would receive deputations and distribute flags for the National Guard. The ceremony was fixed for the earliest possible date, the 26th May. Even so, there would be no time to hold elections after the ceremony if Napoleon was to carry out his intention of opening the Chamber of Representatives before leaving

12 Text in Duguit and Monnier, *Les Constitutions*, pp. 369–76.

Paris to attack the Allied armies in Belgium. He decided to anticipate the results of the plebiscite as he had done in 1800. On 30 April he announced that the Chambers would meet immediately after the acceptance of the *Acte Additionnel* at the Champ de Mai; the electoral colleges were therefore convoked for 4 May to elect their Representatives, who were invited to accompany them to the Assembly of the Champ de Mai.[13]

These various pronouncements, coming hard on each other's heels, caused a certain amount of misunderstanding. An elector of the department of the Vosges wrote to the Minister of the Interior complaining that on reading the decree of 22 April he had hurried to Paris to be in readiness for the Champ de Mai, only to read when he got there the decree of 30 April telling him that he was needed at the chief town of his department to take part in elections. He could not get back home in time for the meeting of his college, yet everybody told him, he said, that there was no point in staying in Paris, since the Champ de Mai had become a useless exercise and would probably not take place. Prefects were besieged with enquiries, not least from electors who wondered whether there was still to be a coronation of the Empress Marie Louise and whether they should buy ceremonial dress for the occasion. Some prefects appear to have thought that the decree of 30 April cancelled the decree of 22 April, and that only Representatives were entitled to attend the Champ de Mai.[14]

It seems fairly certain that Napoleon had never considered the sheer practical difficulties involved in taking a plebiscite, holding elections, and summoning electors to an Assembly of the Champ de Mai in the extraordinary circumstances of the Hundred Days. The administrative personnel, on whom all three operations largely depended, changed with startling rapidity. Only 8 departments kept the same prefect throughout the period; 30 had three or more incumbents, and some as many as five or six. Some departments were without a prefect for weeks on end. Government commissioners were sent into the provinces to examine the conduct of sub-prefects, mayors, and subordinate officers and if necessary dismiss them; in consequence about 60 of the sub-prefects and 40 of the secretaries-general were replaced. In the middle of the crucial period Napoleon allowed the smaller communes to choose new mayors by election. Bureaucratic processes were seldom modified on account of the emergency. The prefects, for instance, were still expected to provide lists of electors of all the colleges. Names of those who wished to attend the Assembly of the Champ de Mai had to be sent beforehand to the Minister of the Interior. The vast amount of documentation needed for the opening of a college was sometimes not ready when the electors assembled, and the president had to hold the

13 *Moniteur*, 23 Apr. 1815; Napoleon, *Correspondance*, no. 21854.
14 *Arch. nat.*, F^{IC}III Nord (4), Vosges (5), Calvados (4).

members together as best he could until the prefect or sub-prefect arrived with the papers.[15]

Political discontents were advertised at large in the press, particularly in an avalanche of brochures. Royalists denied the right of Napoleon to rule under any conditions and urged their supporters to abstain from participation in any of the voting. Jacobins, republicans and democrats were disillusioned by the scant respect shown to the constituent powers of the nation and hostile to the creation of a Chamber of Peers: out of 402 surviving regicides, 80 voted in favour of the *Acte Additionnel* and 321 abstained. There were some Bonapartists who thought that Napoleon had given away too much of his power to an elected assembly. Even liberals were not wholly enthusiastic. Broglie claimed in his memoirs that he took the *Acte* seriously but that many people paid insufficient attention to its wise and liberal measures. Guizot, too, thought afterwards that the *Acte* was given less credit than it deserved.[16]

The plebiscite attracted a much smaller poll than had been the case in previous exercises: out of an estimated electorate of seven and a half million, slightly more than one and a half million had signed the registers.[17] The voting at elections was also sparse. Out of a total of 79,000 electors inscribed on the register of arrondissement colleges, barely 33,000 voted, and out of 20,000 members of departmental colleges, about 7,700 appeared. The smallest polls were in the departmental colleges of the south, where wealthy royalists boycotted the elections: at Marseilles 13 electors out of a total of at least 200 voted, at Montpellier 35 out of 233, at Bordeaux 38 out of 284. Even the more famous candidates did not inspire large numbers of electors to come to the polls: Flaugergues was elected by 45 votes out of 48 in an arrondissement college in Aveyron, and Raynouard by 26 votes out of 36 at Brignolles. [18]

The positive aspects of the achievement should not be underestimated, however. Signs of enthusiasm were not lacking, especially in colleges near the eastern frontier, where participation in the new political system was seen as a gesture of defiance in the face of the enemy. 'Inhabitants of the Department of the Nord! You are situated on the extreme frontier. Whatever may be your political opinions, when the enemy threatens your homeland and your fortifications, your patriotism will raise up insurmountable barriers. The electoral college of the department will meet at 11 a.m. on 10 May in the concert hall.' So ran a poster devised by the prefect at Lille, where the poll reached about 50 per cent. The prefect of the Haut-Rhin received disconsolate letters

15 Bluche, *Le Plébiscite*, p. 10–11; Richardson, *The French Prefectoral Corps*, pp. 56–7, 104–5.
16 Le Gallo, *Les Cent-Jours*, pp. 226–45; Radiguet, 'Les Votes des Conventionnels'; Broglie, *Souvenirs* I, pp. 303–4.
17 1,552,942 yes, 5,740 no (Bluche, *Le Plébiscite*, pp. 36–7).
18 Le Gallo, *Les Cent-Jours*, pp. 428–31.

from former members of the departmental college living in areas which had been given over to Prussia, begging him to allow them to take part in the elections; residents in Belgium wrote similarly to the Minister of the Interior appealing to be admitted to the colleges of the Nord. An element of liveliness was added to the business of the colleges at the last minute by a decree allowing them to elect their own presidents, a move which Lafayette believed helped to make the parliament of the Hundred Days more genuinely representative of public opinion than the Chambers of the Restoration. There was no shortage of candidates: nine competed for one seat at Avesnes. In some colleges illustrious candidates competed against each other: Lafayette and Lebrun defeated Fouché in the departmental college at Melun. Broglie tried in vain to get himself elected, both at Bernay and Evreux. Thibaudeau was done down, or so he believed, by more ambitious men than himself in the departmental college of the Vienne: he nevertheless agreed to carry the banner of the college at the Champ de Mai and to give a dinner for the electors afterwards. Looking back over the electoral period as a whole, Thibaudeau could not ignore the smallness of the vote, but he nevertheless decided that: 'For such a critical situation the national movement was sufficiently imposing. The electors were eager to attend the ceremony of the Champ de Mai and to fulfil their mission with zeal and devotion, in spite of everything that was done to damp their enthusiasm.'[19]

The total number of electors present at the Champ de Mai has never been accurately computed. Some of the prefects sent in impressive lists: 53 were travelling from the Nord, according to the prefect: 22 from the Vosges, including the Comte d'Alsace and the Comte de Choiseul de Stainville. Napoleon wrote to the princes, ministers and grand officers of the crown requesting them to keep open house for the visitors each evening from when they started to arrive in Paris. Twenty thousand places were provided for them in the amphitheatre. Thibaudeau put the number of *bona fide* electors attending at about 10,000. Spare tickets sold at quite a price on the black market, and in the end, to judge by eye-witness accounts, all Paris was there.

The ceremony was put off from 26 May to 1 June, a move which critics did not hesitate to attribute to Napoleon's reluctance to proceed with constitutional practices. More than 400 electors met in committee at the Palace of the Legislative Body the day before to count the votes. After a short speech by Cambacérès the figures for each department were read out, and a number of secretaries added them up. While this process was going on, the idea arose of framing an address to deliver to the Emperor. Carrion Nisas vigorously commended a draft put forward by the electors of Herault; this was adopted unanimously and a deputy from Marne-et-Loire, Duboys, was chosen on account of his stentorian

19 *Arch. nat.*, F^{IC}III, Nord (4), Haut Rhin (3); Lafayette, *Mémoires* v, pp. 429–32; Broglie, *Souvenirs* I, pp. 304–5; Thibaudeau, *Mémoires*, pp. 490–93.

voice to read it out next day. The ceremony itself, like all big outdoor events, was tiring and in large measure tedious for those taking part. Hours were spent in waiting about; without amplification there was difficulty in hearing what was going on. The Emperor arrived in his coronation coach, wearing white satin robes embroidered with gold: some eye-witnesses thought that these trappings were inappropriate in view of France's serious situation, others found the spectacle impressive. Napoleon's increasing flabbiness and look of ill-health were commented upon by many people in the crowd. After the results of the plebiscite had been read out, the Emperor swore loyalty to the Constitution, and speeches were made, Duboys bellowing like a mad bull and Napoleon replying with calm and dignity. This was followed by the most important part of the ceremony as far as the electors were concerned, when the delegation from each department approached the steps of the throne and received from the Emperor's hands a flag to be taken home for the National Guard. Thibaudeau was astounded at the 'candid egoism' of many of the electors, who seized the opportunity to ask for personal rewards from the Emperor, in the way that deputations from the colleges had so often done in the past, as though these were still the palmy days of the Empire.[20]

The Chamber of Representatives began its meetings on 3 June, though the membership of the Chamber of Peers had not yet been announced and the official opening of parliament by Napoleon was not scheduled to take place until the 7th. Thibaudeau described the prevailing attitude among the members as 'anti-Bourbon, defiant towards the Emperor, hostile to the court, bourgeois, slightly democratic, eminently national . . . favourable to Bonaparte the military and revolutionary leader [but] embarrassing to Napoleon the Emperor'. This was Thibaudeau's own attitude, and he probably regretted all the more his failure to get elected. The Chamber of Peers to which he found himself nominated by the Emperor was an uncongenial gathering which Napoleon had arrived at by writing round to various ministers, relatives and friends asking for suggestions. All former Senators who had entered Louis XVIII's Chamber of Peers were included, although twenty-seven of them had voted for the deposition of Napoleon in 1814; Grégoire and Lambrechts were still excluded. The four Bonaparte brothers headed the list, followed by the majority of the marshals, a large number of generals, all the ministers, five archbishops, a few members of the former Council of State such as Molé and Roederer (though the former took care not to attend the meetings), a few members of the former nobility, and the leaders of the conspiracy which had brought Napoleon back to France: 119 members in all. Apart from the general embarrass-

20 Barère, *Mémoires* III, p. 217; Champollion-Figéac, *Mémoires*, pp. 276–8 (the author was one of the secretaries at the committee meeting); Cesena, *Notice sur Duboys*, pp. 43, 62–5; Broglie, *Souvenirs* I, pp. 307–8; Villemain, *Souvenirs* II, pp. 188–9; La Siboutie, *Souvenirs d'un médecin de Paris*, pp. 158–9.

ment it aroused, the chief public criticism was that it contained too many military men.[21]

In the Chamber of Representatives, about 70 per cent of the members were new to parliament. Some were men who had fought in the wars for twelve years and perhaps supported Napoleon now out of esprit de corps or because they saw in him the revolutionary soldier who would once again assert France's right to the natural frontiers. Others were among the twenty-three representatives of industry and commerce (who seem, incidentally, to have been uniformly silent in debate; one of them applied at once for leave of absence for personal reasons but was told that absence would be unpatriotic). A great many were sub-prefects and minor officials who probably got their first and only chance, now that arrondissement colleges, with no property qualification, could elect Representatives directly: 17 per cent were men who had been presented as candidates on one or more occasions and passed over by the Senate.[22] Others, however, were men who had had successful careers under the Empire and arrived at the position of *procureur-impérial* or *conseiller à cour*: these men had much to lose if the Napoleonic venture failed, though as it turned out not all were deprived of their posts at the second Restoration. Some of the newcomers were young men who would not be able to enter parliament again for many years because of the advanced age required by the Charter: many of these reappeared as liberals in the later parliaments of Charles X's reign, a few of them (Manuel, Benjamin Delessert, Laffitte, Bérenger fils) playing a prominent role in liberal politics. A surprising number of the Representatives, however, never sat in parliament again, perhaps because of the property qualification imposed by the Bourbons.

Another group, about 10 per cent, were men who had sat in the parliaments of the Revolution and Directory but had left the political scene after Brumaire. A few (Barbeau Dubarran, Calès, Cambon, Drouet, Beaugard, Bonnesoeur, Garnier, Barère) were regicides, whose election was believed to be due to the influence of Fouché and his police in the electoral colleges.[23] It should not be assumed that they had all been hostile to the Napoleonic régime. The majority had occupied legal or administrative posts of varying importance. Only a few, like Bigonnet who had tried to expel Napoleon from the council chamber of the Five Hundred at the time of the *coup d'état* had actually retired into private life: these now formed a group of *réintégrés*, of whom the most notable was Lafayette. Napoleon viewed them with a mixture of satisfaction and apprehension. He offered Lafayette a peerage, but was probably not surprised when he refused it.[24]

21 Thibaudeau, *Mémoires*, p. 496; Napoleon, *Correspondance*, no. 21924; list in *Moniteur*, 6 June 1815.
22 This figure is from Beck, *French Legislators*, p. 41.
23 Boulay, *Boulay*, p. 272; Villemain, *Souvenirs* ii, p. 224.
24 Lafayette, *Mémoires* v, p. 435.

The Chamber began its career by electing Lanjuinais as President instead of the candidate thought to be favoured by the Emperor, Merlin de Douai. It had long been an open secret that Lanjuinais as a member of the Senate had opposed Napoleon's divorce of Josephine and had supported Lainé's commission in its liberal stance at the end of 1813. Napoleon summoned Lanjuinais to a private interview, in an attempt either to win a promise of loyalty from him or at least to give the impression that he had done so; but he could hardly do other than consent to the nomination. He afterwards wished that Carnot had become President, and thought he might have done so if he had not been made Minister of the Interior.[25]

The election of Lanjuinais was one of the more worthwhile gestures made by the Chamber in its defiance of Napoleon. Others were brash, and showed the members in no better light than their opponent. A good deal of time was wasted on the subject of an oath of loyalty to the Emperor, not because members disliked the oath itself, but because Napoleon assumed that it would form part of the opening ceremony as it had done in the past, whereas the members said that a law was required before an oath could be exacted. None of Napoleon's tactless moves were allowed to go by without protest. Some of this belligerence may have been a result of playing to the gallery, for crowds turned up daily to listen to the debates. Broglie said that he scarcely left the Chamber. A revival of Jacobin oratory gave a spice to the proceedings, as when Barère spoke upon the advantages and disadvantages of an hereditary peerage, and Garnier proposed sending Representatives on mission to the armies.[26]

Amid these superficial excitements it was easy to lose sight of the really important point established by the Chamber of Representatives – its right to act as a constituent assembly. When Napoleon presented the *Acte Additionnel* to the nation he undoubtedly intended it to be a definitive document. In the course of the following weeks, however, he was persuaded by some of his advisers, notably Carnot and Thibaudeau, that the *Acte* was unpopular. Unwilling to admit that a greater degree of liberty was required, he seized upon a somewhat minor criticism – that people could not easily understand which of the provisions of previous constitutional enactments remained in force. When addressing the electors at the Champ de Mai he promised the French people that when he had repulsed foreign armies 'a solemn law, made in the forms prescribed by the constitutional act, will collect together the different dispositions of our constitutions which are now scattered.' This gave no real grounds for supposing that the Chamber of Representatives would be allowed to take part in the process, which was in any case envisaged as collation rather than revision, but a large number of members interpreted the

25 Lafayette, *Mémoires* v, p. 441; Bertrand, *Cahiers, 1816–17*, p. 246; Duvergier de Hauranne, *Histoire* ii, pp. 5–6.
26 Broglie, *Souvenirs* i, p. 309.

words to mean that the *Acte* was purely provisional and that its only valid purpose was to produce an elected assembly which would draft a new constitution. When Napoleon appeared at the opening ceremony on 7 June supported by the Council of State and the Chamber of Peers there were murmurs from some of the Representatives, who refused to regard these bodies as validated. Napoleon in his opening speech repeated the promise made at the Champ de Mai. The Chamber of Representatives in its reply thanked the Emperor for recognizing that 'the task of collecting our scattered constitutions and co-ordinating them was one of the most important occupations reserved for the legislature' (he had recognized no such thing), and promised that the Chamber would faithfully fulfil its mission. It demanded, further, that its deliberations on the subject should take place in public, in order to fulfil the hitherto blighted hopes of the nation to be consulted. Napoleon countered with a sarcastic reference to the example of the late Empire, which made itself the laughing stock of posterity by debating abstract problems while the barbarians battered at the gates: public discussion, he said, would merely undermine confidence in the Constitution, which ought to be France's 'rallying point and polar star' in the coming crisis. The Chamber nevertheless decided to hold a public discussion on how to proceed. This took place on 20 June, when most Frenchmen believed that Napoleon, who had left Paris on 11 June to join his armies, had followed up his early successes in Belgium and secured control of Brussels. The debate reflected the need to achieve as much liberty as possible before Napoleon returned to France amid public rejoicing. Jay referred to the promises made at Lyon; Duchesne described 'wholesale revision' of the *Acte Additionnel* as the unanimous wish of the French people. It was decided that the Representatives from each department should choose one of their members to form a commission which could report to the Chamber on the changes required.[27]

The shattering news of Napoleon's return defeated from the field of Waterloo prevented the commission from meeting. On one subject only is it possible to suggest the lines on which subsequent discussion might have developed. The Chamber had already protested against the arrangement whereby ministers of state without portfolio were sent by the government to sit in parliament. Manuel and Jay had spoken in favour of the British system whereby responsible ministers sat in the House, and the Chamber had decided to set up a special commission to examine the problem. It is possible that steps might have been taken towards a more genuine responsibility of ministers to Parliament if more time had been available.

27 Napoleon, *Correspondance*, nos. 21997, 22023, 22039; Thibaudeau, *Mémoires* ii, pp. 36–7; Lafayette, *Mémoires* v, pp. 445–7; Chaboulon *Mémoires* ii, pp. 36–7. There seems to have been some doubt among contemporaries as to which historical episode Napoleon was referring to as 'l' exemple du Bas-Empire'. Jay said he was talking about Greece; Broglie said he was referring to 'the monks of Constantinople' (*Souvenirs* i, p. 311). The point was taken, however.

The parliament of the Hundred Days ended its brief life in a drama which few of its members were ever likely to forget. In the early hours of 21 June, Napoleon arrived back in Paris without an army but full of hysterical plans for raising more troops. The deputies were fairly sure that he would seize dictatorial power in a determination to fling every ounce of strength into a battle for personal survival. In the paralysis of mind which seized most of them they were grateful for the initiative of Lafayette, who entered the Chamber of Representatives at 10 a.m. in a mood of exhilaration and got the members to agree unanimously that the Chamber should remain in permanent session, that any attempt to dissolve it should be counted as treason, and that the ministers should be summoned to concert measures for the safety of the country. As an afterthought the resolutions were communicated to the Chamber of Peers. The latter had hitherto tried hard to escape public censure by tagging along behind the lower house, and it now associated itself with the resolutions to save itself from extinction. They were, as Thibaudeau pointed out, strictly unconstitutional, but who could care about constitutions when the country was in danger?[28]

Napoleon had not, in fact, seriously considered carrying out a *coup d'état*, though the idea had crossed his mind. He had fondly imagined that the Chambers would vote him more men and more materials and then give him dictatorial powers to continue the war, instead of which they were determined to sacrifice Napoleon in the hope that the Allies would allow France to keep a government of her own choice. They were afterwards criticized by Napoleon for their lack of patriotism, but they could not believe that even a levée en masse would long delay the British and the Prussians, who would simply wait for the Austrians and the Russians to come up and then attack in greater strength. A report by Davout, Minister for War, to the effect that the defeat at Waterloo had been exaggerated and that France still had an army of 60,000 men capable of resisting the enemy was denied by Ney in an impassioned speech in the Chamber of Peers: 'It is false! You are being deceived all along the line. The enemy is victorious at every point. All is lost!' In the Chamber of Representatives Duchesne – the same Duchesne who had been obliged to resign from the Tribunate in 1802 – took the lead in demanding the abdication of Napoleon.[29]

During the next few days the ground shifted rapidly as the members of both Chambers tried to secure their own constitutional position, either by proclaiming Napoleon II as Emperor or offering the throne on terms to the Bourbons. Attempts were made to galvanize the constitutional commission into producing its revisions at once. Meanwhile Prussian and British troops were advancing on the capital. To save Paris from the vengeance of the Prussians, Wellington would accept the

28 Duvergier de Hauranne, *Histoire* ii, pp. 35–48.
29 Napoleon, *New Letters*, pp. 347–8; Broglie, *Souvenirs* i, p. 312; Duvergier de Hauranne, *Histoire* ii, pp. 67–8.

surrender of the garrison only when Louis XVIII had been proclaimed king. On 8 July Louis re-entered the capital. Decazes, restored to the position of prefect of police, locked the doors of the Palais Bourbon and left the deputies peering in through the bars of the grille. The Charter was restored without revision, and neither the Chamber of 1814 nor the Chamber of the Hundred Days was called upon to serve again.[30]

30 Broglie, *Souvenirs* i, p. 310; Duvergier de Hauranne, *Histoire* ii, pp. 66–83.

Bibliography

Archives nationales

Police reports:
AF^{IV}1329, 1490–98, 1504
F^{7}3701–5, 3746, 3829–35

Electoral lists, proceedings of electoral colleges, etc:
F^{IC}II, 33–46
F^{IC}III
AF^{IV}1420–42
CC 28–49

Proceedings of parliamentary assemblies:
C 160–62 (Tribunate)
CC 173–80 (Legislative Body)

Proceedings of the Senate:
CC 972, 976

Beugnot papers:
AB XIX 340, 341, 351, 353

2 Published documents

ANGLÈS, J. J. B. (Comte): *Royauté ou Empire: la France en 1814 d'après les rapports inédits du Comte Anglès.* Edited by G. Firmin-Didot, Paris, 1879.

Archives parlementaires: recueil complet des débats législatif et politiques des Chambres Françaises de 1800 à 1860. Paris, 1862–7 (referred to as *Arch. parl.* in footnotes, followed by the date of the session). Vols I–XIII cover the period 1800 to 1815.

AULARD, F. V. A.: *Paris sous le Consulat: recueil de documents pour l'histoire de l'esprit public à Paris.* Paris, 1903–9, 4 vols.
Paris sous le Premier Empire: recueil de documents pour l'histoire de l'esprit public à Paris. Paris, 1912–23, 3 vols.

Bulletin des Lois, 1799–1815.

DUGUIT, A. and MONNIER, H.: *Les Constitutions et les principes lois politiques de la France depuis 1789*. 6th edn, Paris, 1943.

HAUTERIVE, E. d': *La Police secrète du Premier Empire: bulletins quotidiens adressés par Fouché à l'Empereur, 1804–7*. Paris, 1908–13, 3 vols.
  La Police secrète du Premier Empire: . . . nouvelle série, 1808–10. Paris, 1963–4, 2 vols.

LAINÉ, J. H.: *Rapport de la Commission extraordinaire fait au Corps législatif le 28 decembre 1813*. Paris, 1814.

LOCRÉ DE ROISSY, J.-G.: *Napoléon au Conseil d'État: notes et procès-verbaux inédits de Jean-Guillaume Locré*. Paris, 1963.

Newspapers
The following sets were consulted:
Clef du Cabinet des Souverains
Décade Philosophique, littéraire et politique
Journal de Paris
Journal des Défenseurs de la Patrie
Journal des Hommes Libres de tous les pays
Journal du Soir, de politique et de littérature des frères Chaignieau
Moniteur
Rédacteur
Other newspapers referred to in footnotes were consulted in isolated numbers.

4 Contemporary pamphlets
ANON.: *Collection des quatre philippiques*. Paris, 1814.
  De la fin de la Révolution française et de la stabilité possible du gouvernement actuel. Leipzig, 1800.
  De la monarchie française et de sa constitution, par un juris-consulte. Paris, 1814.
  Idées d'une française sur la constitution faite ou à faire. Paris, 1814.
  Le cri de l'honneur français, ou coup d'oeil rapide sur la constitution des nouveaux tyrans. Paris, 1800.
  Un mot sur la constitution, par un vicaire de Paris. Paris, 1814.

BRUGIÈRE, J. T.: *Constitution de l'an VIII*. Paris, 1800.

CAILLON, E. M. E.: *Deux mots sur la nouvelle constitution*. Paris, 1800.

DESPRADES, G.: *De la constitution qui convient au peuple français*. Paris, 1814.

GAUDIN, J.: *Réflexions politiques sur la constitution de l'an VIII*. Paris, 1800.

GILBERT, C.: *Du Pacte Social*. Paris, 1800.

JARRY-MANCY: *Qu'avons-nous besoin d'assemblées primaires?* Paris, 1799.

JORDAN, C.: *Vrai sens du vote national sur le Consulat à vie*. Paris, 1802.

JULLIEN, M. A.: *Entretien politique sur la situation actuelle de la France et sur les plans du nouveau gouvernement*. Paris, 1799.

MONIER: *Considerations sur les bases fondamentales du nouveau projet de constitution, par M. Monier, juge-suppléant au Tribunal civil de Lyon*. Lyon, 1814.

MONTYON, A. J. B. R. Aguet de: *Examen de la constitution de France de 1799*. London, 1800.

5 Letters and journals

Une année d'une correspondance de Paris, ou Lettres sur Buonaparte, sa famille, ses agens, et sur le gouvernement consulaire, extraites du Courier de Londres. London, 1803.

BERTRAND, H. G. (Général): *Cahiers de Sainte-Hélène: Journal, 1816–17*. Edited by P. Fleuriot de Langle, Paris, 1951.
Cahiers de Sainte-Hélène: Journal, janvier 1821-mai 1821. Edited by P. Fleuriot de Langle, Paris, 1949.

BURNEY, F.: *The Journals and Letters of Fanny Burney, Madame d'Arblay*. Edited by J. Hemlow, Oxford, 1975, 6 vols (vols v and vi only).

CAMBACÉRÈS, J. -J. (Prince, Duc de Parme): *Cambacérès: Lettres inédites à Napoléon, 1802–14*. Edited by J. Tulard, Paris, 1973, 2 vols.

CAZENOVE, A. de: *Journal de Mme de Cazenove d'Arlens*. Paris, 1903.

COCKBURN, G.: *Extract from a diary of Rear-Admiral Sir George Cockburn, with particular reference to General Napoleon Bonaparte, on passage from England to St Helena in 1815, on board HMS Northumberland*. London, 1888.

DUCHÂTEL, C. N. (Comte): *Correspondance inédite du Comte Duchâtel, 1751–1844*. Paris, 1918.

FIÉVÉE, J.: *Correspondance et relations avec Bonaparte*. Paris, 1836, 3 vols.

GREATHEED, B.: *An Englishman in Paris: the Journal of Bertie Greatheed*. Edited by J. P. T. Bury and J. C. Barry, London, 1953.

KERRY, Earl of: *The First Napoleon; some unpublished documents from the Bowood Papers*. London, 1925.

MAINE DE BIRAN: *Journal intime de Maine de Biran, 1792–1824*. Edited by A. de la Valette-Monbrun, Paris, 1927–31, 2 vols.

MALCOLM, Lady C.: *A Diary of St Helena: the Journal of Lady Malcolm, containing the conversations of Napoleon with Sir Pulteney Malcolm*. Edited by A. Wilson, London, 1899.

NAPOLEON I: *Correspondance de Napoléon I, suivie des oeuvres de Napoléon à Sainte-Hélène*. Paris, 1858–70, 32 vols.
Dernieres Lettres inédites de Napoléon 1er. Edited by L. de Brotonne, Paris, 1903, 2 vols.
Lettres inédites de Napoléon 1er. Edited by L. de Brotonne, Paris, 1898.
Lettres inédites de Napoléon 1er, an VIII-1815. Edited by L. Lecestre, 2nd edn, Paris, 1897, 2 vols.

Lettres au Comte Mollien, ministre du Tresor Public. Edited by J. Arnna, Paris, 1959.

Napoléon inconnu. Edited by F. Masson Paris, 1895, 2 vols.

New Letters of Napoleon I. Edited by Lady Mary Loyd, London 1903.

NAPOLEON and MARIE LOUISE: *My Dearest Louise*. Edited by C. F. Palmstierna, translated by E. M. Wilkinson, London, 1958.

PICTET, M. A.: *Journal d'un Genevois à Paris sous le Consulat*. Geneva, 1893.

REICHARDT, J. F.: *Un hiver à Paris sous le Consulat, 1802–3, d'après les lettres de J.-F. Reichardt*. Edited by A. Lacquiante, Paris, 1896.

REINHARD, Christine: *Une Femme de diplomate: Lettres de Mme Reinhard à sa mere, 1798–1815*. Edited by Baronne Wimpffen, Paris, 1901.

ROEDERER, P.-L. (Comte): *Autour de Bonaparte: Journal du Comte P.-L. Roederer*. Paris, 1909.

YORKE, H. R.: *France in 1802, described in a series of contemporary letters by Henry Redhead Yorke*. Edited by J. A. Sykes, London, 1906.

6 Memoirs and works by contemporaries

ABRANTÈS, Laure Junot (Duchesse d'): *Mémoires de la Duchesse d'Abrantès: souvenirs historiques sur le Consulat*. Paris, 1929–30, 4 vols.

BARÈRE, B.: *Mémoires*. Paris, 1824–4, 4 vols.

BEUGNOT, A. (Comte): *Mémoires du Comte Beugnot, 1783–1815*. Paris, 1866.

BOULAY DE LA MEURTHE, A. J. C. J. (Comte): *Théorie constitutionnelle de Sieyès, extraits des mémoires inédites de M. Boulay de la Meurthe*. Paris, 1836.

BOULAY DE LA MEURTHE, F. J.: *Boulay de la Meurthe*. Paris, 1868.

BOURRIENNE, L. A. F. de: *Mémoires de Bourrienne, ministre d'état, sur Napoléon*. Stuttgart, 1829–30, 10 vols.

BROGLIE, A. L. V. C. de (Duc): *Souvenirs, 1785–1870*. Paris, 1866, 4 vols.

CAULAINCOURT, A. A. L. de (Duc de Vicence): *Mémoires du Général de Caulaincourt*. Paris, 1933, 3 vols.

CHABOULON, P. A. E. Fleury, de; *Mémoires de Fleury de Chaboulon, ex-secrétaire de l'Empereur Napoléon et de son cabinet*. Paris, 1901, 3 vols.

CHAMPOLLION-FIGÉAC, J. J.: *Fourier et Napoléon, l'Egypte et les Cent-Jours: mémoires et documents inédits*. Paris, 1844.

CHAPTAL, J. A. C. (Comte de Chanteloup): *Mes Souvenirs sur Napoléon*. Paris, 1893.

CHASTENAY-LANTY, Victorine de (Comtesse): *Mémoires de Mme de Chastenay, 1771–1815*. Paris, 1896, 2 vols.

CHATEAUBRIAND, F. A. R. de (Vicomte): *Mémoires d'outre-tombe*. Edited by M. Levaillant, Paris, 1948, 4 vols.

CHAZET, A. R. P. Alissan de: *Mémoires, souvenirs, oeuvres et portraits*. Paris, 1837, 3 vols.

CONSTANT, B.: *Cours de politique constitutionnelle, I: Principes de politique*. 3rd edn, Brussels, 1831.

Mémoires sur les Cent-Jours. Paris, 1829.

CORNET, M. A. (Comte): *Souvenirs sénatoriaux*. Paris, 1824.

DUVEYRIER, H. (Baron): *Anecdotes historiques*. Paris, 1907.

FAURIEL, C.: *Les Derniers Jours du Consulat*. Paris, 1886.

FOUCHÉ, J. (Duc d'Otrante): *Mémoires de J. Fouché, ministre de la police générale*. Paris, 1824, 2 vols.

GIRARDIN, L. S. C. X. de (Comte): *Discours et opinion, journal et souvenirs de S. Girardin*. Paris, 1824, 4 vols.

GOHIER, L. J.: *Mémoires*. Paris, 1824, 2 vols.

GRÉGOIRE, H. B. (Comte): *Mémoires*. Paris, 1837, 2 vols.

JOSEPH (Bonaparte): *Mémoires et correspondance politique et militaire du Roi Joseph*. Edited by A. du Casse, Paris, 1854–5, 10 vols (vol. I only).

LAFAYETTE, M. J. (Marquis de): *Mémoires, correspondance et manuscrits du Général Lafayette*. London, 1837, 6 vols.

LANJUINAIS, J. D. (Comte): *Constitutions de la nation française avec un essai de traité historique et politique sur la Charte*. Paris, 1819.

LAS CASES, E. de (Comte): *Le Mémorial de Sainte-Hélène*. Edited by La Pleiade, Paris, 1956, 2 vols.

LA SIBOUTIE, F. L. Poumiès de: *Souvenirs d'un médecin de Paris, 1789–1863*. Paris, 1910.

LEMAISTRE, J. G.: *A Rough Sketch of modern Paris*. London, 1803.

MARMONT, A. F. L. V. de (Duc de Raguse): *Mémoires du Maréchale Marmont, 1792–1841*. 3rd edn, Paris, 1857, 9 vols.

MÉNÉVAL, C. F. de (Baron): *Bourrienne et ses erreurs*. Paris, 1830.

Mémoires pour servir à l'histoire de Napoléon I er. Paris, 1894, 3 vols.

MERCY-ARGENTEAU, F.: *Memoirs of the Comte de Mercy-Argenteau, Napoleon's Chamberlain*. New York, 1917, 2 vols.

METTERNICH-WINNEBURG, C. W. N. L. von (Prince): *Memoirs of Prince Metternich*. Edited by Prince Richard Metternich, translated by Mrs A. Napier, London, 1880–82, 5 vols.

MIOT, A. F. (Comte de Melito): *Mémoires*. Paris, 1858, 3 vols.

MOLÉ: *see* NOAILLES

MORELLET, A.: *Mémoires inédites de l'abbé Morellet*. Paris, 1823, 2 vols.

NOAILLES, H. de (Marquis): *Le Comte Molé, 1781–1855: sa vie, ses mémoires*. Paris, 1922–30, 6 vols.

NAPOLEON I: *Manuscrits inédits, 1786–91*. Edited by F. Masson and G. Biagi, Paris, 1912.

Mémoires pour servir a l'Histoire de France sous Napoléon, écrits à Sainte-Hélène sous la dictée de l'Empereur, par les généraux qui ont partagé sa captivité. Paris, 1829–30, 9 vols.

Napoleon's Memoirs. Edited and translated by Somerset de Chair, London, 1945.

PASQUIER, E. D. (Duc): *Mémoires du chancelier Pasquier.* 3rd edn, Paris 1893–5, 6 vols.

PELET DE LA LOZÈRE, J.: *Opinions de Napoléon.* Paris, 1833.

PONTÉCOULANT, L. G. le Doulcet (Comte de): *Souvenirs historique et parlementaires, 1764–1848.* Paris, 1861–5, 4 vols.

RÉMUSAT, C. de: *Mémoires de ma vie.* Paris, 1958–62, 5 vols (vol. I only).

ROEDERER, P.-L. (Comte): *Mémoires sur la Révolution, le Consulat, et l'Empire.* Paris, 1942.

ROVIGO: *see* SAVARY

SAINT-HILAIRE, E. M. de: *Souvenirs intimes du temps de l'Empire.* Paris 1860, 6 vols.

SAVARY, A. J. M. R.: *Memoirs of the Duke of Rovigo, written by himself.* Translation, London, 1828, 4 vols.

SÉGUR, P. P. de (Comte): *Histoire et mémoires.* Paris, 1873, 7 vols.

THIBAUDEAU, A. C. (Comte): *Mémoires sur le Consulat, 1799–1804.* Paris, 1827.
   Mémoires, 1799–1815. Paris, 1913.

VILLEMAIN, A. F.: *Souvenirs contemporains d'histoire et de littérature.* Paris, 1854–5, 2 vols.

VITROLLES, E. F. de (Baron): *Mémoires et relations politiques du baron de Vitrolles.* Paris, 1884, 3 vols.

7 Secondary works

BASTID, P.: *Sieyès et sa pensée.* Paris, 1939.

BECK, T. D.: *French Legislators, 1800–1834.* California, 1974.

BELLANGER, C. et al.: *Histoire générale de la presse française.* Paris, 1969, 2 vols.

BENAERTS, L.: *Le Régime consulaire en Bretagne.* Paris, 1914.

BERGERON, L.: *Banquiers, négociants et manufacturiers parisiens du Directoire à l'Empire.* Lille, 1975, 2 vols.
   L'Épisode napoléonien: aspects intérieurs, 1799–1815. Paris, 1972.

BETTS, R. F.: 'Dupont de Nemours in Napoleonic France, 1802–1815'. *French Historical Studies* v (1967).

BLUCHE, F.: *Le Plébiscite des Cent-Jours.* Geneva, 1974.

BOURDON, J.: *La Constitution de l'an VIII.* Paris, 1942.
   Napoléon au Conseil d'État. Paris, 1963.

BOURLETON, E., COUGNY, G. and ROBERT, A.: *Dictionnaire des parlementaires français.* Paris, 1889–90, 5 vols.

BRAUN, J. P. M.: *Nouvelle Biographie des députés, ou statistique de la chambre de 1814 à 1829.* Paris, 1830.

BROSSE, J. and LACHOUQUE, H.: *Uniformes et costumes du Premier Empire.* Paris, 1973.

BROTONNE, L. de: *Les Sénateurs du Consulat et de l'Empire.* Geneva, 1974.

BRUGUIÈRE, M.: *La Première Restauration et son budget.* Geneva, 1969.

BURY, J. P. T.: 'The End of the Napoleonic Senate'. *Cambridge Historical Journal* IX (1969), pp. 165 ff.

CABANIS, A.: *La Presse sous le Consulat et l'Empire*. Paris, 1975.

CAMPBELL, P.: *French Electoral Systems and Elections, 1789–1957*. London, 1958.

CESENA, A. de: *Notice biographique sur M. J. J. Duboys*. Angers, 1846.

CHARLES-ROUX, F.: *Bonaparte, Governor of Egypt*. London, 1937.

CHAVANON, J. and SAINT-IVES, G.: *Le Pas-de-Calais de 1800 à 1810*. Paris, 1907.

CONNELLY, O.: *Napoleon's Satellite Kingdoms*. New York, 1965.

CONTAMINE, H.: *Metz et la Moselle de 1814 à 1870*. Nancy, 1932.

CRONIN, V.: *Napoleon*. London, 1971.

DE SOTO, J.: 'La constitution sénatoriale du 6 avril 1814'. *Revue internationale d'histoire politique et constitutionnelle*, 1953.

DURAND, C.: *Le fonctionnement du Conseil d'État napoléonien*. Gap, 1954.

'L'Exercice de la fonction législative, 1800–1815'. *Annales de la Faculté de Droit d'Aix en Provence*, new series, no. 48 (1955).

DURAND, R.: *L'Administration des Côtes-du-Nord sous le Consulat et l'Empire*. Paris, 1925, 2 vols.

DUTRUCH, R.: *Le Tribunat sous le Consulat et l'Empire*. Paris, 1921.

DUVERGIER DE HAURANNE, P.: *Histoire du gouvernement parlementaire en France*. Paris, 1857–71, 10 vols (vols I to III only).

FALMY, S. N.: *La France en 1814 et le gouvernement provisoire*. Paris, 1934.

FRAYLING, C. (ed.): *Napoleon Wrote Fiction*. London, 1967.

FULFORD, R.: *Samuel Whitbread, 1764–1815*. London, 1967.

GEYL, P.: *Napoleon, For and Against*, London, 1949.

GOBERT, A.: *L'Opposition des assemblées pendant le Consulat, 1800–1804*. Paris, 1925.

GODECHOT, J.: *La Grande Nation*. Paris, 1956, 2 vols.

Les Institutions de la France sous la Revolution et l'Empire. Paris, 1951, 2 vols.

GOODSPEED, D. J.: *Bayonets at St Cloud: the Story of the 18th Brumaire*. London, 1965.

GRUNER, S.: 'Destutt de Tracy, a Forgotten *Idéologue*'. *Durham University Journal* LXIII (1970–71), pp. 186–95.

GUÉRARD, M. B.: *Notice sur Daunou*. Paris, 1855.

GUERRINI, M.: *Napoleon and Paris: Thirty Years of History*. Paris, 1970.

GUILLOIS, A.: *Le Salon de Madame Helvetius, Cabanis et les idéologues*. Paris, 1970.

HALL, H. F.: *Napoleon's Notes on English History*. London, 1905.

HEALEY, F. G.: *The Literary Culture of Napoleon*. Geneva, 1959.

HERIOT, A.: *The French in Italy*. London, 1957.

HOUSSAYE, H.: *1814*. 25th edn, Paris, 1899.

1815. 25th edn, Paris, 1898, 2 vols.

KITCHIN, J.: *La Décade, 1794–1807, un journal 'philosophique'*. Paris, 1965.

KUSCINSKI, A.: *Les Députés au Corps législatif, de l'an IV à l'an VIII*. Paris, 1905

LEAN, E. Tangye: The Napoleonists. London, 1970.

LEFÈBVRE, G.: *Napoléon*. 5th edn, Paris, 1965.

LE GALLO, E.: *Les Cent-Jours*. Paris, 1924.

LEUILLIOT, P.: *La Première Restauration et les Cent-Jours en Alsace*. Paris, 1958.

LEWIS, M.: *Napoleon and his British Captives*. London, 1962.

L'HUILLIER, F.: *Recherches sur l'Alsace napoléonienne*. Paris, 1947.

LYONS, M.: *France under the Directory*. Cambridge, 1962.

MACCUNN, F. J.: *The Contemporary English view of Napoleon*. London, 1914.

MARKHAM, F.: *Napoleon*. London, 1963.

MASSON, F.: *Le Sacre et le couronnement de Napoléon*. 4th edn, Paris, 1908.

MEURIOT, P.: *La Population et les lois électorales en France*. Paris, 1916.

MYERS, A. R.: *Parliaments and Estates in Europe to 1789*. London, 1975.

OLLIVIER, A.: *18 Brumaire*. Paris, 1959.

PALMER, R. R.: *The Age of the Democratic Revolution*. Princeton, 1959–64, 2 vols.

PERCEVAL, E. de: *Le Vicomte Lainé*. Paris, 1926.

PICAVET, F.: *Les Idéologues*. Paris, 1891.

PIÉTRI, F.: *Napoléon et le Parlement, ou le dictature enchaîné* Paris, 1955.

PONTEIL, F.: *Napoléon et l'organisation autoritaire de la France*. Paris, 1956.

RADIGUET, L.: *L'Acte additionnel aux constitutions de l'Empire*. Caen, 1911.

'Les votes des Conventionnels en 1795 et en 1815'. *Revue des Études napoléoniennes*, 1912.

RÉVÉREND, A.: *Armorial du premier empire: titres, majorats, et armoiries concédés par Napoléon 1er*. Paris, 1894–97, 4 vols.

RICHARDSON, N.: *The French Prefectoral Corps, 1814–30*. Cambridge, 1966.

ROBIQUET, J.: *La Vie quotidienne au temps de Napoléon*. Paris, 1963.

ROCQUAIN, F.: *L'État de la France au 18 Brumaire*. Paris, 1874.

SAINT-IVES, G. and FOURNIER, J.: *Le Département des Bouches-du-Rhône de 1800 à 1810*. Paris, 1899.

SCHAMA, S.: *Patriots and Liberators: Revolution in the Netherlands, 1780–1813*. London, 1977.

STUART, D. M.: *Dearest Bess: the Life and Times of Lady Elizabeth Forster*. London, 1955.

TAILLANDIER, M. A. H.: *Documents biographiques sur P. C. F. Daunou*. Paris, 1841.

THIRY, J.: *La Première Abdication de Napoléon 1er*. Paris, 1948.
La Première Restauration. Paris, 1943.
La Seconde Abdication de Napoléon 1er. Paris, 1945.
Le Sénat de Napoleon, 1800–1814. Paris, 1932.

THOMPSON, J. M.: *Napoleon Bonaparte, his Rise and Fall*. Oxford, 1952.

TULARD, J.: *Bibliographie critique des mémoires sur le Consulat et l'Empire*. Paris, 1971.

TULARD, J. and DAINVILLE, F. de: *Atlas administratif de l'Empire français d'après l'atlas rédigé par ordre du Duc de Feltre en 1812*. Geneva, 1973.

VANDAL, A.: *L'Avènement de Bonaparte*. Paris, 1907, 2 vols.

VIALLES, P.: *L'Archichancelier Cambacérès, 1753–1824*. Paris, 1908.

VIARD, P.: *L'Administration préfectorale dans le Départment de la Côte-d'Or sous le Consulat et le Premier Empire*. Paris, 1914.

VIDALENC, J.: *Le Département de l'Eure sous la monarchie constitutionnelle 1814–48*. Paris, 1952.

VILLEFOSSE, L. de and BOUISSOUNOUSE, J.: *The Scourge of the Eagle: Napoleon and the Liberal Opposition*. London, 1972.

WARLOMONT, R.: La Représentation économique dans l'Acte additionnel aux constitutions de l'Empire'. *Revue internationale d'Histoire politique et constitutionnelle*, 1954.

WEIL, G. D.: *Les Élections législative depuis 1789*. Paris, 1895.

WELSCHINGER, H.: *La Censure sous le premier empire*. Paris, 1882.

WILSON, A.: *Fontanes*. Paris, 1928.

WOLOCH, I.: *Jacobin Legacy: the Democratic Movement under the Directory*. Princeton, 1970.

Index

(Periods of service are indicated for members of Napoleon's parliaments)

Helmut Böhme
(Translated by W. R. Lee)

**An Introduction to the Social and
Economic History of Germany: Political
and Economic Change in the Nineteenth
and Twentieth Centuries**

Wilfred Fest

Dictionary of German History 1806-1945

William Fest

**Peace or Partion: The Habsburg
Monarchy and British Policy 1914-1918**

J. M. Salmon

**Society in Crisis: France in the
Sixteenth Century**

R. T. Thomas

**Britain and Vichy: The Dilemma of
Anglo-French Relations, 1940-42**